Torture and the Military Profession

D1542152

Torture and the Military Profession

Jessica Wolfendale
Research Fellow
Centre for Applied Philosophy and Public Ethics
Department of Philosophy
University of Melbourne, Australia

First published 2007 by
PALGRAVE MACMILLAN
Houndmills, Basingstoke, Hampshire RG21 6XS and
175 Fifth Avenue, New York, N.Y. 10010
Companies and representatives throughout the world

PALGRAVE MACMILLAN is the global academic imprint of the Palgrave Macmillan division of St. Martin's Press, LLC and of Palgrave Macmillan Ltd. Macmillan® is a registered trademark in the United States, United Kingdom and other countries. Palgrave is a registered trademark in the European Union and other countries.

ISBN-13: 978-0-230-00182-4
ISBN-10: 0-230-00182-3

This book is printed on paper suitable for recycling and made from fully managed and sustained forest sources. Logging, pulping and manufacturing processes are expected to conform to the environmental regulations of the country of origin.

A catalogue record for this book is available from the British Library.

Library of Congress Cataloging-in-Publication Data
Wolfendale, Jessica, 1973-
    Torture and the military profession / Jessica Wolfendale.
        p. cm.
    Includes bibliographical references and index.
    ISBN 0–230–00182-3 (alk. paper)
    1. Military ethics.   2. Torture.   I. Title.
U22.W64 2007
172'.42—dc22   2007016442

10   9   8   7   6   5   4   3   2   1
16   15   14   13   12   11   10   09   08   07

Printed and bound in Great Britain by
Antony Rowe Ltd, Chippenham and Eastbourne

Contents

Preface

This book developed out of research undertaken for my PhD thesis at Monash University. There are many people I would like to thank for their support and encouragement during the writing of this book. I am deeply indebted to Jeanette Kennett and Justin Oakley, my supervisors at Monash University, who provided constant guidance and encouragement throughout the writing process. Both Justin and Jeanette provided detailed and incisive feedback at all stages of writing, helping me to refine and develop my arguments. Dirk Baltzly undertook the daunting task of reading the entire work from beginning to end, and his input and insights were invaluable.

Michael Walzer and Garrett Cullity kindly provided perceptive and helpful suggestions for refining the arguments in this book. Early versions of some of the chapters of this book were read to several audiences over the last few years. I received extremely useful comments from the staff and students at Monash University, the Centre for Applied Philosophy and Public Ethics, and from two anonymous reviewers at *Social Theory and Practice*. The feedback I received contributed greatly to the writing of this book.

I also wish to express my heartfelt appreciation and thanks to my mother Lynne for her unfailing love and support, my sister Zoë for her great forbearance and kindness, Trish for her constant love and encouragement, and Dan for his patience and support during the final months of writing.

JESSICA WOLFENDALE

Acknowledgements

Sections of the following chapters draw on previously published material, as indicated. Permission to adapt and use parts of that material has been kindly granted by the publishers, as noted. I would also like to thank David Owens for allowing me to refer to his unpublished paper 'The Authority of Practical Judgement'.

Chapter 4, Chapter 6: 'Military Obedience: Rhetoric and Reality', in Igor Primoratz (ed.), *Politics and Morality* (Basingstoke, UK: Palgrave Macmillan, 2006). Copyright © Palgrave Macmillan 2006.

Chapter 5, Chapter 7: 'Training Torturers: A Critique of the "Ticking Bomb" Argument', *Social Theory and Practice*, 32 (2006): 269–87. Copyright © 2006 by the Department of Philosophy, Florida State University.

Chapter 7: 'Stoic Warriors and Stoic Torturers: The Moral Psychology of Military Torture', *South African Journal of Philosophy*, 25 (2006): 62–77. Copyright © 2006 by the Philosophical Society of Southern Africa.

Publication of this work was assisted by a publication grant from the University of Melbourne.

Introduction

Torture is banned in international conventions governing the conduct of war. It is publicly condemned by military and government officials alike. Yet military torture is widespread. Amnesty International has identified over 150 countries that use torture, many of whom are signatories to the above conventions.[1] This discrepancy between rhetoric and reality has widened further in the war against terrorism that began after 11 September 2001, with evidence suggesting that the United States (signatory to several conventions banning the use of torture) has been systematically using torture against terrorism suspects in Afghanistan, Iraq, Guantanamo Bay and elsewhere.[2] This discrepancy between rhetoric and reality demands explanation.

In most Western nations the modern military claims to be an honourable profession serving the good of national security. The importance of protecting national security is taken to provide the military with special moral permission to perform acts of great destructive power – to kill, to maim, and to destroy cities. However, the military also claims to be bound by the laws of war and important broad-based moral values. The ideal of the good military professional is a highly moralized ideal involving a list of military virtues including honour, integrity, loyalty, and valour.

Yet despite this emphasis on moral values and military virtues, the systematic use of torture is closely linked to the military profession. Most torturers are military personnel acting with explicit or implicit authorization from military superiors, and attempts by governments and military officials to justify the use of torture often appeal to the military's role as protector of national security. Implicit in these arguments is the belief that the military has a special moral permission to use torture in extreme circumstances, a permission arising from the unique role of the military as protector of the nation-state. Torture of this kind is a

1

'crime of obedience': 'a crime that takes place not in opposition to the authorities, but under explicit instructions from the authorities to engage in an act of torture, or in an environment in which such acts are implicitly sponsored, expected, or at least tolerated by the authorities.'[3]

The prevalence of systematic institutionalized torture shows that combating torture requires more than making it illegal: it requires understanding the context in which it occurs. Institutionalized torture is inextricably linked to the military profession, yet an analysis of this connection has been lacking from debate on this topic. The aim of this book is to provide such an analysis.

This book examines the military's claim to be a profession, and in particular the claim that in extreme circumstances the military has special moral permission to use torture. I show that the claim for special moral permission to torture is unjustified and furthermore that the use of torture is incompatible with the military's claim to be a profession. Professional status brings with it constraints on what may be done in pursuit of professional goals. If it is a legitimate profession, the military must be bound by the laws of war and must strive to minimize the harms of war. If military personnel are professionals then they must aim to embody the professional military virtues and they must be guided by a conception of professional integrity that best serves the ends of the military. Military rhetoric supports this view. Public statements and the writings of military ethicists portray the combatant's role as an honourable role bound by high moral standards in the service of an important moral good. The good combatant is a person of courage, integrity, honour, and discipline. According to military rhetoric, such a person would never become a torturer. Yet in most cases it is military personnel who are the torturers. Military personnel are involved in activities that violate not only the laws of war but the stated values of the military profession. There is a clear discrepancy between military rhetoric and the behaviour of real military personnel. Why are military personnel becoming torturers? What is wrong with the military profession?

The reason for the discrepancy between military rhetoric and real military behaviour lies in the nature of modern military training. As I will demonstrate, the moral psychology cultivated through modern military training aims to undermine combatants' moral agency and instils dispositions that are associated with crimes of obedience. The reason that most systematic torture is performed by military personnel acting under orders is not because of human weakness or an innate tendency to obey authority but because military training at both basic and elite levels deliberately instils the dispositions linked to crimes of obedience. Far from being a mark of barbaric unprofessional military forces, the moral psychology of torture is cultivated and enhanced through the training methods of the most sophisticated military forces. Furthermore, this moral psychology is aided by a version of professionalism that perverts the concepts of professional integrity and professional detachment. By undermining the ability of military personnel to be reflective moral agents and by instilling the dispositions of destructive obedience, this training seriously undermines the military's claim to be a profession.

Chapter 1 offers an account of professional ethics. I explain the definition of a profession and the moral significance of professional status, particularly the common claim that professional status justifies departures from broad-based moral constraints. I argue that professional status should be constrained by broad-based moral ideals and that special professional moral permissions are best considered as a sub-set of broad-based morality. However, as professionals encounter unique moral issues they need specific moral guidance tailored to their professional duties. Virtue ethics, with its emphasis on human flourishing and character, is the most useful approach to take to professional ethics.

Chapter 2 outlines Justin Oakley and Dean Cocking's virtue ethics approach to professional roles. This approach is superior to competing accounts of professional ethics because of the central role given to reflective moral agency in the Aristotelian concept of the virtues. Under the virtue ethics approach to professional roles professionals are governed by the regulative ideal of their profession – the conception of excellence in professional functioning that best serves the ends of the profession. This ideal sets appropriate limits on professional activity and incorporates the acts, roles, and character traits that best promote the ends of the profession. Like ordinary virtues, professional virtues are not simply emotional dispositions or habits but are traits governed by reflective moral agency – the capacity to rationally deliberate about the conception of the good and to act on one's deliberation. Good professionals must therefore be reflective moral agents. The virtue ethics approach to professional roles gives rise to a conception of professional integrity that has important implications for when professionals can and sometimes ought to refuse their services when providing them would violate the ideals of their profession.

In Chapter 3 the virtue ethics approach is applied to the military profession. Despite some doubts arising from the military's problematic role as the agent of the civilian authority, the military fulfils the essential criteria of a profession and so there is a *prima facie* reason to accord it professional status. Having made the case for the military's professional status,

I then establish the military's regulative ideal, from which derives a list of military virtues that best enable military personnel to serve the goal of the military profession – the protection of national security. Of the military virtues, obedience and integrity are often considered to be the most important. Because the military's regulative ideal is the conception of excellent professional functioning, this gives rise to a conception of military professional integrity that delineates when military professionals should disobey orders and refuse to provide their services on the grounds that to do so would violate important military professional ideals. While obedience is a central military virtue, the military's regulative ideal sometimes requires disobedience. Obedience in the military therefore has certain restrictions.

Chapter 4 explores the limits of the military obedience. Because obedience involves substituting another's judgement for one's own it can only be a virtue if it is reflective obedience. Blind obedience can never be virtuous. For obedience to be a military professional virtue, it must contribute to the ends of the military and must be governed by practical wisdom. This view is supported by the legal obligation of military personnel to disobey illegal or immoral orders. In theory selective disobedience is justified by the military's own claims about ideal military obedience. Furthermore, it is only reflective obedience that is consistent with the military's claim to be a profession, a claim which commits the military to a regulative ideal that provides strong grounds for disobedience of illegal orders. Good military personnel should therefore never obey orders that involve the commission of war crimes. However, the prevalence of torture now and in the past indicates that military personnel can and do obey illegal and immoral orders. Torture seems to be obviously immoral and illegal. Can the military justify the use of torture?

Chapter 5 demonstrates that common justifications for the use of torture, such as the popular 'ticking bomb' argument, fail. Furthermore torture is banned unconditionally in all national and international conventions governing conduct in warfare. The military cannot claim a special moral permission to use torture. An order to perform torture is therefore illegal and immoral and good military personnel should refuse to obey such an order. Why, then, are military personnel involved in the use of torture? After considering possible explanations for the real-life involvement of military personnel in torture, I show that this involvement cannot be explained by appeals to the horrors of war or individual human weakness. In addition, the military's treatment of personnel who disobey illegal or immoral orders reveals an inconsistency in the military's attitude towards obedience.

Chapter 6 explores the reasons for this inconsistency. The inconsistency apparent in the military's treatment of personnel who embody the ideal of reflective obedience is a symptom of a far more serious problem in military training. Basic military training builds on the pre-existing tendencies towards unreflective obedience identified by psychologist Stanley Milgram and sociologists Herbert Kelman and V. Lee Hamilton in their work on obedience to authority. Military training does not merely allow these dispositions to come to the surface; it deliberately enhances them. Modern military training aims at undermining combatants' moral agency and makes it virtually impossible for them to truly embody the military virtues. Reflective moral agency – which is necessary for reflective obedience – requires the capacities for moral reflection and empathy, and it is these capacities that are deliberately undermined by basic military training. This training explains why military personnel sometimes obey illegal orders or interpret ambiguous orders illegally – why situations like the abuse of prisoners at Abu Ghraib occur. However, this training is not sufficient to explain the difference between the untrained inept torturers at Abu Ghraib and the 'professional' torturers employed in the supposedly justified torture of terrorist suspects at Guantanamo Bay and elsewhere.

Chapter 7 explains how professional torturers are created. Far from being unprofessional sadistic 'bad apples', professional torturers are obedient, loyal military personnel often trained in elite Special Forces units. The training processes used in these units enhance the dispositions cultivated during basic combat training, leading to psychological dispositions that enable the move from ordinary combatant to torturer. This training appeals to combatants' professional pride and by doing so provides a veneer of legitimacy to the professionalization of torture. Far from training military personnel to be reflective moral agents – one of the ways that innate dispositions towards destructive obedience might be combated – military training at both elite and basic levels not only inhibits the expression of the capacity for reflective moral agency; it undermines the capacity itself and further entrenches the dispositions of destructive obedience. The moral psychology of torture and the moral psychology of ordinary military personnel are on a continuum.

The discrepancy between military rhetoric and military reality is therefore indicative of widespread institutional processes that undermine combatants' capacities for reflective moral agency. These processes produce a perverted form of professionalism that helps cultivate the moral psychology of torture.

In conclusion I argue that military training as it currently stands undermines the moral agency of military personnel and produces dispositions connected with crimes of obedience. These training methods are morally abhorrent for two reasons. First, these methods harm military personnel by deliberately undermining their capacity for reflective moral agency. Second, these methods undermine the military's claim to be a legitimate profession. The military's professional status requires military personnel to be reflective moral agents and requires that military actions are constrained by important broad-based moral standards and the laws of war. Yet current military training undermines the ability of military personnel to embody the military's professional virtues. If we find the training of torturers to be morally reprehensible and the justifications for the use of torture unsound, then we have reason to be equally uneasy about basic military training techniques that produce essentially the same kind of moral psychology and that are supposedly justified by the same appeals to the military's role as protector of the nation-state.

If the modern military wishes to maintain the status of a profession and the special moral permissions that status implies, then it must train military personnel to be reflective moral agents and it must maintain a genuine commitment to the laws of war. This involves far more than adding ethics classes and reiterating military rhetoric about the military virtues; it requires a serious rethinking of the nature of the military profession and military training. If crimes of obedience such as torture are not to become institutionalized, military training must be changed.

1
Professions and Professional Ethics

The modern military institution refers to itself as a profession and military personnel are frequently referred to as professionals. Is the military justified in using the term 'profession' and if so, what is the moral significance of that status? Is there a morally significant distinction between professional and non-professional occupations? Does professional status justify departures from the constraints of broad-based or ordinary morality within professional practices?

In this chapter I summarize the defining characteristics of a profession and explain why professional status is claimed to be morally important. Often, professionals claim to have special moral permission to perform acts that would be morally wrong outside the professional context. Lawyers, for example, claim special permission to represent clients whose cases might be unjust. Doctors claim special permission to maintain their patient's confidentiality even when doing so might harm others. This idea of special moral permissions carries particular weight in the case of the military, given the military's great destructive power. The military claims permission to kill people, destroy cities, and endanger the lives of military personnel. Whether special moral permissions are justified by appealing to professional status is the core issue in professional ethics.

I consider two arguments in support of this claim: the argument from expertise and the argument from friendship, and show that these arguments fail to ground the existence of special moral permissions. It is far from clear that role-relative morality should be distinct from broad-based morality, or that professionals have special moral permissions that cannot be explained by reference to professional expertise.

What is a profession?

The distinctive characteristics of a profession are by no means uncontroversial. Writers on professional ethics list a wide range of different and sometimes incompatible criteria that are claimed to be the defining features of a profession. While debate continues over the status of occupations such as journalism and business, there are two occupations that are universally agreed to be professions – medicine and law. The consensus on the professional status of these occupations allows some agreement about the essential criteria of a profession. The most important (and least controversial) criterion of a profession is that it serves an important human need. In *Virtue Ethics and Professional Roles*, for example, Justin Oakley and Dean Cocking define a good profession as one that: 'involves a commitment to a key human good, a good which plays a crucial role in enabling us to live a humanly flourishing life.'[1]

To count as a profession an occupation must do more than provide a service that satisfies a desire: it must provide a service that addresses a need central to a flourishing human life,[2] or at the very least central to the functioning of modern human society.[3] It is clear, then, why medicine and law are professions: they serve the goals of health and justice, both of which are essential for a flourishing human life. It is also clear why occupations such as florist, plumber, and gardener do not count as professions. These occupations cater to desires that are not central to a flourishing human life, even if they might be important for other reasons.

It is not clear whether the good that a profession serves must be an agent-neutral good such as justice or health. Common sense ideas of professions seem to tally with the view that a profession's goal should be an agent-neutral good linked to the good of human society, not just to the good of certain people. Indeed, one of the reasons why some writers claim that business is not a profession is because the goal of business is not an agent-neutral good at all, but the businessman's self-interested gain.[4] However, so long as a profession serves a good that is important for human flourishing and is not simply the good of some arbitrarily defined group of people, then the good need not be agent-neutral, although it could be expressed in agent-neutral terms or as a universal value.[5]

However, serving an important human good, agent-neutral or otherwise, is not sufficient to make an occupation a profession. Chefs and builders serve important human needs, but it is debatable whether these occupations count as professions. Other criteria need to be met.

Beyond serving an important human need, most writers agree that professions differ from other occupations in at least two significant ways. For example, Michael Bayles argues that, as well as providing an important service, professions are characterized by specialized and high-level training – training that is not just skill-based but involves a significant intellectual component – and by significant autonomy within professional roles. Professionals are not mere technicians for hire or automata carrying out rote tasks – their roles require judgement, reflection, and wisdom. Professionals are reflective moral agents who must make informed decisions about when and how to apply their professional knowledge, decisions involving significant responsibility for their client's wellbeing and interests.[6] Paul Camenisch adds that, because of the importance of the service they provide, professions often have a monopoly on provision of that service, a monopoly that is governed by professional organizations and regulatory bodies.[7] For example, lawyers and doctors need a licence to practise medicine, and their behaviour is regulated by codes of conduct set by an association of members. Such codes of conduct usually include a set of standards (that may or may not be legally enforceable) by which members of the profession are judged. Members failing to abide by these standards can be excluded from practice.[8]

A further, less well accepted, criterion of a profession is the importance of moral character. Professionals, it is claimed, must be more than good at their job; they should be good people too. Because professionals provide a service that individuals cannot provide for themselves and that is central to an individual's wellbeing, professionals must be of good moral character; must be trustworthy, honest, wise, and have integrity. The conception of the good lawyer and the good doctor is not simply a conception of technical ability, but is a highly moralized conception, and so professionals are expected to be under a more intense moral spotlight than other workers.[9]

The moral importance of a profession's goal has further implications for the defining features of a profession. Not only is the professional's moral character under greater scrutiny, but the profession as whole invites greater moral analysis than other occupations.[10] Some professions (such as law) have been subject to much criticism on the grounds that the profession *as a whole* fails to serve the moral good it claims to serve. Criticisms of the adversarial legal system, for example, focus on the fact that lawyers are permitted to perform acts (impugning witness integrity, defending wealthy companies from legitimate suits) that seem very far from serving justice. Of course, there are many and ingenious justifications for such departures from the stated goal of the legal profession, some of which I will discuss later. For the moment it is enough to note that praise and criticism of professions and professionals often focuses on how well professionals and particular professional practices further the stated moral good that the profession exists to serve.

The essential criteria of a profession can be summarized as follows. A profession serves an important human good necessary for a flourishing human life. Professionals are required to undertake a high level of training and are expected to exercise significant autonomy in their work. A profession, by virtue of the importance of the service it provides, has a monopoly on the provision of that service and is subject to internal checks and balances, usually through a code of practice and/or licensing boards, regulatory bodies, or associations of professional members. Finally professionals are expected to display more than technical competence; they are also expected to maintain a high moral character and to use their skills wisely – to exercise reflective moral judgement in carrying out their roles.

Defining what a profession is does not, however, tell us why professional status is morally significant.

The moral importance of professional status

Why do so many occupations seek the 'official' status of professions? What moral work does the term 'profession' do?

Professional status is generally appealed to for two reasons. First, as noted above, professions claim to serve important human goods, and so the moral character of professions and of individual professionals is particularly important. Given the consequences of surgeons as opposed to, say, hairdressers 'going bad' it is far more important for surgeons to be morally good. Recovering from a bad haircut is far less traumatic than recovering from botched surgery. So claiming professional status for an occupation is intended to indicate both the serious nature of the goal of the profession, and the importance of the professional's good moral character.

Second, and most important, professional status is appealed to in order to justify departures from the standards of everyday or broad-based morality. Professional roles, it is argued, are best thought of as involving distinct obligations and responsibilities that a broad-based morality will be unable to capture.[11] If it can be shown that professional roles and the actions permitted within those roles genuinely further the profession's goals then, it is claimed, those roles and actions are perhaps better judged by internal standards than by the standards of ordinary morality.[12]

If this view is accepted then being a professional is claimed to provide a kind of special 'moral permission' to perform acts that would be impermissible, or at least morally reprehensible, in ordinary life. For example, while it would be immoral for an ordinary citizen to impugn another's reputation, it is not considered immoral for a defence lawyer to do so in order to defend her client.

This idea of special moral permissions is often taken to mean that certain acts are no longer morally wrong when done within the bounds of a profession, if they can be shown to be necessary for the achievement of professional goals. The justification for the profession's existence (that it serves an important human need) supposedly 'trickles down' both on to professional roles (for example, the role of defence lawyer) and on to the acts permitted within those roles (cross-examination of witnesses), even if those roles and acts would normally be considered morally wrong. Supporters of the idea of special permissions often justify the discrepancy between professional role demands and the demands of ordinary morality by appeal to the overall good that the profession serves. The importance of that moral good is held to provide sufficient grounds for overriding the demands of ordinary morality in certain situations, and is claimed to be the source of the special moral permissions.

The question most theories in professional ethics try to answer is how to ground these moral permissions and how these permissions are related to broad-based morality. Should professional morality be seen as a different kind of morality or is it a sub-set of ordinary morality? Certainly it is not obvious that special moral permissions should automatically follow from professional status. Given that a profession's goal is usually the promotion or protection of an agent-neutral moral good, it is far from clear how the pursuit of an agent-neutral good gives rise to permissions to perform actions that conflict with broad-based morality. Why should professionals have permission to perform acts that would normally be wrong? What gives them that permission? We want a very strong reason to permit the creation of roles or acts that violate ordinary moral constraints. The burden of proof lies with those who claim that such special permissions exist and that there is a justifiable distinction between professional morality and broad-based or ordinary morality.[13]

Before addressing this issue let us consider whether some professional activities really do conflict with the demands of ordinary morality, or whether they can be accommodated within broad-based morality. Is the conflict real or apparent?

Professional roles and professional morality

At first glance professional acts and roles seem to conflict frequently with ordinary moral standards. Michael Bayles notes that role-related norms could conflict with ordinary morality by, for example, requiring behaviour that is not permitted by ordinary morality or prohibiting behaviour that is required or permitted by ordinary morality.[14] Certainly professionals (particularly doctors) are permitted to do serious and life-threatening acts that non-professionals are not permitted to do. Professionals, by virtue of their expertise, can perform actions that would not only be wrong but quite possibly dangerous if done by a non-professional. A doctor can perform emergency surgery on an unconscious individual, can decide to withdraw treatment when she judges it to be futile, and can even in some cases withdraw a patient's life support. However, this is not the kind of special permission that conflicts with ordinary morality. Any impartial moral theory will agree that acts that involve a high degree of risk, are particularly complex, or involve someone's crucial interests (health, legal status etc.) should only be done by people who are properly trained. The fact that only doctors can perform surgery does not point to a conflict with ordinary morality – it makes perfect sense within ordinary morality. Professional expertise and the monopoly on professional services are justified not only on the grounds of impartial morality but also through common sense. It is not here that the conflict lies.

The feature common to most professional roles that is most likely to conflict with ordinary morality is professionals' strong partiality towards their clients' interests. Most professional roles require professionals to give more weight to their clients' interests than to the interests of others, even others who might benefit more from the professional's services.[15] However the existence of such partiality may not necessarily conflict with the demands of ordinary morality. Ordinary morality does after all permit certain kinds of partiality (that of parents towards their children for example),[16] so there is no necessary conflict between a professional's partiality towards her clients and the demands of ordinary morality. On the face of it, it seems quite justifiable for a doctor to be partial towards her patients. So it is not a professional's partiality towards her clients *per se* that conflicts with ordinary morality, but what she is permitted to do in pursuit of her clients' interests. When pursuing professional goals on behalf of her clients she may perform acts that harm the interests and wellbeing of others without their consent. While this is perhaps more apparent in the lawyer's role than in other roles, other professionals such as engineers might pursue a client's interests when doing so damages the environment, for example. It is here that the idea of special moral permissions is most apparent. The professional claims to have permission to give more weight to her client's interests (and ignore other competing moral claims) than would be justified in a non-professional setting. As Richard Wasserstrom argues, the nature of the professional–client relationship is governed by role-specific concerns that make it appear appropriate for the professional to put aside considerations that might ordinarily weigh against certain courses of action.[17] For example, a lawyer not only has permission to give more weight to her client's interests than would be justified outside the professional role, she also has permission to give *less* weight to moral considerations that might normally guide her actions. So long as her client is not pursuing an illegal course of action the lawyer is permitted to ignore the consequences of fulfilling her client's wishes, even when those consequences might seriously harm others. A lawyer defending a client accused of rape, for example, can in some countries require the complainant (the rape victim) to undergo a psychiatric evaluation before the trial. Indeed, as Wasserstrom points out, a good defence lawyer not only *can* pursue this option, but *should* – despite the pain and distress it would cause the rape victim.[18]

At first glance it is hard to see how such preferential treatment and the harm it can cause could be justified under impartial moral considerations. Indeed, lawyers' unsavoury reputation points to a sense of unease about the moral justifications for the tactics lawyers are permitted to use in pursuit of their clients' cases. Yet the professions of law and medicine clearly serve important human needs and are generally accepted as necessary and legitimate professions by the wider community.[19] Furthermore, the roles of lawyer and doctor and the duties they involve seem to *require* strong partiality. How could doctors, lawyers, or indeed any professionals do their job effectively without being partial to their clients' interests? It is also plausible that many professional roles just cannot be performed without the possibility of some harm to others. Sometimes defending or carrying out one person's legitimate claims will unavoidably be at the expense of another's. If you are a lawyer and your client wins a lawsuit, then their win is at the financial (and probably emotional) expense of the other side.[20] It is perhaps inevitable that in the pursuit of a client's interests, the interests of others will be adversely affected.

Because of these features it is often claimed that professional roles cannot adequately be judged by the standards of broad-based morality, but instead should be judged by some internally generated role-based moral standards. Furthermore, in some cases of conflict, such role-generated reasons for action should take priority over the demands of broad-based morality. The pursuit of the profession's goal justifies departures from the constraints of ordinary morality in certain ways.

An example will highlight the common-sense appeal of this approach. If my friend tells me that she has a serious and life-threatening sexually transmitted disease but has no intention of telling her long-term boyfriend, I might feel it my duty to break her confidence and inform her partner and previous partners. I might weigh up my duty as a friend against the harm caused by keeping her secret, and I might decide that the harm is too great – I should tell.

However, if I am a doctor and she is my patient, I am bound by confidentiality not to inform my patient's current or previous partners, even if there is significant doubt about her willingness to inform them. For me as a doctor, the value of maintaining patient trust and confidentiality outweighs the impartial moral considerations that might otherwise indicate that those partners and ex-partners should be told.[21] The agent-neutral good of patient health gives me permission (in this case) to maintain my patient's confidentiality. As a doctor I have special moral permission to give more weight to the duty of confidentiality than could be justified were I not a professional. This special moral permission derives from consideration of the overall goal of doctoring. Maintaining patient confidentiality serves patient health because patients can be assured that I will not reveal their medical histories to other people. If doctors did not maintain patient confidentiality, patients would be less likely to be truthful about their conditions, and might refuse important tests (for example, HIV tests) or even refuse to see a doctor at all if they had a condition they did not want others to know about.

But the above example does not really seem to present a conflict with broad-based morality. The justification for doctors' special moral permission to give more weight to patient confidentiality seems straightforwardly consequentialist – doctors are permitted to give more weight to their clients' interests because to do otherwise would undermine the goal of the profession. Such permission is firmly grounded in the good of doctoring and would be withdrawn if it turned out that it did not in fact contribute to serving patient health. This example does not show a striking conflict with ordinary morality, but there is another aspect to many professional roles that presents a far more serious gap between professional permissions and broad-based morality. Many professionals are agents for others.

The problem of serving others: lawyers and doctors

There is a significant difference between the kind of moral permissions claimed by doctors and those claimed by lawyers, a difference that brings out the main sources of conflict between professional permissions and broad-based morality. Unlike doctors, lawyers act as agents for others (their clients, or possibly also the court, depending on the view one takes about where lawyers' main loyalties should lie). Through the pursuit of her client's interests a lawyer's actions might impact negatively on others' interests and wellbeing without their consent. A lawyer is expected to represent all her clients with the same degree of professionalism, to leave aside her own personal beliefs about their guilt or innocence and the justness or morality of their cases.[22] The good lawyer is meant to be neutral on the morality of her client's case, so long as the client is acting within their legal rights. As the Victorian Bar Association Rules of Conduct state: 'A barrister must seek to advance and protect the client's interests to the best of the barrister's skill and diligence, uninfluenced by the barrister's personal view of the client or the client's activities, and notwithstanding any threatened unpopularity or criticism of the barrister or any other person, and always in accordance with the law including these Rules.'[23]

Similarly the American Bar Association states that: 'A lawyer should seek to be excused from [court or bar appointments] only for "compelling reasons"' and these 'do not include such factors as the repugnance of the subject matter of the proceeding, the identity or position of a person involved in the case, the belief of the lawyer that the defendant in a criminal proceeding is guilty, or the belief of the lawyer regarding the merits of the civil case'.[24]

While such guidelines are not legally enforceable, they do indicate the widespread acceptance of the belief that good lawyers should not pass judgement on the moral value of their clients' cases.

This aspect of the lawyer's role has two crucial implications. First, implicit in the ideal lawyer's character is the ability to put aside one's personal opinion and judgement about the moral worth of a client's case. Being a good lawyer requires a commitment not to allow one's moral judgement about the justness of the case or the guilt or innocence of the client to interfere with the committed pursuit of that case. Second, being a good lawyer is likely to involve the pursuit of cases that, if successful, will sometimes seriously adversely affect the interests of others. One has only to think of the consequences of a previously convicted rapist's acquittal on a new charge to see that this is true. The lawyer's duties can therefore conflict with the demands of ordinary morality in two ways: a lawyer might defend a client who is likely to be guilty, and a lawyer may pursue a client's case when doing so will adversely affect the interests and wellbeing of others. This is a very different matter from the doctor's professional permissions. When she accepts a patient a doctor does so as a consultant to that patient; she is not hired to represent her patient's interests or carry out her patient's wishes.[25] The exercise of her duties in no way allows her to affect the health and wellbeing of others at her patient's behest. However, like lawyers, doctors do have a duty not to turn away patients on the basis of personal preferences. The Australian Medical Association's Code of Ethics states that a doctor must 'Refrain from denying treatment to your patient because of a judgement based on discrimination.'[26]

A doctor is not an agent for another's intentions and motives but an autonomous practitioner who may choose whom she helps with her skills. This does not mean that doctors *never* work as agents for others – there are many doctors who work for non-medical organizations, such as insurance companies, and consider themselves loyal to those organizations. The point is that doctors who put their client's (be it an individual or an organization) interests above the guiding concerns of doctoring are no longer acting as good doctors. Unlike the conception of a good lawyer it is no part of the conception of a good doctor to act as an agent for a client or to be agnostic as to the moral value of that client's wishes.

Indeed, if a doctor puts loyalty to a non-medical institution above loyalty to medical ideals, they could be construed as a bad doctor. The case of David Spaulding is a perfect example of this. In 1956 David Spaulding sued John Zimmerman, the driver of a car that had been involved in an accident in which Spaulding, who had been a passenger, was severely injured. Zimmerman's insurance company sent a doctor in their employ to examine Spaulding. During the course of this examination, this doctor discovered that Spaulding had a life-threatening aortic aneurysm – a condition that Spaulding was unaware of. Instead of telling Spaulding or informing Spaulding's doctors, the doctor called Zimmerman's lawyer, who (along with the insurance company and the doctor) decided to conceal this information.[27] The doctor in this case clearly put his duty as an agent of the insurance company above his duty *as a doctor* to inform Spaulding that his life was in immediate danger. In a discussion of this case, Arthur Isak Applbaum argues that this doctor failed to act as a good doctor and violated important tenets of the medical profession: 'On this view, one says in response to the insurance company doctor that he cannot coherently claim to be a doctor and then fail to attend in the right way to Spaulding's condition. No agreement with the insurance company or Zimmerman ... can release the doctor from the obligations of his natural role.'[28]

The importance of retaining professional autonomy when employed by an institution is noted in codes of medical ethics. For example, the Australian Medical Association's Code of Ethics states that: 'If you work in a practice or institution, place your professional duties and responsibilities to your patients above the commercial interests of the owners or others who work within these practices.'[29]

If a doctor does act as an agent for an institution and places that institution's interests above those of her patients, then she is no longer a good doctor. However, in the case of lawyers, putting the clients' interests first is part of what it means to be a good lawyer. A lawyer who failed to do this would be a bad lawyer. It is worth noting that when Spaulding discovered the deception he successfully appealed the settlement that he had made with Zimmerman. However the court that granted the appeal also argued that Zimmerman's *lawyer* was acting within his professional rights. The court claimed that there was 'no canon of ethics or legal obligation' that required the lawyer to inform Spaulding of his condition.[30] Zimmerman's lawyer did what a zealous advocate should do despite the fact that his actions posed a significant threat to Spaulding's life.[31]

Unlike a lawyer's normal professional duties, a doctor's normal professional duties are unlikely to involve pursuit of unjust or immoral causes. The legitimate exercise of a doctor's professional duties does not and should not result in the harming of the interests of other unwilling individuals. If such harm occurs it is most likely to arise when doctors are putting the interests of their employers above the ideals of the medical profession.

In summary, the lawyer's role involves quite different kinds of special permissions from the doctor's. The special moral permissions claimed by lawyers, and indeed by other professionals who act as agents (for example, engineers) are far more likely to conflict with broad-based morality than the doctor's special permissions, and are more serious because they involve the likelihood of harm to non-consenting individuals. Can these kinds of permissions be successfully grounded by appeal to the guiding ideals of the legal profession? We should be cautious about accepting this justification at face value. After all, there have been many professionals who justified serious violations of ordinary moral standards by claiming that such violations were necessary for the pursuit of health, or justice.[32] So we must ask if appealing solely to the profession's goals is the best way of grounding such permissions. How persuasive are claims that the pursuit of professional goals should outweigh important competing impartial moral considerations?

Grounding moral permissions

The problem of justifying special moral permissions such as those claimed by lawyers, and the question of how best to characterize the relationship between professional norms and those of ordinary morality are probably the most debated issues in professional ethics. Many writers argue that subsuming professional ethics entirely into broad-based morality fails to make sense of the role-specific obligations and considerations that emerge from and partly define professional life. While most writers reject the strictly relativist approach that would make professional norms entirely separate from broad-based moral norms[33] many still argue that professionals face moral issues that are unique to the professional context.

It is argued that in order to carry out their professional duties effectively professionals are justified in limiting the scope of their moral outlook to a more specific role-based morality.[34] In *Virtue Ethics and Professional Roles,* Justin Oakley and Dean Cocking offer an argument for such role-restricted moral reasoning based on a comparison with friendship. In the following section, I argue that this approach fails to justify role-restricted moral reasoning.

Professional roles and friendship

How does the example of friendship illuminate the morality of professional relationships? It is helpful to consider this question in relation to the concept of a regulative ideal. Oakley and Cocking define a regulative ideal as follows: 'To say that an agent has a regulative ideal is to say that they have internalized a certain conception of correctness or excellence, in such a way that they are able to adjust their motivation and conduct so that it conforms – or at least does not conflict – with that standard ... A regulative ideal is thus an internalized normative disposition to direct one's actions and alter one's motivations in certain ways.'[35]

Given this definition, the regulative ideal of friendship is the conception of the character traits, motives, and acts that best promote the aims of friendship. Good friends would guide their actions by reference to this ideal, and try to internalize it so that they are motivated to act in accordance (or not in conflict) with it.[36] What is of interest in the case of friendship is that the regulative ideal of friendship gives rise to agent-relative reasons for action. If I internalize the regulative ideal of friendship then as a good friend I should be governed by agent-relative concerns. My friends are valuable to *me* because they are *my* friends, not because having friends contributes to some agent-neutral good. Therefore the concept of being a good friend is agent-relative in a way that the regulative ideal of broad-based morality is not. So it is possible that being a good friend – being governed by the regulative ideal of friendship – might give rise to reasons for action that could conflict with the reasons for action arising from broad-based moral considerations. Furthermore, at times it may seem right that the reasons arising from friendship should override those arising from broad-based morality. Being a good friend might, within limits, mean that I violate certain broad-based moral values.[37]

Oakley and Cocking claim that professional relationships share both friendship's characteristic agent-relativity and the conflict with broad-based morality. As they explain: 'not only have both friendship and professional roles been thought to license departures from what impartialist ethical theory would ordinarily require of us, but friendship has been appealed to as a model to explain how such departures might be justified in professional life'.[38]

The strength in this comparison lies in the undeniable common-sense appeal of the belief that you might (and should) do things for your friend that you would not do for others. You might lie for your friend, for example, even though lying is normally morally wrong. It seems true that being a good friend sometimes requires being less than good, according to broad-based moral standards: 'True and good friends, that is, will have a motivational disposition which involves a preparedness to act for the friend, such that the claims of friendship will sometimes trump the maximization of agent-neutral value.'[39]

So our common-sense ideas of friendships agree with the claim that a good friendship generates agent-relative reasons for action that may, at least in some cases, legitimately override the demands of impartial morality.[40] According to Oakley and Cocking, this agent-relativity is also characteristic of professional relationships. Like a good friend, a good professional is expected to act *for* the sake of their client, not simply out of a regard for duty or consequences. Professional relationships, like friendships, generate agent-relative reasons for action that may sometimes override broad-based moral standards. The appropriate motives that govern both friendship and professional relationships are to a large extent agent-relative and so the value of these relationships is not best expressed as a function of agent-neutral value.[41]

However, Oakley and Cocking do think that just as there are limits to what we may do in the name of friendship, there are limits to how far the agent-relative reasons arising from professional relationships may override broad-based moral standards. The characteristic partiality of professional roles and the consequent departures from the demands of ordinary morality are justified only so far as they promote the profession's aims – aims that are justified under broad-based morality. So doctors are justified, under this account, in maintaining confidentiality even when doing so violates impartial moral considerations because confidentiality and trust are essential to promoting patient health.[42] However, as I noted earlier, a doctor would not be justified in maintaining confidentiality if doing so did not serve patient health and wellbeing.

While many of us might agree with Oakley and Cocking's claims about the nature and good of friendship, it is far from clear that the comparison with professional relationships succeeds. There are two main problems with the comparison. First, the conflict between friendship and broad-based morality is not a conflict between different kinds of *moral* reasons – it is a conflict between non-moral reasons (those generated by friendship) and moral reasons – between friendship and morality.[43] On the other hand the reasons for action arising from professional relationships and obligations are distinctly moral. Professionals claim special *moral* permission to give more weight to the reasons for action arising from professional relationships and duties than to those arising from broad-based morality. Professionals, it is argued, should be able to weigh moral values differently. The conflict between friendship and morality does not parallel the conflict between professional relationships and broad-based morality because it is a different kind of conflict. In the one case the non-moral demands of friendship can conflict with the demands of morality *per se*. In the other, professional special moral permissions can conflict with other moral demands – those arising from broad-based morality.

The second problem is identified by Dean Cocking and Jeanette Kennett. Cocking and Kennett agree that there are certain overt similarities between friendship and professional relationships and similarities in the conflict that might arise between these and the demands of broad-based morality: 'There are distinctive role-generated obligations and sensitivities across the range of roles in which we might engage. Important agent-relative attachments and loyalties develop in these contexts, such as to one's partner as a police officer or one's patients as a general practitioner ... which may on occasion bring us into conflict with some broadly accepted moral requirement.'[44]

Both professionals and good friends are motivated by a particularized concern for the needs and wellbeing of the client in one case and the friend in the other.[45] Cocking and Kennett argue, however, that the superficial similarities between the kinds of conflict that can arise from competing role-generated reasons and the reasons given by broad-based morality mask a fundamental difference between the reasons for action generated by friendship and those generated by professional roles.[46] The main difference lies in the kinds of motives that appropriately govern these roles.

Unlike friendship, the partiality characteristic of professional relationships is regulated not by feelings of affection but by the profession's overall goal. Professional partiality is justified only so long as it promotes a broad-based (usually impartial) moral good such as justice or health.[47] This means that a profession's regulative ideal is not agent-relative; it is a conception of professional excellence that best serves an agent-*neutral* good and that gives rise to agent-neutral reasons for action. On the other hand, friendship's regulative ideal gives rise to agent-relative reasons for action. My friend is valuable to me not because of the connection between friendship and the promotion of an impartial moral good, but simply because she is my friend. However, a professional's relationship with their client is not agent-relative in the same sense. As a professional it is my duty to serve my client's interests *regardless* of my feelings for them. The value of my relationship with my client is not a value that is derived from its being relative to *me*. Instead, its value is derived from the contribution that it (and my partiality and particularized concern) makes to the overall good the profession claims to serve.

This means that while friendship's partiality and agent-relativity is intrinsically valuable, this is not the case with professional partiality. As Cocking and Kennett point out, professional partiality is *extrinsically* valuable. It is valuable because of how it promotes excellence in the proper performance of the professional role and thereby furthers the ends of the profession.[48] If professional partiality for clients were shown to inhibit or undermine professional goals, then such concern would not be considered valuable (or not in the professional context at least), and would be actively discouraged.

Of course professional relationships can be very valuable to both professionals and their clients. As a doctor I may develop a friendly relationship with a particular patient that is characterized by particularized concern and feelings of affection and regard. Such a relationship may have great personal importance for me. But the value arising from such a relationship is neither central to nor necessary for the professional relationship. Of course *some* care and concern is essential for a good doctor–patient relationship. I would not be a good doctor if I was callous and cold-hearted towards my patients. But the appropriate extent of that concern is strictly limited by my professional goals. Being too empathetic would undermine my ability to do my job well. Being too uncaring would have the same effect. As a good doctor I should try to cultivate a position between those two extremes in order to better serve my patient's wellbeing. However, feelings of care and concern for a *particular* patient that go beyond professional empathy are not central or even necessary for the doctor–patient relationship, and so the value of that particular relationship to me is distinct from the value of the doctor–patient relationship considered more generally. Agent-relative feelings of affection may arise out my professional relationship with my patients – the fact that they are *mine* might ground such feelings – but these feelings are constrained by the boundaries of the doctor–patient relationship. As Kennett and Cocking point out, it would probably be considered a professional *failure* if I became too attached to such relationships – my professional, objective judgement about the best interests of my patient might be undermined by my affection for them.[49]

Therefore the kind of partiality a doctor is reasonably permitted to engage in and still remain within the bounds of a professional relationship is quite limited: 'tightly governed by the guiding concerns appropriate to her role as a doctor'.[50] The aspects of this kind of doctor–patient relationship that qualify as intrinsically valuable are aspects which are distinct from the professional relationship, and which *should* be distinct if the professional relationship is not to be compromised.

A further dissimilarity between friendship and professional relationships lies in the manner in which these relationships are entered into and ended. A professional's relationship with her client is a governed by quite different 'acceptance and terminating conditions' from those of friendship.[51] The professional enters ('accepts') the relationship with the client as a contract: she undertakes to provide a certain service to the client to the best of her ability. The relationship is terminated when her services are no longer required. The relationship between client and professional is 'maximally structured' – strongly governed by the respective social roles of the participants and by strict legal and conventional guidelines – in stark contrast to the loose ('minimally structured') nature of friendship.[52] Unlike professional relationships, friendships are, as Cocking and Kennett put it: 'voluntary, egalitarian, and *open-ended* in a way that these other social and professional roles are not'.[53]

Finally, the conditions that define a professional relationship have little to do with whether the professional feels 'particularized concern' for her client. In many professional relationships the professional and her client never meet (engineers, architects, accountants, and lawyers may be in this situation), and the client may not be an individual but an organization or corporation. The professional role requires impartiality in the degree and kind of partiality appropriately shown towards clients; a good professional should treat each client with the *same* degree and *same* kind of partiality. Arthur Isak Applbaums' term 'role-relative'[54] better describes the motives and feelings that appropriately govern professional roles than the term 'agent-relative'.[55] Applbaum points out that: 'The professions characteristically put forth *role-relative* but *person-neutral* prescriptions: the lawyer faces the role-relative prescription of zealous advocacy, and so is obligated to serve unsavoury clients and their unsavoury ends with a zeal that, outside of the role, would be wrong. But she is to exclude completely reasons for action that might otherwise flow from the particularities of her person: her extra-professional projects, values, commitments, relationships.'[56]

A professional conducts her relationship with her clients (whether they are individuals or organizations) according to a set of standards or governing conditions relative to her role. These standards are justified as long as they do not violate important broad-based moral constraints (such as the client's autonomy or rights) and as long as they enable the professional to best fulfil her professional goals. It is unclear then why such standards could be considered *agent*-relative, given that they apply not to the agent *qua* agent but to the agent *qua* occupier of a particular role. Any occupant of that role would be subject to the same governing conditions. A professional relationship is governed not by *agent*-relative feelings of affection but by *role*-relative concerns, and the value of such concerns (unlike the value of friendship) can be captured by impartial moral considerations. It is impartial moral considerations that justify the profession's existence, status as a profession, and the level of concern appropriate in professional relationships. Any occupant of a specified role, be it a professional or an occupational role (doctor, lawyer, car mechanic) has role-relative permission to perform certain kinds of actions that would be impermissible if performed by someone outside the role; impermissible not because of the agent-relativity of the role relationship, but because of impartial moral considerations about how best to protect the client's wellbeing and serve the ends of the profession. Not being a car mechanic or a doctor means that I do not have permission to tamper with my friend's car without her permission, just as I do not have permission to perform open-heart surgery.

This difference between professional partiality and friendship undermines Oakley and Cocking's argument. They use the comparison with friendship to draw certain conclusions about the reasons for action that govern professional roles and professional relationships. They argue that the reasons for action generated by professional relationships (like the reasons for action generated by friendship) are agent-relative, intrinsically valuable, and in some cases can justifiably override the demands of impartial morality. But, as I have argued, the parallel with friendship is an illegitimate one. There is no reason to suppose that professional partiality and the partiality characteristic of friendship are agent-relative and intrinsically valuable in the same way. There is therefore no *prima facie* reason to believe that the reasons for action arising from professional partiality should override the demands of impartial morality when the two conflict. The claim that professional relationships generate reasons for action that might justifiably override the demands of impartial morality therefore needs further argument, given that such partiality is importantly distinct from the partiality characteristic of friendship.

Professional morality as part of broad-based morality

Comparing relationships such as friendship with professional relationships does not succeed in grounding professionals' special moral permissions. At this point the claim that broad-based morality cannot encompass professional special moral permissions seems doubtful. The example of patient confidentiality is easily explained by reference to the goal of medicine and can be comfortably accommodated by broad-based morality. Yet the special permissions claimed by lawyers are harder to explain in reference to broad-based morality and the goal of the legal profession. Lawyers can do many things that seem to conflict with the goal of promoting justice: they can pursue cases that are legal but patently unjust, they can impugn witnesses' credibility, and they can (and some argue should) do everything they can to defend their client even if there is a strong likelihood that their client is guilty. In fact, these aspects of the legal profession have prompted some writers to deny that lawyers should be able to do such things precisely because these actions fail so extravagantly to promote justice.[57] The fact that lawyers might be *legally* permitted to engage in tactics that seem very far from promoting justice does not mean that such tactics are morally justifiable or that they promote the ends of the legal profession. An appeal to the ideals of the law or indeed of any profession as a justification for gross violations of broad-based moral standards should be treated with scepticism. If special moral permissions are to legitimately override competing moral concerns they must be shown to be genuinely necessary for the pursuit of professional ideals. There needs to be a further argument to support the claim that such permissions should override important broad-based moral standards.

Some writers deny that there is any legitimate justification for professional special moral permissions and deny that there should be any moral distinction between professional demands and the demands of ordinary morality. If maintaining patient confidentiality in the example given earlier is not justified under broad-based morality then it is not justified, full stop. Supporters of this theory argue that professional standards must be based on broad-based ethical theories and that professionals should be guided by such theories when acting in their professional lives.[58] Robert Veatch, for example, claims that: 'the use of a professionally generated ethic ... makes no sense in theory or in practice.'[59]

Richard Wasserstrom argues that while role-based morality certainly makes moral reasoning within a professional context easier, simplicity of application is not a sufficient reason to justify the creation of an overriding role morality.[60] He points out that: 'The behaviours that are justified by or within a role do, it is conceded, come within the domain of morality. Even if role-restricted reasoning makes good moral sense, it is not at all clear what, on moral grounds, the role and its redescription of moral outlook should come to ... More importantly, I think the burden of argument and proof rests upon those who seek to justify the differential consideration and treatment of members of the moral community that takes place as a result of role-defined reasoning.'[61]

Why, he argues, should we accept the claim that role morality gives a strong reason to override the demands of impartial morality in either the weight given to the interests involved or the weight given to the harm caused by professional acts?[62] To allow role morality to override impartial morality can lead to the justification of morally suspect acts and what Gerald Postema calls the narrowing of the professional's moral 'vision', which can lead to the neglect of important broad-based principles.[63] The Tuskegee syphilis study demonstrates the serious consequences that can result when professionals are so focused on their professional goals that they neglect broad-based moral considerations altogether. The study lasted from 1932 to 1972 and involved the monitoring of more than 400 African-American syphilitic men in order to study the course of the disease. The men were not told they had syphilis and were not given treatment when an effective one was discovered in 1947.[64] The study involved hundreds of doctors, nurses, and other health care practitioners, none of whom saw fit to question the ethics of not treating the men, even though it was clear that they would die of the disease and would pass syphilis on to their sexual partners as well. The goal of 'contributing to medical research' was taken to override all other moral considerations. This case is illustrative of the problems that can arise when professionals are encouraged to adopt a role-differentiated moral outlook that gives more weight to professional concerns than those of broad-based morality. While in theory professional concerns are not meant to override very important broad-based moral considerations, in practice they can be seen as overriding simply because professionals have learned to view them that way – to view their professional goals as all-important. The result is a distorted version of professional detachment.

Of course some professional detachment is necessary for good professional functioning, but it must be strictly regulated. For doctors and other health care professionals, for example, a degree of detachment is required because of the emotional (and sometimes physical) distress caused by dealing with death, dying and illness. Such desensitization is a normal and necessary reaction to the environment in which doctors work. But this detachment is the mean between being overcome by one's emotional responses and not having any emotional responses at all – doctors must try to find a balance between over-sensitivity and hard-heartedness.

However, there is a significant difference between becoming detached from the *emotionally* troubling aspects of one's work and becoming detached from the *morally* troubling aspects of one's work. A good doctor attempts to become emotionally detached, not morally detached. She attempts to detach her feelings from her work, but not her moral judgement or moral sense. Some emotional detachment does not necessarily indicate anything problematic about the mindset of the doctor who develops it, but we don't want doctors to be so detached they cease to react at all to their patients' distress and illness, and we don't want health care professionals to become *morally* desensitized to the issues that arise from their work. As in the Tuskegee syphilis case, the results of such moral detachment can be truly chilling. This case is illustrative of the intuitive belief that professionals might need to develop *more* moral sensitivity and moral awareness rather than less because the consequences of moral blindness can be so serious. The danger in adopting a role-differentiated moral outlook is that important broad-based moral considerations are not only weighed differently but overlooked altogether.

Given these concerns and given how important it is that professionals are attentive to broad-based moral considerations, I argue that professional morality is best conceived of as a *subset* of broad-based morality and that professional actions should not be evaluated differently simply because they are undertaken in a professional context. The professional context serves to *focus* broad-based moral principles in a very specific context – quite possibly a context unique to the profession – but the professional context does not provide a *prima facie* reason to supersede those principles.[65] This view of professional morality avoids the not inconsiderable danger of professional moral 'blindness' and avoids the danger of internally justified special moral permissions. Special moral permissions do not represent a distinct class of moral reasons that can override 'ordinary morality'. Instead they are context- and role-dependent permissions that are justified only so far as they contribute to a profession's guiding ideals, and only so far as those guiding ideals serve important human needs. Such permissions may well conflict with competing moral considerations because there is simply no way to avoid all conflict within morality. In such (inevitable) cases of conflict, professionals sometimes have special permission to weigh the considerations differently to a non-professional (doctors can give more weight to confidentiality, for example) if doing so genuinely contributes to the profession's goals, but these professional special moral permissions are not a *different* form of morality.

Conclusion

Given my view of the basis of special moral permissions, it might appear that there would be no room in my argument for a distinctive professional morality. This is not the case. As I noted above, professional relationships, obligations, and duties can present professionals with unique moral issues and situations. Because of this it is important for professionals to understand and prepare for the kinds of moral issues they are likely to face in their professional lives. A professional morality can provide this guidance. But which moral theory best captures the needs of a professional ethic? In the next chapter I argue that Oakley and Cocking's virtue ethics approach provides the most useful ethical guidance for professionals. I show that, compared to a competing dispositional rule-consequentialist approach to professional ethics, virtue ethics is particularly well suited to dealing with the relationships, responsibilities and obligations that are generated by and unique to professions and professional roles. The central role of reflective moral agency in the virtue ethics' character-based approach is not only compatible with Kantian views about virtuous action (and indeed with any plausible ethical theory) but can encompass both the impartial moral good of professional ideals and can provide a useful way of generating distinctive moral standards by which professional conduct and professionals' moral character may be judged.[66] Furthermore, virtue ethics avoids the partial-compliance problem that a rule-consequentialist approach to professional ethics must overcome. Virtue ethics is therefore well suited to clarifying the idea of professional special moral permissions constrained by and contained within broad-based morality and it is well suited for deriving the character traits that are most appropriate for professionals in light of their professional goals.[67]

2
Virtue Ethics and Professional Roles

The virtue ethics approach to professional morality is most fully developed by Justin Oakley and Dean Cocking in *Virtue Ethics and Professional Roles*. Using the Aristotelian account of virtue ethics – an account that places central importance on the exercise of reflective moral agency[1] – this approach provides a useful way of delineating professional responsibilities and professional morality. Aristotelian virtue ethics is particularly well suited to professional ethics because it ties virtuous behaviour to the concept of good functioning in particular roles. Oakley and Cocking claim that 'virtue ethics' teleological approach to right action in terms of good functioning relative to appropriate ends makes it especially well placed to capture the special roles and sensitivities of particular professions'.[2]

The Aristotelian approach to professional role morality is a two-tier approach: professions are defined by their connection to excellence in human flourishing – *eudaimonia* – and professional virtues are then derived from the profession's regulative ideal; the conception of excellence in professional functioning. First, a profession must provide a service that addresses an important human need, a need essential or at least very important for a flourishing human life. Second, the particular professional roles, actions and character traits that professionals should adopt are then determined or regulated by that goal. The good professional in a good professional role would develop traits and virtues appropriate to the promotion of the ends of the profession.[3] So the regulative ideal is used to delineate both good professional roles and good professional character. As I will demonstrate, the regulative ideal also sets the limits of appropriate professional behaviour, indicating not only when professionals should provide their services but also when they should refuse. Professionals sometimes have a positive moral duty to refuse their professional services when providing them would violate important professional ideals.

Virtue ethics and dispositional rule-consequentialism

Before describing the virtue ethics approach to professional roles, I will consider a plausible character-based alternative: dispositional rule-consequentialism. Brad Hooker defines dispositional rule-consequentialism as the view that: 'accepting rules is a matter of having certain desires and dispositions ... an act is morally right if and only if it is called for by the set of desires and dispositions the having of which by everybody would result in at least as good consequences judged impartially as any other'.[4]

Under this view, an act is morally right if it conforms to the set of general rules or dispositions that lead to the best consequences if they are accepted by all or most people, and it is morally wrong if it fails to conform to those rules or dispositions.[5]

Applying this theory to professional ethics would have the following result. Rather than appealing to good consequences in a general sense, we would consider what counts as good consequences in the professional context. An ideal (or optimific, as Hooker puts it) set of professional dispositions would be those dispositions the having of which by all or most professionals would best promote the ends of the profession, where the profession serves an important moral good by consequentialist standards.

At first glance it is clear that a dispositional rule-consequentialist approach and a virtue ethics approach to professional ethics would be likely to reach many of the same conclusions regarding what counts as good professional behaviour and good professional character. For example, both approaches would recommend trustworthiness as a virtue appropriate to doctors, in light of the ends of the medical profession. However, important differences between the two approaches indicate that virtue ethics is the more appropriate approach to apply to professional ethics. First, rule-consequentialism, as an ethical theory, must overcome what is known as the partial-compliance objection. Hooker describes the objection as follows: 'Following a moral code that would be optimal in a world in which everyone accepted it can be (in Brandt's words) "counterproductive or useless" in the real world where there is actually only partial social acceptance of that code.'[6]

While, as Hooker points out, there may be different interpretations of this objection, the most plausible (and most serious) interpretation claims that the rule-consequentialist might be committed to following a rule in a situation where doing so causes great harm because of others' non-compliance.[7] Given that we live in a world where any set of ideal rules or dispositions will only ever be partly complied with, this is a serious concern. Addressing this concern is a task that rule-consequentialists must overcome if rule-consequentialism is to be a viable ethical theory, let alone a viable approach to professional ethics. One solution could be to 'build in' exceptions to general rules in order to cover cases such as that mentioned above. However J. J. C. Smart argues that the practice of making exceptions to rules in cases where following the rule would lead to very bad consequences (either through others' non-compliance or for other reasons) leads rule-consequentialism to collapse into act-consequentialism.[8] Hooker has a different concern. He considers Richard Brandt's solution of adding in a 'standing disposition to prevent great harm'[9] that might override the standing motivation to obey moral rules in some cases, and worries that this solution would lead to rule-consequentialism being excessively demanding, a problem that is a common criticism of conse-quentialist theories in general.[10] The difficulty in overcoming the par-tial-compliance objection in a way that is not excessively demanding and that does not effectively collapse into act-consequentialism pro-vides a strong reason to prefer the Aristotelian virtue ethics approach to professional ethics.

A second reason for preferring the virtue ethics approach to profes-sional ethics is how the virtues are defined. Under a dispositional rule-consequentialist approach, the ideal set of dispositions that a professional would cultivate would be derived from considering the dispositions that would best promote the ends of the profession were they adopted by all or most professionals. Whether a particular disposition (say, the disposi-tion to be loyal to one's clients) counts as a professional virtue is there-fore based on considering the consequences that would follow if most or all professionals adopted the character trait in question. However, under the Aristotelian virtue ethics approach the criteria of a virtue are inde-pendent from judgements about the consequences that would ensue if all or most professionals were virtuous. Instead, as will become apparent, the criteria of a virtue derive from a consideration of what is needed for human functioning and, more specifically, good professional func-tioning. So the first step in deriving a set of virtues is not to ask, what virtues would bring about the best consequences were all or most profes-sionals to possess them? Instead, we ask what constitutes excellent human functioning and then what constitutes good professional func-tioning in light of the aims of the profession. This, in the Aristotelian approach, leads to the centrality of practical wisdom as the capacity that must ground all the virtues. As Rosalind Hursthouse explains: 'they [the concepts of the individual virtues] are interconnected ... by the role that *phronesis* or moral wisdom – which enables its possessor to grasp the correct application of concepts such as *good* and *evil, worthwhile, trivial* – plays in each of them'.[11]

As I demonstrate in this chapter, in the Aristotelian approach the importance of practical wisdom is crucial in determining which dispositions are virtues and which are not, independent of which dispositions bring about the best consequences. Embodying the virtues therefore means different things under the dispositional rule-consequentialist view and the Aristotelian view. Being loyal, for example, need not be reflective loyalty under the dispositional rule-consequentialist view (indeed it is not clear whether the dispositional rule-consequentialist approach can provide a clear definition of what loyalty actually entails in relation to the agent's motivations). Whether loyalty should be reflective would depend on whether reflective loyalty would bring about the best consequences if most or all people possessed it. Depending on how this empirical question is answered, it may well turn out that blind unthinking loyalty is actually better from a dispositional rule-consequentialist perspective than reflective loyalty. However, under the Aristotelian account only one kind of loyalty would count as virtuous: loyalty governed by practical wisdom. Any other form of loyalty, even if it leads to as good or better consequences than reflective loyalty, would simply not be virtuous.

Given the high stakes involved in military professional activity, I argue that the Aristotelian account is more appropriate as an account of professional virtues. It evades both the partial-compliance problem and it grounds the criteria of a virtue on a concept of good human and good professional functioning in which reflective moral agency plays a central and defining role. This avoids the possibility that unreflective dispositions could be virtues.[12]

Aristotelian virtue ethics[13]

What are the virtues? According to Aristotle the moral virtues are derived from 'what we need, or what we are, *qua* human beings.'[14] The virtues are states of character connected to, and indeed partly constitutive of, good human flourishing – *eudaimonia*.[15] Human flourishing refers to the distinctive features of human nature – the distinctive ends and functions (the *telos*) of human life.[16] Excellent functioning must relate to the ends being sought. For example, the end of medicine is health, and a good medical practitioner aims at excellence in pursuit of this end. Similarly, good human functioning aims at the production of happiness.[17] What is necessary for good human functioning and the production of happiness? Aristotle argues that the distinctive characteristics of good human functioning are not 'the life of nutrition and growth' (which is shared by plants and animals) but the exercise of our rational capacities, as the capacity for reason is distinctive to human beings. He claims that 'The function of a man is an activity of the soul which follows or implies a rational principle.' So a flourishing human life requires the 'good and noble performance' of actions that imply the rational principle.[18]

This concept of human flourishing is largely objective; it is independent from what we might think is good for us and what we might happen to desire. It does not merely refer to what brings us pleasure. Instead, *eudaimonia* refers to a broad sense of flourishing, a view of what counts as a good life for a human being that is largely independent of an individual's conception of the good.[19] A virtue, then, is a state of character that contributes to living a good distinctively human life, and a vice is a character trait that inhibits such flourishing.[20] Given that extremes of character and behaviour (such as bad temper, vanity, depression, meanness, and crippling shyness) are detrimental to good functioning, the virtues are generally states that pave a way between such extremes of feelings or attitudes.[21] For example, the virtue of pride is a mean between vanity and excess humility, and the virtue of courage is a mean between confidence and fear.[22]

But not just any character state or personal quality counts as a virtue, even if it does contribute to a good human life. To understand this claim requires an understanding of the connection between virtue and practical wisdom – *phronesis*. Far from being unthinking emotional dispositions, the virtues are manifestations of rational deliberation: they are expressive of the agent's voluntary choice. As Aristotle says; 'Moral virtue implies that the action is done by choice; the object of choice is the result of previous deliberation.'[23] The virtues do involve an emotional aspect but it is an emotional aspect that is felt correctly. As Rosalind Hursthouse explains, the virtues are felt 'on the *right* occasions, towards the *right* people or objects, for the *right* reasons', and to know when such emotional dispositions are correct requires practical wisdom.[24] Christine Korsgaard describes the kind of deliberation that underlies this view of choice. Chosen actions, she explains, are ones that result from rational deliberation about whether an action is good, when the concept of the good is also a result of deliberation.[25] Richard Sorabji makes the same point: practical wisdom requires deliberation of two kinds, deliberation about the correct action in a particular case, and deliberation about what is required in a more general sense from the conception of the good life.[26] In other words, *phronesis* refers not simply to the ability to deliberate about the best means to achieve one's immediate aims; it also involves the ability to deliberate about what things (pursuits, behaviours, etc.) best lend themselves to living a good life.[27] These two kinds of deliberation are connected: 'It [practical deliberation] enables a man, in the light of his conception of the good life in general, to perceive ... more generally what virtue and *to kalon* require of him in that particular case, and it instructs him to act accordingly.'[28]

This means that our chosen actions reveal our character because they reflect our conception of the good.[29] But does practical wisdom have to be part of a virtue? Why can't the virtues be *any* emotional state that promotes a good life?

The reason for the importance of practical wisdom lies in human beings' distinct nature. Adult humans have the capacity for reason. This means that we have the capacity to deliberate about the nature of a good life and about what actions would promote that good. The exercise of this capacity for practical wisdom is what makes us distinctively human and it is only through exercising this capacity that we truly act as human beings, rather than as animals. So good human functioning involves, and is partly constituted by, the exercise of rational deliberation. Without such deliberation we cannot be said to act from choice and our actions cannot be virtuous even if they are actions that a virtuous person would perform. To be virtuous requires more than doing the right actions; it requires acting from the right state – from choice.[30]

The claim that the virtues must be manifestations of practical wisdom makes sense of two common intuitions we have about moral responsibility. The first is that we cannot be held morally responsible for actions or traits over which we have no control, even if they contribute to our living a good life. So being incredibly good-looking will certainly make it easier for me to make friends, and friendship is certainly part of a good life. However, my fabulous bone structure is not something that I can be morally praised for because it is not a manifestation of my choice. I did not become fabulously good-looking through exercising practical wisdom, and so being good-looking does not reflect on my moral character either positively or negatively.

Similarly, I might be born with a particularly benevolent temperament. I just happen to love giving to homeless people, caring for animals, and volunteering for charities. Yet this naturally kind disposition is not sufficient for me to have the virtue of benevolence. Instead, my benevolence is what Aristotle calls a *natural virtue*. Such natural traits are valuable because they can be trained in the right way, but in and of themselves they are not real virtues because they do not arise from any understanding or deliberation – and this means they can easily be led astray.[31] So while the natural virtues are good to have because they form positive 'raw material' that can be guided correctly and that can make it easier to do the right thing, they *must* be used wisely. Without wise guidance, they can be all too easily corrupted.

Furthermore, if I act thoughtlessly from such natural inclination then I am not acting in a distinctly human way: 'For both children and brutes have these natural dispositions, but without reason they are evidently hurtful.'[32] Children and puppies might be naturally kind, trusting, and sweet tempered, but they are not virtuous because, Aristotle claims, they lack the deliberative capacity necessary to make a choice.[33] Children and puppies lack practical wisdom and so they are unable to form a conception of the good life by which to judge when kindness is appropriate.

This distinction between acting from inclination and acting from reason makes sense of a second intuition we commonly hold about the attribution of moral responsibility. Even when they do act kindly or loyally, animals and children (and perhaps the severely mentally impaired) do not act as moral agents: they are not morally responsible for what they do. Animals and children may sometimes act in accordance with virtue but it does not make sense to say that they are virtuous or that they are morally responsible for their actions. The reason for this is the same reason why they are not responsible for their actions: they lack the requisite capacity for choice. They may act voluntarily, but because they lack practical wisdom they cannot act from choice because choice requires 'rational deliberation and thought'. Their actions are the result of unreflective dispositions.[34]

Kantians can also endorse a virtue ethics approach to moral action. Aristotle's definition of virtuous actions is very similar to Kant's discussion of moral action in *The Groundwork of the Metaphysics of Morals*. While there are important differences between them, both Aristotle and Kant agree that natural dispositions cannot be called morally good unless they are governed by wisdom or what Kant calls the good will.[35] As Kant writes: 'Understanding, wit, judgement and the like, whatever such talents of mind may be called, or courage, resolution, and perseverance in one's plans, as qualities of temperament, are undoubtedly good and desirable for many purposes, but they can also be extremely evil and harmful if the will is not good.'[36]

This is strikingly similar to Aristotle's comments on natural virtue. Kant and Aristotle both place great importance on the role of rationality in virtuous action. Korsgaard describes the similarities between them: 'Aristotle and Kant both believe that in human beings, reason can be practical ... Both of them believe that the moral value of an action is a function of the way in which it is chosen.'[37]

Hursthouse also demonstrates that for both Aristotle and Kant it is the exercise of reason that makes us truly human. According to Kant, humans' capacity for rationality means that we are the embodiment of the moral law: 'the will of a rational being, in which … the highest and unconditional good can be found'.[38] So just like the virtuous Aristotelian, the virtuous Kantian does not act solely from inclination. Acts done simply from inclination, however amiable, have no moral value; they are not acts of a moral agent. Natural sympathy and benevolence alone are insufficient for virtuous action.[39] For Kant as for Aristotle, the problem is that natural sympathies are unreliable – compassion can be misguided, sympathy can fail.[40] While these traits are useful – '[they are] conducive to this good will itself and can make its work much easier' – they must be directed by the good will or 'they can become extremely evil'.[41] If I act from inclination my actions have no moral value even if they are in conformity with duty, because I am not acting from recognition of the moral law.[42] My actions do not involve the exercise of my capacity for reason – the capacity that is essential for moral agency.

For both Kantians and Aristotelians therefore, virtuous action requires not merely the possession but the exercise of reflective moral agency.[43] Possessing the capacity to reflect on our actions makes us moral agents, but it only through exercising that capacity that we can act virtuously. Indeed, the crucial role of the capacity for reflective moral agency in moral responsibility, moral agency, and the practice of praising and blaming, is recognized by many writers on moral responsibility. For example, Randolph Clarke argues that 'in order to be a morally responsible agent, one must be capable of appreciating and acting on moral reasons'.[44] This connection between responsibility and the ability to rationally reflect on one's reasons for action and to act according to one's judgement is also central to our everyday conceptions of agency and responsibility. Karen Jones describes the normative conception of moral agency as involving: 'capacities to step back from any actional impulse and inquire whether the desire really reflects anything choiceworthy in the action … to be able to respond to reasons as reasons, an agent requires critical reflective ability, dispositions to bring that ability to bear when needed, and dispositions to have the results of such reflection bear on their behaviour'.[45]

The conception of reflective moral agency that is central to Kantian and Aristotelian accounts of virtuous action is therefore compatible with a broad range of ethical theories.

In summary, the essential features of a virtue are as follows. First, a virtue is a character state that promotes human flourishing. Second, as has become clear from the discussion of Kant and Aristotle, a virtue is not just an emotional disposition; it is a manifestation of rational deliberation. Even emotions such as kindness that are conducive to a good life must be guided by wisdom if they are to be virtuous. The exercise of practical deliberation is partly constitutive of excellent human functioning and so being virtuous involves, by definition, rational deliberation about when one should act and how one should act. The virtues are therefore intrinsically valuable not simply because they are expressions of emotions or dispositions, but because they involve the best forms of human functioning.

Having established the meaning of a virtue, how does this definition apply to the concept of professional virtues? Oakley and Cocking base their virtue ethics approach to professional roles around the concept of a profession's regulative ideal.

The regulative ideal of professional roles

In the virtue ethics approach, a profession's regulative ideal is the conception of excellent professional functioning that best promotes the ends of the profession. This is a tiered approach. Professions contribute to human flourishing by providing a service essential to people's wellbeing, and then the regulative ideal incorporates the ideal roles, practices, character traits, and behaviours that best promote the ends of the profession. For example, the end of the legal profession is justice – an important human need. As such, the legal profession is a good profession. The role of lawyer is necessary to promote the ends of the legal profession, and so the regulative ideal tells us that the role itself is a morally good role under this account.[46] A profession is justified if it serves an important human need – one necessary for excellence in human functioning. The profession's regulative ideal is then contained within that larger concept of good human functioning.

The regulative ideal of a profession is not solely determined by how the profession contributes to human flourishing. A profession's goals must be acceptable and indeed morally admirable by the standards of broad-based morality. Professional activities in pursuit of those goals must be constrained by important broad-based moral standards: 'actions in the professional context are not immune from broad-based moral values, such as justice and respect for personal autonomy'.[47] Professionals do not have free rein in how they serve the ends of their profession, even if their profession serves an important human need. The medical research undertaken by the Nazis certainly was intended to serve the goals of medicine, yet experimenting on unwilling patients violates important broad-based moral standards and for that reason (amongst many others) it is not part of what a good doctor should do. A profession's regulative ideal therefore incorporates many important broad-based moral standards which act as side-constraints on the kinds of acts in which professionals can legitimately engage. The regulative ideal will not simply be a conception of professional excellence independent from broad-based moral ideals. It will be informed and constrained by such ideals.

How should a profession's regulative ideal guide the behaviour of professionals?

Once part of a good profession that contributes to human flourishing, a good professional should strive to achieve excellence in professional functioning; the standard set by the regulative ideal. The regulative ideal guides the professional in her professional activities. Rather than appealing to a broad conception of virtuous behaviour, the professional can be guided by a role-specific conception of virtue.[48] A good lawyer, for example, need not merely appeal to what a good person would do when deciding how to behave in a professional context. Instead, she should be guided by a conception of the 'good lawyer': a standard of excellence (involving character traits, behaviours, attitudes, etc.) that best enables her to serve justice. Such a conception is normative: it guides her behaviour and motivations in specific ways that best fit the conception of the good lawyer.[49] But this conception of excellence need not be always foremost in her mind. Ideally, a lawyer would have internalized the conception in such a way that it guided her behaviour and motives so that she became disposed to act in ways consistent with the ideal. As Oakley and Cocking explain; 'A regulative ideal can guide us in our actions, without becoming one of our *purposes* in acting.'[50]

Because a profession's regulative ideal sets limits on appropriate professional behaviour, the concept of a regulative ideal governing professional actions and roles also makes sense of the idea of 'professional integrity', a concept that has important implications for when professionals might justifiably refuse to provide their services, a point I explore in section 5 of this chapter.

In summary, the concept of a professional regulative ideal serves two main functions. It gives an account of what constitutes a morally good profession, and it then allows some distance between the demands of everyday morality and the standards of professional excellence – the responsibilities and obligations that properly guide the actions of professionals within their professional roles. Once the regulative ideal is determined (and fulfils the requirements stated above), professionals are then justified, according to this account, in using that ideal (rather than just broad-based or impartial moral principles) to govern their actions and determine what kind of character they should develop. For example, a doctor might appeal to a conception of serving patient health when deciding whether or not to inform a patient of a distressing diagnosis. He need not appeal to impartial moral concerns to derive an answer. Instead of asking 'What would a good person do?' he can ask himself what action would best serve medicine's regulative ideal: 'What would a good *doctor* do?' Telling the patient the diagnosis is the appropriate answer to this question. Furthermore, by not withholding information that the patient needs to make decisions about her future, the doctor also respects her autonomy. This example shows how the regulative ideal can function to guide action within certain side-constraints imposed by autonomy and the importance of consent.

   Just as the concept of human flourishing gives rise to the moral virtues that best promote excellence in human functioning, so the regulative ideal of a profession is used to derive a set of professional character traits best suited to promoting excellence in professional functioning.

Professional virtues

Oakley and Cocking connect specific professional virtues to the ends of the profession. As we have seen, a profession's goals must contribute to human flourishing – it is this criterion that connects the concept of distinct professional virtues to the neo-Aristotelian notion of *eudaimonia* – and the professional virtues are then those traits that allow the professional to best serve the ends of the profession. They are traits that are partly constitutive of good professional functioning. As such they form part of the profession's regulative ideal. Oakley and Cocking use the example of the doctor to illustrate the process of deriving professional virtues from the goals of a profession.

The good doctor

According to Oakley and Cocking, a good doctor should strive to develop character traits and dispositions that will enable her to best serve the goal of promoting patient health: 'being a good doctor, on this account, involves having appropriate dispositions, emotions, and sensitivities in a medical context, as well as performing appropriate actions, and those elements of a doctor's character have ethical value in their own right, apart from the virtuous actions they issue in'.[51]

They argue that a good doctor would develop the following traits: beneficence (the disposition to focus on patients' psychophysical needs); truthfulness (serves patients' health by giving them the information they need to make informed decisions about their health); trustworthiness (helps patients feel comfortable); courage (for example, when dealing with infectious diseases); humility (being able to admit to errors and seek advice); and a sense of justice (for example, in relation to issues of distribution of care and medical aid).[52] These traits both enable a doctor to serve the goals of medicine, and are intrinsically valuable. A virtuous doctor has reason to develop these character traits not just because of how they will lead her to act but because they are valuable 'in their own right'.[53] Just as cultivating the virtues is constitutive of living a good life, cultivating professional virtues is partly constitutive of being a good professional.

Oakley and Cocking do not explicitly state what must be a consequence of adapting Aristotelian virtue ethics to professional ethics: the importance of reflective moral agency to virtuous action. Just like ordinary virtues, professional medical virtues must be manifestations of the doctor's rational choice. They must be based on deliberation about the ends of the profession and about the acts and character states that best promote those ends. A doctor who had an instinctive ability to diagnose patients – who had a good diagnostic 'nose' – and who was exceptionally nimble-fingered, would not be displaying professional virtues because her talents would not arise from deliberation and choice. Like the connection between natural virtues and true virtues, these traits would be useful because they are conducive to good professional functioning, but unless they are governed wisely they cannot be virtuous. A doctor's natural talents could easily be misused unless she deliberates about when it is most appropriate to use them. She could easily use her talents to serve immoral ends – using her diagnostic 'nose' to diagnose patients who could then be used in medical experiments, for example. Only through experience and reflection would she learn how best to use her natural abilities to serve the ends of medicine.

The regulative ideal therefore generates a conception of professional integrity that not only indicates when and what kind of professional behaviour is appropriate, but also indicates when it is appropriate to refuse one's professional services. In order to be a good professional one should not simply assume that the current legally permitted professional roles and actions are in fact best suited to serving the ends of the profession. A good professional should, if they are to act virtuously, be reflective about their role and their duties. It is precisely this kind of rational reflection that enables professions to stay true to their goals, and it is this kind of reflection that has led to professional developments such as codes of ethics, whistle-blowing guidelines, and (in the case of medicine) research guidelines.[54]

Regardless of whether one wishes to dispute the finer points of Oakley and Cocking's list of the virtues of the good doctor, there is an interesting point to note. The virtues noted above could easily be those of the good *person*. Someone who displayed these character traits outside the context of medicine would be an admirable person, one whom many of us would do well to emulate. They are virtues that anyone has good reason to develop. These virtues might be *particularly* suitable for a doctor to cultivate and they might be cultivated and expressed differently in a medical context than in a non-medical context, but they remain good character traits nonetheless. Could there be a case where the virtue ethics approach must praise as a virtue in a professional context a trait that would ordinarily be a vice? If so, would this be a problem for a plausible virtue ethics approach?[55]

Professional virtues and ordinary vices

Oakley and Cocking claim that a professional might be justified in cultivating traits that are neutral or even vicious in everyday life, but they do not give a clear example of this or explore the claim in any detail.[56] If this claim is true, it seems to open the way for a conflict with broad-based morality. Take callousness, for example. This is certainly not a virtue in everyday life but could it be professional virtue? Should trauma doctors, for example, strive to harden themselves to the suffering of their patients and the gruesome sight of those patients' injuries? Wouldn't they be able to do their job more efficiently if they didn't react to their patients' pain and distress? If so, then this case would be a counter-example to my claim in Chapter 1 that professional morality is a subset of broad-based morality – it would seem that professional moral virtues might be different from and not just a subset of ordinary virtues. However, this conflict is only apparent.

As I explained in Chapter 1, good professional detachment is a mean between two extremes: callousness and over-sensitivity. In the medical context this kind of detachment is not a vice because it serves the ends of the profession and is governed by wisdom. A doctor who puts aside her own feelings so that she can help her patients is not being callous – she has not completely ceased to respond to her patients' distress – instead, she is wise enough to see that the best way to help them is not to give in to her own distress but to leave it to one side while she is working.

This kind of detachment is also an appropriate response to certain kinds of non-professional situations. There are times when all of us have to put aside our normal emotional responses so we can deal with a crisis – a car crash, a sick child, a distraught friend. Yet controlling one's emotional responses so that one can more effectively help another is not callousness. A callous person does not feel distress in the first place. Good professional detachment therefore requires doctors to find the mean between callousness and over-sensitivity and this requires reflective deliberation. It requires that they govern their emotional responses by practical wisdom.[57] It does not require them to try to eradicate their responses altogether.

Similarly a trait such as ruthlessness might have a place in both ordinary and professional contexts. Lawyers might need to be ruthless (or at least appear to be so) when cross-examining witnesses, and mothers might need to be ruthless when taking their unwilling child to their first day of school. In both cases this apparent ruthlessness is necessary in order to further the ends of the legal profession in one case, and the child's own welfare in the second. In both cases ruthlessness must be used wisely. A lawyer who was ruthless just out of habit – without even thinking – would no longer be a good lawyer, and a mother who became so inured to her child's distress that she ruthlessly ignored its cries and didn't even think about whether her responses were helpful would not be a good mother. Habitual unreflective dispositions are not virtuous in any context.

So Oakley and Cocking's claim that professional virtues could be ordinary vices rests on a misunderstanding of the connection between virtuous action (in professional and non-professional contexts) and wisdom. The very definition of a virtue precludes the possibility of a professional virtue that is an ordinary vice. The examples above showed that even when there appears to be an ordinary vice that could be a professional virtue, this conflict is merely apparent.

This does not mean that professional virtues are expressed in the same way as ordinary virtues, or that cultivating professional virtues may not conflict with ordinary virtues. Professional virtues are expressed in different contexts than ordinary traits – doctors might need to practice detachment more often than people who are not doctors, for example – and cultivating professional virtues might require a trade-off with other professional and ordinary virtues.[58] For example, a doctor might find that her sense of justice conflicts with her beneficence. She may not be able to justify performing an expensive procedure on a very ill patient when there is little likelihood of success and when others would benefit more from the procedure. As I noted in Chapter 1, there is no possibility of avoiding all conflict within morality. But this conflict occurs in non-professional contexts as well – mothers, friends, and lovers might find themselves torn between being kind and being honest, for example. Conflict between competing moral reasons and virtues is inevitable and does not support the claim that professional virtues could be ordinary vices. Professional virtues are not a different kind of virtue and they are not ordinary vices. They are governed by practical wisdom and must further the ends of the profession.

There can of course be professional virtues that are neither virtuous nor vicious in everyday life. In relation to the medical profession, for example, Oakley and Cocking claim that: 'In a medical context, an action would be right if and only if it is what a virtuous doctor would do in the circumstances, and the character of the virtuous doctor would be constituted by dispositions which serve the goal of health in appropriate ways. Thus ... something can be a virtue in professional life – such as a doctor's acute clinical judgement in making a correct diagnosis from a multitude of symptoms – which might be thought neutral in ordinary life.'[59]

Such a case is not problematic for my view because there may well be unique aspects of a professional's duties that require very specific kinds of traits like good clinical judgement that are not needed in ordinary life, or at least not to the same extent. But, as I pointed out in section 1, even 'acute clinical judgement' does not count as a professional virtue unless it is used wisely.

In summary, professional virtues form part of the conception of excellence that is a profession's regulative ideal. They are partly constitutive of excellent professional functioning. Professional virtues, like ordinary virtues, must be governed by rational deliberation and must be expressive of the professional's rational choice. The regulative ideal encompasses these virtues and so gives rise to the concept of professional integrity. When asked to perform a professional service a good doctor must ask herself if providing that service is what a virtuous doctor (one governed by the regulative ideal of the medical profession) would do, or if a good doctor would refuse. A profession's regulative ideal thus has a further role. It delineates the virtues appropriate for professionals in relation to the ends of their profession, and it also sets limits on appropriate professional behaviour. Professionals guided by their profession's regulative ideal would not be mere technicians for hire. Instead, they would sometimes refuse to provide their professional services. Refusal of service can happen in two ways: through conscientious objection or because of a commitment to professional ideals.

Professional integrity and conscientious objection

In the literature on professional ethics, discussion about refusal of professional services has focused primarily on conscientious objection. Conscientious objection is a refusal to provide a professional service on the grounds that to do so would violate deeply held personal moral or religious views. For example, a doctor might refuse to carry out abortions because, as a devout Catholic, she believes they are immoral.[60] Such decisions can be controversial, as was the case in South Australia when nurses refused to carry out second trimester abortions because they found the operations greatly distressing.[61] Note, however, that the scope of justifiable conscientious objection is not unrestricted. If a doctor refused to administer antibiotics for life-threatening cases out of a personal belief in a 'vitalist' conception of health, she could be legitimately criticized because her objection on personal grounds to practices that are central to medicine raises the question of why she became a doctor in the first place.[62] A second restriction concerns the availability of the professional service in question. One of the main criticisms of the nurses' action in South Australia was that it forced women needing second trimester abortions to travel interstate (travel that many could not afford), since there was only one practitioner in the state who would perform such abortions. Yet second trimester abortions were legal in South Australia, so the nurses' action resulted in both a significant health risk to women needing such abortions and denied them their legal rights. In a discussion of this case, Leslie Cannold argued that the nurses' action was impermissible: 'because the risk to which they subjected abortion patients outweighed the benefits ... of the nurses exercising their autonomy-based right to act on conscience'.[63]

To avoid cases like this, conscientious objection in the medical profession is usually considered to be legitimate only when the service in question is not central to the practice of medicine and the patient can obtain the service elsewhere without undue hardship.[64] Such limitations would apply to legitimate conscientious objection in other professions. However, while the limits of legitimate conscientious objection are an important issue, Oakley and Cocking argue that there is another kind of refusal of service that has not been widely discussed: refusal of professional services on *professional* grounds. They claim that there are appropriate limits to what a professional should do within their professional role and those limits are at least partly set by the regulative ideal of the profession.[65] Reference to a profession's regulative ideal provides grounds on which professionals might refuse their services because of a commitment to the values of their profession.

Refusal of service on the grounds of professional integrity is different from conscientious objection because the professional believes that the act required violates certain *professional* values rather than her own personal values. So a doctor might refuse to agree to a patient's request for euthanasia not because performing euthanasia conflicts with her religious or personal views, but because it conflicts with her beliefs about what *as a doctor* she should do. She might believe that performing euthanasia violates the legitimate goals of medicine, particularly the goal of promoting patient health.[66] Similarly, a lawyer might refuse to represent a client whose case she believed to be manifestly unjust on the grounds that to represent that client would violate the regulative ideal of the legal profession; the promotion of justice.[67]

This kind of refusal of service is based on a conception of professional integrity that is importantly distinct from what a professional might legally be permitted to do. In some countries it may be quite legal for doctors to perform euthanasia at a patient's request. In several countries it is legal for a lawyer to reveal a rape victim's past sexual history in court[68] and in some countries military personnel are permitted to torture people suspected of terrorism. The fact that certain actions are legally permitted within a professional practice does not mean that those actions serve the profession's stated values. There are some practices that only doctors can legally perform that are only very loosely connected with the goal of promoting health. For example, doctors in the United States often supervise the administration of lethal injections,[69] and only doctors are permitted to perform elective cosmetic surgery such as liposuction and breast implants.[70] Indeed there might be some grounds for claiming that doctors who choose to practice only elective cosmetic surgery no longer count as doctors (in the usual sense) at all. As Arthur Isak Applbaum points out, doctors who choose not to be guided by the traditional goals of medicine might no longer be doctors in the traditional sense of the word since they serve quite different ends from the traditional ends of medicine. Doctors who are employed by insurance companies, for example, could conceivably view themselves as members of a different profession serving different ends from those of medicine – perhaps they could call themselves 'schmoctors' instead of doctors, so people would know what ideals guide their work.[71]

A profession's regulative ideal not only sets the appropriate limits for refusal of professional services, but also provides grounds for criticizing professionals who provide their services in situations where doing so seems to violate professional ideals. A professional who provides a professional service that she objects to on personal grounds might seem weak-willed and might blame herself for failing to abide by her personal moral or religious beliefs, but she has no positive moral duty to refuse her services on conscientious grounds. Conscientious objection is an important right, but it is not a professional's moral duty. But if a professional is asked to use her professional expertise in a way that violates the ideals of her profession, then she has a moral duty to refuse. Because they are members of professions that protect people's vital interests, professionals' special moral permissions are only justified as long as those permissions promote the ends of the profession. If professionals use their professional expertise in ways that violate the ideals of their profession they are guilty of far more than failing to live up to high standards: they have betrayed the ideals of their profession and the public welfare that their professions exist to protect.

I am not simply claiming that doctors and lawyers *can* refuse their services on professional grounds if they choose to do so; I argue that in some cases they *should*. The option to refuse professional services is not just one option among many available to professionals. The Nazi doctors who experimented on and murdered prisoners and the doctors who participated in torture sessions in Latin America were not merely failing to exercise their option to refuse their services when they had grounds for doing so; they were using their medical skills to actively violate medicine's guiding ideals. One of the many reasons why these doctors are particularly blameworthy and why their actions are so horrendous is because they were *doctors*, who should have been motivated by a concern for patient health. A doctor's participation in torture or in the abuse and killing of prisoners is a double betrayal; a betrayal of the patient and a betrayal of the doctor's professional duties and professional values – a corruption of the proper ends of medicine.[72] Similarly, a lawyer whose sole business is to represent a Mafia family is blameworthy not only because of the consequences of protecting criminal interests, but also because he is providing his services for ends that undermine his profession's stated ideals. A lawyer who knowingly devotes his skills to keeping organized crime in business seems particularly reprehensible because of the high moral professional standards that he is meant to uphold, standards that are determined to an extent by the regulative ideal of the legal profession.

A profession's regulative ideal therefore delineates the legitimate and central goals of the profession. It provides a way of clarifying when professionals should refuse to provide their professional services and provides grounds for determining when professionals no longer adequately serve the goals of their stated profession.

Conclusion

In summary, Oakley and Cocking's virtue ethics approach to professional ethics uses Aristotelian virtue ethics as a basis from which to derive a distinctive conception of professional virtue ethics tied to a profession's regulative ideal. Professions are justified by their connection to human flourishing and a profession's regulative ideal is the conception of excellence in professional functioning. The regulative ideal incorporates professional virtues and delineates the appropriate limits of professional activity, thereby giving rise to a clear conception of professional integrity. This account makes sense of the intuition that professionals who use their professional services in ways that violate the values of their profession are particularly morally reprehensible.

However, while the virtue ethics account seems plausible when applied to the traditional professions of law and medicine, Oakley and Cocking do not discuss how the concept of a regulative ideal would apply to professions that involve the use of violence against others. It is not clear from their discussion whether professions that use violence against others (and in the case of the military, extreme violence) can count as good professions and, if so, what the professional virtues of these professions would be.

In the next chapter I apply Oakley and Cocking's approach to the military profession. If the military counts as a legitimate profession then it will be possible to establish the military's regulative ideal and from this ideal derive a set of professional military virtues. Applying the virtue ethics approach to the military profession will draw out a conception of professional integrity that will provide grounds for refusal of military service. If it turns out that the regulative ideal of the military is one that cannot be upheld without serious violations of the moral integrity and agency of military professionals, or that can be used to illegitimately justify torture and other atrocities, then we have good reason to doubt the legitimacy of the military's claim to be a profession and the plausibility of the military's claim to have special moral permission to use violence. Does the military qualify as profession?

3
Professional Ethics and the Military

'... a true member of the military profession must also be a humanist'.[1]

Having established the criteria of a profession and clarified the concept of the regulative ideal of a profession and the associated professional virtues, we are now in a position to apply these concepts to the military. By claiming to be a profession, the military claims special moral permission to perform acts of extreme violence and destruction. Unlike most professionals, military personnel are permitted to kill, to destroy the infrastructure of enemy states, and to endanger the lives of military personnel under their command. If it is a profession, then the military warrants greater moral scrutiny and military personnel can be expected to meet high moral standards. Professional status brings with it special moral permissions but also imposes moral constraints: professionals must guide their actions by the regulative ideal of their profession, and they must respect important broad-based moral standards. Professional special moral permissions to violate ordinary moral standards or to weigh moral values differently within the professional context are only justified if the profession genuinely serves an important human need, and only if the special permissions are necessary to serve that need. Given that the military claims special permissions of a very serious nature, we certainly want it to be a profession governed by high professional standards and professional responsibilities. Without such status the military would be no better than a mercenary army. Is the modern military a legitimate profession?

In this chapter I present the strongest case for the professional status of the military, a case that provides a strong *prima facie* reason to believe military special permissions to be justified. Although there are aspects of the military's role as agent of the civilian government that do not fit easily

47

with its claim to professional status, the military does fulfil the main criteria of a profession. Using Justin Oakley and Dean Cocking's virtue ethics approach, it is possible to derive the military's regulative ideal and the set of appropriate military professional virtues. This regulative ideal gives rise to a conception of professional integrity such that disobedience on both an individual and an institutional scale is both justified and a positive moral duty under certain circumstances. By claiming professional status, the military is bound by strong moral constraints (imposed by the regulative ideal, the laws of war and broad-based moral standards) on what it may do in pursuit of professional goals. As I will demonstrate, there are situations where the military should refuse to provide its services on the grounds that do so would violate important professional ideals.

Is the military a profession?

Can the military count as a profession given that it is an authoritarian hierarchical organization? This fact does not disqualify it from constituting a profession. At most, it means that not every role in the military would count as a professional role. The profession of medicine also involves a hierarchy of roles involving differing levels of responsibility and skill. There are health care workers who can legitimately call themselves professionals and those who cannot, yet there is no doubt that they all form part of the medical profession and as such they are all governed by professional standards and professional ideals. In these hierarchical settings what distinguishes the professional from non-professional role is largely increasing decision-making autonomy, responsibility and skill-levels. This is one reason why nurses' professional status has been the subject of some debate. But even if there is doubt about whether or not nurses are professionals, there is no doubt that nurses are bound by similar professional standards as doctors because they are part of the same profession. Similarly, while autonomy and responsibility vary greatly between the ranks that constitute the military profession, all military personnel are part of the same organization and are therefore bound by the same professional ideals. Furthermore, it is often the lowest ranks in the military that carry out the most destructive acts. Because of this it is crucial that they are bound by the same professional standards as higher-ranking military personnel. We want even the lowliest combatant to obey the laws of war, maintain a good moral character, and fight for a good cause. The presence of low-ranking and less autonomous roles does not imply that an organization is not a profession. The military organization is a candidate for professionalism even if not every military role counts as a professional role to the same degree.

Working within the military complex are doctors, lawyers, engineers, and many others who count as professionals in their own right. For the purposes of this discussion I will restrict my analysis to military personnel who are not also members of other professions and whose role is primarily defined by their skills and training in the use and management of military force. This includes all ranks in the military hierarchy. I will accept the distinction drawn by Samuel Huntington, who describes roles such as military doctor or engineer as auxiliary roles that, while necessary for effective military functioning, are secondary to the central military goal.[2] Huntington describes the central and distinctive feature of the military professional to be the 'management of violence'.[3] He describes the scope of the military professional's duties as follows: 'The direction, operation, and control of a human organisation whose primary function is the application of violence is the peculiar skill of the officer ... It distinguishes the military officer *qua* military officer from the other specialists which exist in the modern armed services.'[4]

Unlike Huntington, however, I argue that officers are not the only professionals in the military profession. Because of the nature of military special permissions military personnel of *all* ranks should be bound by professional ideals and professional moral constraints. After all, foot soldiers and officers both claim special moral permission to kill. Officers bear greater responsibility and possess greater professional expertise than lower-ranking personnel, depending on their rank. So an infantry squad leader has less professional expertise than an officer in charge of an airborne division, who in turn has less professional expertise than the officer in charge of directing large-scale operations involving the Navy, Air Force, and Army.[5] But despite these degrees of professional expertise, all military personnel can be described as members of the military profession.

The criteria of a profession

A profession serves an important human need

What is the goal of the military? What human need does it exist to serve? The military is entrusted with a monopoly on weapons of great destructive capacity. In most societies the military is one of only two institutions permitted to perform acts of extreme violence and destructiveness in the pursuit of national security.[6] Military personnel are expected to subsume their personal interests to the military ethos and must also be prepared to sacrifice many of their political rights, such as the right to free speech and other political freedoms. Most importantly, military personnel must be prepared to kill, to be killed, and to send others to their deaths. The military's demands on its members are extreme.

The military is controlled by the civilian authority of a nation-state and exists to carry out that civilian authority's defence policies. The military is not an independent policy-making body, but an institution authorized to use extreme force to further and protect the nation's interests, as decided by the legitimate government of that nation. Does protecting and pursuing national interests constitute serving an important human need? It seems clear that when a country is under attack or under direct threat of attack, the military protects the very survival of the nation and the survival of individual citizens. As Anthony Hartle puts it, in such a situation the military, 'stands as the line of defence in protecting the quality of life in society'.[7] It could plausibly be argued that in such cases the existence of the military serves the most important human need of all – the need for physical security, without which no human can live a flourishing life.

But it is far from clear that the military exists *solely* to serve such an important good. Many of the military's activities (peacekeeping, for example) do not directly impact on the nation-state's physical security or political integrity. Using the military to invade another nation or to support the military activities of an ally does not clearly further the human need for security. Such actions are often *justified* by appeal to certain values (democracy, freedom, etc.) that are claimed to be essential to the wellbeing of humanity but, first, it is simply not clear that such justifications are in fact the real motives for the use of the military in those circumstances and, second, the connection between these kinds of military action and national security is often extremely tenuous at best. The military exists to serve the needs of the nation-state, and there is no *prima facie* reason to suppose that the needs of the nation-state as interpreted by the nation's leaders are morally valuable needs – or even 'needs' at all. In the past some military forces fought in the name of universal religious values, such as in the Crusades, but the modern military has a far more modest goal: 'it is defending a particular political and social order in the face of threats to it by other militaries in the service of other states'.[8]

The problem is clear: we cannot assume that a given social-political order is morally justified, or that a nation-state's civilian government will only use its military forces for morally good ends.

Perhaps, however, we can avoid this problem by claiming that protecting the interests of the nation-state means more than protecting the *physical* security of the nation: it means protecting *all* the nation's most important interests and values. In that case serving as allies for another nation is a way of ensuring a *quid pro quo* situation of protection – we help them because they will help us – thereby ensuring a greater level of protection for the nation. Similarly, intervening in the affairs of another country could be justified if the actions of that country threatened certain important national interests such as trade interests, or important political interests crucial to the political survival of the nation. Therefore the claim that the military exists solely to serve the human need for national security should not be defined only as protecting the physical security of the nation but should be interpreted fairly broadly: the military exists to protect the interests (physical and otherwise) of the nation from serious threats. However this claim, if true, does not alter the fact that these interests (as interpreted by the nation's leaders) may not be morally valuable. Given this problem, is there another ideal that might serve as the military's *raison d'être*?

Attempting to find an impartial moral goal above and beyond the goal of protecting the nation-state is highly problematic. Is it plausible to suppose that there is a single overarching ideal common to all military forces that is not the protection of their respective nations? Could there be a more universal meaning of protection not linked so strongly with individual nation-states?[9] Given that organizations such as the United Nations are able to authorize the use of different nations' military forces to protect vulnerable populations (for example, in East Timor, Haiti, Somalia, and the former Yugoslavia), perhaps the military's guiding ideal should be the protection of basic human rights, or even the promotion of universal human goods such as freedom.[10]

Certainly, military intervention for humanitarian purpose is now seen as a valid use of military force. The belief that military intervention in the affairs of another country is a 'violation of the right to sovereignty'[11] has given way to the belief that the right to sovereignty (and non-intervention) is dependent on the protection of basic human rights. This means that a state's legitimacy and its right to non-interference may depend upon how it treats its population.

Given this claim, can we then say that the military's primary role is not just to protect the nation-state, but to protect or promote basic human rights? Perhaps we can say that each nation's military force has a duty to protect human rights above and beyond the protection of national security. Indeed, the rise of peacekeeping missions and humanitarian interventions during the 1990s points to a view of the military as being bound to protect not only national interests but also universal interests such as world security and the protection of human rights.[12] Unfortunately, while there are good grounds for claiming that humanitarian intervention should be a part of the military's duties, it is far from clear that such a duty is or should be the overriding goal of the military.

It is true that the United Nations can and does use different nations' military forces for the purposes of humanitarian intervention, but the use of military force in this way has not fundamentally changed the military's primary function. The military forces of a nation-state become involved in United Nations' military activity only with that nation's express permission. A nation's military forces participate only because the civilian authority of that nation has ordered it – not because of an overriding duty to human rights. Military forces are *absolutely* subordinate to the authorities of their nation of origin. They exist to protect and further the interests of that nation, and participation in international peacekeeping missions (participation conditional on the permission of that nation's government) in no way changes that.

Despite the often dubious uses of the military and the difficulty of establishing an impartial military ideal, writers in military ethics and in philosophy often simply assume that the existence of the military serves an essential human need. Elizabeth Anscombe takes this view: 'For society is essential to human good; and society without coercive power is generally impossible.'[13]

Under this view, without the military there could be no society in which human life could flourish. However, given that the modern military force has many duties that are not directly connected with such an important moral good, such a rationale for the existence of the military, if it is accepted, needs to be accepted cautiously. The difficulties in establishing whether or not the military serves an important human need are serious and affect the legitimacy of the military's claim to be a profession. That said, even if one rejects such a pessimistic view of the nature of human society, it is certainly true that in the world of today the military is *perceived* to be essential to national security. A substantial defence budget is standard in modern Western societies. Indeed, in some countries the proportion of defence spending is greater than the budget for services such as the health and justice systems.[14] Anthony Hartle makes a similar point: 'That a strong and capable military force is considered essential to national interests seems undeniable since World War II, if one considers the huge budgetary appropriations for defence expenditures ... Despite wishes to the contrary, the prevailing view in Western society seems to be that the use of force is an inherent aspect of the human condition.'[15]

We might wish that we did not live in a world that required armed intervention and armed protection, but we *do* live in such a world. Even if we wish we did not need a military force to protect us (just as we might wish that we did not need a police force or a prison system), that does not make it any the less important for human flourishing in today's world.

Even if the military does not serve an agent-neutral human good such as justice and health, it is plausible to claim that the military exists to serve a vital human need – a need that has arisen because of unfortunate but perhaps inevitable facts about modern human society and the existence of nation-states with competing interests.[16]

For the purposes of making the best case for the military's status as a profession, we can accept the assumption that the military is necessary for national survival and the assumption that this counts as serving a morally important human need. The military arguably fulfils the first criterion of a profession.

A profession has a monopoly on the provision of service

The second criterion commonly claimed to be a defining feature of a profession is a monopoly on the provision of the service. The military uncontroversially fulfils this requirement. It alone in society has the authorization to, as Richard Gabriel puts it, 'legitimately carry out the systematic application of violence in the service of the state'.[17] In most societies only the police force has a similar permission to use force against others, and then only on a far more limited scale. The military's monopoly on the use of force and its independence from the normal legal constraints on the use of violence is strengthened by internal regulations and an internal justice system that monitors the behaviour of military personnel and punishes the misuse of force.[18]

Autonomy and proficiency

The military fulfils the requirements of autonomy in two ways: it is an autonomous organization and many roles within it require autonomous decision-making. Depending on their rank, military officers are often required to exercise decision-making autonomy as part of their role, and they also undergo a high degree of intellectual as well as technical training. In most countries military officers must complete intense training in both the technical aspects of warfare and the intellectual areas of strategy and theory. In the United States, for example, all officers must attend basic training as well as courses tailored to their areas of expertise and must spend a year at the Command and General Staff College. After many years of experience some will attend the Army War College which specializes in strategy and international relations. This process can take up to twenty years.[19] It is true that military officers of lower ranks have limited decision-making autonomy, but they must still exercise autonomous decision-making within the domain of their authority. Even the lowest-ranking officer must interpret orders, decide strategies and bear responsibility for the wellbeing of those under her command. Collective autonomy[20] as a profession is evidenced by the fact that the military alone is responsible for the training, education, recruitment, and internal standards of the military force.[21] As Major T. L. Stevens points out: 'Through devices such as promotion advisory committees, selection boards, and court martials – the military exercises a degree of self-regulation rare in any other calling.'[22]

The military's self-regulation and self-policing is far more marked than that of other professions. The professional organizations of medicine and law do use review boards, professional associations, and sometimes ethics committees to regulate their professional standards, and in some cases these have the legal power to disbar or censure individuals who fail to meet those standards. However, neither of these professions maintains an internal justice system and police force to monitor professional standards. The military's degree of self-containment from civilian society is unique.

Professional roles involve a moral component

As we saw in Chapter 1, the concept of the good professional implies more than technical competence or mastery of requisite skills; it also implies certain morally laudable character traits such as honesty or trustworthiness.[23] In the military the concept of the good military combatant is highly moralized. Modern descriptions of the ideal combatant include a list of virtues (for example, loyalty, honour, and integrity) that has remained largely unchanged despite the many rapid changes to military technology in the last century.[24] Anthony Hartle argues that it is particularly important for officers to be of good moral character because of their heavy responsibilities – they are not only responsible for the success of their missions but also for the wellbeing and lives of their troops. Military officers of all ranks are therefore expected to develop not only technical expertise but also moral character traits and values such as duty, patriotism, and integrity.[25] While all military personnel are expected to develop such traits it is the officer class that bears the greatest responsibility. Good character is even more important in the military than in other professions because of the military's professional special moral permissions. Given that military personnel may kill and send others to kill, it is crucial that they are trustworthy people of high moral standards.

Rather then being stated explicitly in official codes of ethics, this moral ideal is largely perpetuated through tradition. While there are few formalized codes of ethics for American and Australian military personnel, those personnel are bound both by international treaties (such as the Geneva Conventions) that are based on moral principles such as universal human rights, and by military codes such as the United States' *Uniform Code of*

Military Justice. Military training institutions also have a strongly entrenched customary (if not always formalized) code of conduct, and the guiding aims of most military institutions refer to moral values. For example, the Australian Royal Military College at Duntroon states that 'The charter of the Royal Military College of Australia is to prepare cadets ... for careers in the army, by promoting leadership and integrity, by inspiring high ideals and the pursuit of excellence, and by inculcating a sense of duty, loyalty, and service to the nation.'[26] Members of the military are clearly expected to meet high ethical standards and severe punishment is possible for those members who fail to meet basic professional standards. Military officers' serious responsibilities mean that bad character and incompetence can have deadly consequences. Even the lowliest military personnel are bound by the values of the profession – a soldier who is untrustworthy, immoral, and disloyal endangers not only herself but her fellow soldiers as well.

From the above discussion it is clear that a good *prima facie* case can be made for the military's professional status. Like other professions the military profession imposes special obligations upon its members and claims special moral permission to perform acts that conflict with the values of everyday morality. Not only officers but all military personnel will 'typically claim a moral permission to harm others in ways that, if not for the role, would be wrong.'[27] This conflict is most apparent in the military's role as agent of the civilian authority.

The military as agent of the civilian authority

Like lawyers, individual military personnel and the military as an institution must carry out another's motives and intentions. Low-ranking personnel carry out their commanding officer's orders, officers carry out their superior officer's orders, and the military institution carries out the orders of the civilian authority of the nation-state. The military hierarchy exists primarily, if not solely, to protect and further the interests of the nation-state through the use of violence and the threat of violence. As Samuel Huntington explains: 'The existence of the military depends upon the existence of nation-states capable of maintaining a military establishment ... the justification for the maintenance of employment of military force is in the political ends of the state.'[28]

But is the military the agent of the nation or the state? Are the nation and the state the same entity? David Luban argues that 'nation' and 'state' are not equivalent, although the meanings of the terms are often conflated. He argues that 'nation' indicates a political community, while 'state' refers to 'an on-going institution of rule over, or government of, its nation'.[29] Thus the *nation* of Australia refers to the community of Australian citizens, whereas the *state* of Australia refers to the current system of government.

Luban introduces this distinction in order to discuss the definition of wars of aggression in just war theory. He argues that the common appeal to 'state's rights' as a reason for not interfering in another country's affairs confuses the concept of the nation with that of the state. A state is legitimate only so long as it has the consent of the nation, and it is only legitimate states that can be said to have rights that could be infringed by external military interference from other countries.[30] To an extent, Michael Walzer shares this view. He argues that 'The moral standing of any particular state depends upon the reality of the common life it protects.'[31] However, unlike Luban, Walzer distinguishes a state's legitimacy 'at home' from its legitimacy in the eyes of the international community. The international community may believe that a particular state is tyrannical or otherwise illegitimate, but as long as the government of that state 'actually represents the political life of its people' then intervention is not justified.[32] This means that even if a state is illegitimate it should have 'presumptive legitimacy' in the eyes of the international community. Only the citizens of that state have the right to rebel or overthrow their government if the government no longer represents them or defends their common life.[33] However, there are occasions when foreign intervention may be justified. Foreign states could intervene to overthrown the government of an illegitimate state when it is radically clear that the government does not represent or 'fit' with the community it claims to represent, when, for example: 'the violation of human rights within a set of boundaries is so terrible that it makes talk of community or self-determination or "arduous struggle" seem cynical and irrelevant, that is, in cases of enslavement or massacre'.[34]

While there is disagreement as to the extent of a state's right to non-interference, the distinction between nation and state and between legitimate and illegitimate states leaves room for justified military intervention by outside nation-states in extreme cases involving massacre or genocide. The military interventions in Iraq and the former Yugoslavia were justified largely on these grounds.[35] Given this distinction, is the military the agent of the nation or the state? Where should the military's loyalties lie?

Most writers on professional military ethics agree that the military's subordination to the civilian authority – the state, in other words – is of crucial importance. It is no part of the military's role to make foreign and domestic policy. Instead, its role is to implement those policies at the will of the civilian authority. Thus the military is an agent for a single 'client' – the state. While there is no doubt that the military protects the nation – the community of citizens – it does so by obeying the state.

As an agent of the state, the military has three main functions: to inform the civilian authority of threats to national security, to advise and report on possible courses of action, and to carry out the policies formulated by the civilian authority. However, in order to carry out these functions effectively the military itself must remain politically neutral.[36] This neutrality is required because the military is committed to carrying out the civilian authority's military policy regardless of the political opinions of the individual military personnel and regardless of the civilian authority's political stance. Like lawyers, military personnel must be neutral about the morality of the causes they promote. Such neutrality is considered a mark of a good military professional. Indeed, some American military officers refrain from voting in order to maintain political neutrality and to maintain the ability to give unbiased advice to the current civilian authority.[37] In Australia, the former Australian Defence Force Chief General Peter Cosgrove stated that: 'There is a convention that is well understood that we seek to avoid an overt association of a military person in an image or in any other way with a political activity.'[38]

As Huntington explains, 'The military quality of the professional is independent of the cause for which he fights.'[39] While they may advise the government about the best course of action, military officers must in the final instance withhold judgement on the political and ethical wisdom of the policies they enact on behalf of the nation-state. They must be '"above politics" in domestic affairs'.[40] This requirement means that officers may find themselves carrying out policies that go against their military judgement.[41] The good military officer's character, like the character of the good lawyer, requires an ability to withhold personal judgements about the moral and political value of the civilian authority's use of the military. This is true for all military personnel. Just as high-ranking officers must withhold judgement about the orders they receive, so too must low-ranking personnel withhold judgement about their orders. Furthermore, not only should individual members of the military withhold judgement about the wisdom (political or otherwise) of the policies of the civilian authority, but the military as an institution must also be seen to be politically neutral. While the military may advise the civilian authority and may even strongly urge or advise against certain courses of action, in the final instance the military is expected to obey the civilian authority and to publicly support or at least not criticize the civilian authority's policies.

The upshot of the military's subordination to the civilian authority is that military personnel are likely to encounter ethical issues similar to those encountered by lawyers. Through the normal exercise of her professional duties, a member of the military is likely to carry out policies that (while perhaps legal) are unjust or immoral, and that will cause harm to others on a far greater scale than the harm caused by a lawyer's actions. A military professional is part of a profession that, in the pursuit of professional goals, may kill and injure thousands of people and severely damage the civil structure and environment of other countries. In modern warfare, the deaths of unarmed civilians and the destruction of non-military targets are also probable, if not inevitable, consequences of going to war. Carrying out military missions also unavoidably endangers the lives of the military personnel involved. An officer must sometimes send personnel on missions that are likely to result in their deaths. The military professional's normal professional duties can cause far, far greater harm than that potentially caused by lawyers or doctors.

Because of this feature of the military profession, the military's claim for special professional permissions must be strong enough to counter two massive and interrelated problems: the problem of justification and the problem of harm. First, as we have seen, there is no *prima facie* guarantee that the civilian authority will only use the military for morally justifiable ends. This is a problem that raises serious concerns about how often and under what conditions governments are actually justified in using military force. Second, there is the problem of the massive harm and loss of life caused by military action, including not only harm to individuals but also to the environment, the infrastructure of the society under attack, and military personnel themselves. Even if a state has a *prima facie* justification to use military force in pursuit of a just cause, one must still consider whether the loss of life and destruction that will result is proportional to the value of this end. These two considerations correspond, respectively, to the requirements of just cause and proportionality in the just war doctrine of *jus ad bellum*.

The just war tradition, a tradition dating back to St Augustine, encompasses two separate areas: *jus in bello* and *jus ad bellum*.[42] *Jus ad bellum* refers to the conditions that must be met before a resort to war is permissible, and *jus in bello* governs the actions that are permissible within warfare (for example, the treatment of prisoners of war). Many of these principles are found in national and international laws of war and are intended to minimize the harms of war noted above.[43] An in-depth discussion of these traditions is beyond the scope of this book, but it is sufficient to note that these conditions serve to strictly limit when and how military force can be used. The right of a nation-state to maintain a military force does not imply *carte blanche* in how that force is used. Nor is the military permitted free rein in how it carries out its missions. Just as a defence lawyer may not use illegal means to defend her client, so the military must obey the laws of war in carrying out military actions. As a profession it is bound by professional ideals and the laws of war and these place strict limits on what may be done in the name of protecting national security.

This means that, if the military is to maintain its professional status, the use of military force must be governed by strict principles (when it can be used and how it can be used) if it is to have any strong moral justification at all. Yet while the use of military force must be governed by the laws of war (and the moral principles underlying them), obeying the laws of war is the not the central aim of the military profession. Military institutions are inherently partial to the interests of the nation; they are deeply nationalistic. Their main function is subordination to the civilian authority and protection of the security of the nation-state, as interpreted by the legitimate authority of that nation. This means that the concerns of *jus ad bellum* are outside the military's professional jurisdiction – the decision to go to war is made by the civilian authority and the military profession is subordinate to that authority. This partiality could lead to a tension between obeying the civilian authority and upholding the laws of war – a tension I explore later in this chapter.

Given the harms caused by military action and the partiality inherent in the military profession, it is clear that the moral framework governing the military profession must be robust enough to provide good reason to accept the dangers of military action. We shall now see whether the virtue ethics approach can provide such a framework, and whether it can generate a plausible professional ethic for the military profession.

Virtue ethics and the military profession

As I argued in Chapter 2, the virtue ethics approach to professional roles has advantages over competing theories of professional ethics for two main reasons. It provides a clear framework for articulating professional ideals and a robust concept of professional integrity, and it ties virtuous action to reflective moral agency. Virtue ethics has the further advantage of being an approach that is very popular within the military itself – many writers (for example, Anthony Hartle and Richard Gabriel) in military professional ethics adopt some version of virtue ethics, particularly in reference to the character of good military personnel. The first and most important step in applying Oakley and Cocking's approach to the military profession is to ascertain the military's regulative ideal. This regulative ideal will give rise to the list of virtues appropriate to military personnel, and will delineate the legitimate boundaries of professional military activity.

The regulative ideal of the military

While the military's role as agent of the civilian authority is problematic, a good case can nonetheless be made for the professional status of the military. Under the virtue ethics approach, the military's regulative ideal is the conception of excellent professional functioning that should guide the actions of military personnel, and will also tell us which military roles genuinely promote the ends of the military. The regulative ideal will provide the basis for a concept of military professional integrity that can be used to establish when military personnel should refuse to participate in certain military activities on the grounds that to do so would violate the goals of the military profession.

The military's function is the protection of the interests and security of the nation-state, and so the regulative ideal is the ideal conception of roles, traits, and behaviours that best promote this end. Does the role of military combatant promote the ends of the military? The role of military combatant is unarguably crucial to the successful pursuance of military goals. Depending on rank, military combatants organize, mobilize, and are responsible for the distribution and actions of weapons and other military personnel. No organized military action could take place without combatants. It can be safely stated that, given that the military profession arguably counts as a profession under the virtue ethics account, the role of combatant is a legitimate professional role, one that is necessary for excellence in military functioning.

Having established that the role of combatant can be regarded as a professional role, the next step is to consider what character traits good military personnel should cultivate. As I explained in Chapter 2, there are two constraints on the traits that may count as professional virtues. First, as Oakley and Cocking point out, the actions that professionals may justifiably perform and the character traits they may justifiably develop in pursuit of professional goals are limited by broad-based moral side-constraints such as patient and client autonomy, and by the larger good that their profession serves. Oakley and Cocking describe these constraints in relation to doctors: 'Refraining from unjustifiably interfering with the autonomous decisions and actions of patients is an important side-constraint on what doctors may legitimately do in their role, just as refraining from such interventions is an important side-constraint on any professional in their legitimate dealings with their clients.'[44]

A professional's character traits and actions are formed within and constrained by broad-based moral values and social acceptance and by their profession's guiding ideals.[45] The same limitations apply in the case of the military. The combatant's professional virtues are those traits that best enable her to serve the ends of the military profession, subject to the side-constraints imposed by important broad-based moral values and the laws of war as spelled out in the Geneva Conventions and other such treaties. Constraints imposed by the military's goals and the laws of war not only limit actions that may be taken within warfare (such as deliberately targeting civilians, or destroying important cultural symbols), but also limit the kinds of character traits that military personnel can justifiably develop in pursuit of professional goals. Like all professional virtues, combatants' professional virtues must be governed by reflective moral agency. Good military personnel are not killing machines.

But given the unique requirements of military service and the military profession's unique special moral permissions, isn't it likely that military personnel might need to develop traits that are different from and possibly incompatible with ordinary virtues? After all, lawyers and doctors don't need to systematically kill people or destroy cities as part of their professional duties. Military personnel must be able kill enemy combatants, and so perhaps sadism or a love of killing would make their duties easier – a combatant who was squeamish about killing would be useless. These kinds of traits might well be useful in some aspects of military service but they could not count as professional virtues for two reasons. First, they are morally reprehensible. They are likely to lead to actions that violate important broad-based and indeed professional moral standards. Second, as I argued in Chapter 2, professionals must deliberate carefully about the traits they develop and govern the expression of these traits by a clear understanding of how the traits contribute to the ends of their profession. The fact that a particular trait might make certain professional tasks easier is not a reason to think that it is a professional virtue. Military personnel who cultivated cruelty and sadism might find killing the enemy easier to do – even fun – but cruelty and sadism are not for this reason professional virtues, or indeed virtues of any kind. Like doctors who became callous, military personnel who became cruel and sadistic would no longer be good combatants because they would no longer be properly guided by their profession's regulative ideal. Professional virtues must genuinely serve the ideals of the profession and must be governed by reflective moral agency. Appropriate professional virtues must be more than habitual dispositions or inculcated emotional responses; they must arise from reflective deliberation about how and when the traits promote the ends of the profession. There may be several natural traits that are useful for good professional functioning, but unless those traits are governed wisely they are not virtuous.

However there is no doubt that military personnel must learn to kill. Learning to kill requires military personnel to become detached from the act of killing itself and from the emotional and physical distress caused by killing and witnessing killing. However, like the good doctor's professional detachment, such detachment must be a mean between the extremes of callousness or sadism, and over-sensitivity. Good military personnel would be like Aristotle's melancholy soldier, who 'understood both that his war was just and that killing, even in a just war, is a terrible thing to do.'[46] Developing the appropriate level of professional detachment is even more important for military personnel than it is for doctors, because military personnel who became too habituated to killing would not only be unprofessional; they would be very dangerous.

Given these limitations, the character traits of good military personnel, like those of the good doctor, would be guided by 'an account of what counts as excellence within certain roles'.[47] In this case, an account of what counts as excellence in the role of combatant, determined by what counts as excellence in serving the military profession's ends. This account of excellence includes excellence in the technical aspects of warfighting (use of weapons, strategy, physical strength), and excellence in the character traits that enable military personnel to perform their function within the moral constraints imposed by the military's professional status. What traits would best aid military personnel in promoting the goals of the military profession?

The virtues of the good combatant

According to Anthony Hartle in *Moral Issues in Military Decision-making*, the characteristics of the good combatant arise from three different sources: the functional requirements of the role, the values of the society that the military serves, and the moral and legal principles of international law that that society is bound by.[48]

The character traits arising from the functional requirements of the combatant's role are those traits that aid military personnel in carrying out the duties required for promoting the ends of the military profession.[49] Deciphering the values of society is not so straightforward. The social values expressed by military forces vary greatly over time and between different societies and cultures. For example, the Japanese Samurai had a very strict moral and professional code quite distinct from that of, say, the Prussian army in the eighteenth and nineteenth centuries.[50] There are likely to be strong cultural differences in ideals of military professionalism and the ideal character of military personnel. For the purposes of this chapter the discussion will be limited to the United States and Australian military forces. Some indication of the values of these societies can be found in documents such as the US Constitution and in the writings and speeches of political and military leaders.

The moral and legal principles of international law that legally bind the military reflect certain moral principles that can be inferred from the conventions and treaties to which America and Australia (as well as the UK) are signatories. Documents such as the Geneva Conventions provide a guide to military values because, while there is an important distinction between legal and moral values, the conventions relating to the conduct of warfare are nonetheless based on clear moral values, most commonly rights-based or humanitarian principles.[51] By choosing to be bound by these conventions the United States and Australian governments are signalling their acceptance of the moral principles underlying the conventions and their willingness to bind their military forces by those conventions.

The functional requirements of the role

The military first and foremost plays a functional role. This role can be divided into two parts: carrying out the political and military objectives of the civilian authority, and performing military duties effectively. Fulfilling these roles requires different kinds of character traits.

A. The combatant as servant of the state   The military exists to carry out the orders of the civilian government regarding situations affecting national security. Acting as the agent of civilian authority results in two defining characteristics of the military organization and the military personality: authoritarianism and conservatism. The military must be totally loyal to the nation-state's legitimate government and must fulfil governmental objectives without judgement. To do so effectively, the military requires that military personnel carry out legal orders swiftly and efficiently, and requires that criticism of governmental policies and objectives be mini-mized, if not eradicated altogether. The decision to use military force is ulti-mately a political decision and the military's role is limited to advising on the most effective use of military force and does not extend to considering whether the use of military force is politically or ethically justified in the first place.[52] No members of the military, even if they play an important advisory role, must impose their own political views on the government. Instead, they must faithfully carry out the government's policies regardless of which political party may be in power at any given time.

However, this institutional political neutrality does not lead to a politically neutral military personality. As we have seen, members of the military must be largely non-judgemental about the moral or political value of the policies they are required to carry out. The military cannot allow a plurality of views and conflicting interpretations of orders and so must limit political discussion and impose a strict emphasis on obedience to authority. Individual military personnel must obey promptly and without question the legitimate orders of their superiors – debate and dissent would severely undermine efficiency. Combatants' obedience is reinforced by strong loyalty to the nation-state, the military as an institution, and the combatants' units. These restrictions on political expression, the military's submission to the civilian authority, and the emphasis on group loyalty result in a strong political conservatism. In Huntington's words: 'For the profession to perform its function, each level within it must be able to command the instantaneous and loyal obedience of subordinate levels. Without these relationships, military professionalism is impossible.'[53]

At first glance the combined requirements of political neutrality and efficiency would suggest that a good combatant should develop the character traits of competence, loyalty, discipline, obedience, patriotism, and truthfulness. Competency, loyalty, obedience, and discipline are essential for prompt and effective carrying out of orders and for the prompt decision-making required of military personnel of every rank. Military personnel must also be deeply nationalistic and patriotic. As the combatant's duty is to further and protect the interests of their nation-state ahead of those of competing or threatening states, the good combatant must be deeply loyal both to the current government and to the values of the nation. Hartle argues that protecting the state is the combatant's most important duty: 'The state, which legitimizes the professional military function, provides the ultimate moral and political ideal in the context of professional service.'[54]

Truthfulness is necessary because of the serious nature of military activity – superiors and subordinates' reports must be reliable if military objectives are to be effectively achieved. False reporting can endanger the success of a mission and can endanger the lives of both combatants and civilians.[55] Personal courage is also an essential characteristic. As Hartle puts it, 'The professional commitment is one of "ultimate liability".'[56] The demands of military service are such that all military personnel must be prepared to take command in situations of intense fear and uncertainty and, if need be, make the ultimate sacrifice. The functional requirements of the role of combatant therefore require a person who is competent, courageous, obedient, loyal, trustworthy, patriotic, and disciplined. These virtues enable military personnel to most effectively serve the military's needs.

B. *The combatant as leader*   Unlike the lowest-ranking military personnel, a military officer must not only carry out orders rapidly and efficiently but must also be a leader of others. He must be able to demand immediate obedience to his orders. He must inspire the trust, loyalty, and honesty of his troops if he is to carry out his commission and lead his troops willingly into potentially life-threatening situations. His troops must be able to trust him with their lives. Thus the officer must be a person who can both inspire and maintain such trust and loyalty. Perhaps the most crucial virtue for the officer as leader is integrity. It is not always clear what integrity means in the context of military service. However, given the importance of trust between an officer and his subordinates, integrity is often interpreted as moral integrity or personal honour – the virtue of upholding and living by one's moral principles. Hartle adopts this interpretation. He argues that when a new officer takes the American commissioning oath and swears by 'Duty–Honor–Country', the term 'honor' is interchangeable with 'integrity'.[57] Integrity so defined implies trustworthiness, a consistency both of character and of moral values.[58] The Australian Royal Military College also describes integrity as an essential part of the military ethic: 'There is an absolute requirement for integrity in a military officer and a cadet. Integrity demands the exclusion of lying, cheating, dishonesty and evasion ... Any doubts about the integrity of an officer destroys the trust of superiors and colleagues and the respect of subordinates. The lives of soldiers, the honour of the Army, and ultimately that of the Nation, can be at stake.'[59]

Because trust between officers and their subordinates is so important and the consequences of loss of trust can be so disastrous, integrity is often referred to as one of the most important military virtues.[60] It and obedience are claimed to be the '*sine qua non* of the military institution'.[61] Integrity in the military thus requires a person who is prepared to live up to the standards of the good officer in all parts of their life, not just when they are 'on the job'.

From the above discussion a short list of relatively uncontroversial military virtues can be derived all of which clearly promote the ends of the military profession. I will summarize the list as follows: courage, obedience, integrity, loyalty, honesty, trustworthiness, discipline, and patriotism. These virtues derive from the functional requirements of the combatant's role, and would hold in each of the three services (Army, Navy, and Air Force). To embody these virtues requires a person of exceptional strength of character who is willing to sacrifice their self-interest and (to some extent) their individual freedoms for the military ideals.

However, there are further character traits and moral values relevant to the military that can be derived from the values of the wider society and from the military treaties that that society is bound by.

The military values: society and the laws of war

The values of society

It is difficult to ascertain precisely the influence of society's values on the development of the ideal moral character of military personnel. As I have noted above (pp. 50–1), it is plausible to characterize the military's duty as not only protection of the nation's physical security but also the protection (and sometimes furtherance) of the *values* that the nation claims to embody. Characterizing the military's duty in this way leaves room for a discrepancy and possible conflict between the traditional cultural values of a society and the values of the current government of that society – a discrepancy that has implications for military disobedience that I explore later in this chapter. In this section, I will briefly discuss the values generally held to be representative of American and Australian societies, as espoused by the leaders and traditions of those countries.

In the United States the Constitution is an important indicator of the basic values that have supposedly persisted throughout modern American history. In their commissioning oath, new American officers swear to 'support and defend the Constitution of the United States against all enemies'.[62] This oath involves more than simply a vow to obey the current civilian authority; it involves a commitment to the moral and political values embodied in the Constitution.[63] It is interesting to note that, while the commissioning oath requires officers to swear to 'observe and follow such orders and directions, from time to time, as may be given me ... or by the future President of the United States of America',[64] the appeal to the constitution indicates a loyalty to a value system that might not coincide with that of the current government, creating the possibility of conflict between the military's loyalty to the constitution and loyalty to the current President. As Hartle claims, 'An officer's loyalty is to the principles and values manifested in the Constitution, not to the person of the commander in chief.'[65] However, while Hartle raises the possibility of conflict he does not explore its implications. To see how this discrepancy could arise, it is necessary to have a basic understanding of the values of the Constitution.

Hartle claims that the United States Constitution is characterized by a commitment to a society 'in which citizens can enjoy liberty, justice, and equality'.[66] Given this uncontroversial interpretation of the Constitution we can infer that the American military institution is committed to protecting and upholding the values of individualism, freedom of speech, political assembly, democracy, and equality. The possibility of conflict arises because it is plausible that certain governments of the United States have not protected or enhanced the values embodied in the Constitution.[67] This means that the military could face a conflict between obeying the civilian authority and protecting the values of the Constitution. In such cases it is not clear where the military's loyalties should lie. In practice, given the importance of subordination to the civilian authority and the fact that at no time has the American military refused to obey the orders of the President, it seems that loyalty to the current civilian authority has priority even when ethical and military considerations might argue against a particular policy. During the Vietnam War the American military continued to carry out the government's policies even though many officers believed that the policies were both politically and militarily inefficient and were needlessly endangering the lives of American troops.[68] Yet even with this history of obedience to the civilian authority there might still be scope for legitimate military disobedience of civilian authority, a possibility that I discuss below (pp. 73–5).

How does protecting the values of the Constitution affect the ideal combatant's character? What is clear is that upholding and protecting these values is not equivalent to embodying them. Military personnel must be willing to forego many of their civilian political freedoms (such as freedom of speech and freedom of assembly) in order to serve military ideals effectively. Malham M. Wakin describes how members of the military must forego their civilian freedoms: 'The elemental human rights mentioned in the US Constitution comprise an abbreviated listing of values critical to the way of life worth defending ... Military professionals, however, in order to perfect the instrument of defending these values, of necessity curb their own exercise of some of these freedoms. They accept restrictions on the liberty to speak, they refrain from partisan politics, they are denied political office while on active duty, they accept restrictions on their freedom of movement, and in general subordinate personal preferences to the good of the military unit and the good of the country.'[69]

So the good combatant must develop traits that will enable him to defend the values of society, even if that means he must sacrifice the very freedoms that those values gave him. He must therefore cultivate the trait of self-sacrifice. To protect a society that places great value on the individual and the individual's freedoms, he must subsume his individual freedoms to the military institution.

While the American military profession is committed to protecting values that might, in theory at least, conflict with the values of the current political leadership, there is no obvious such conflict in the Australian military. The Australian military, while similarly traditionally committed to the values of democracy, equality, and freedom, is strongly subordinate to the civilian government. This is evidenced by the fact that the military is controlled and commanded by the Minister of Defence (a civilian position) of the current government.[70] The main difference between Australian and American military values is simply the emphasis placed on the commitment to the current government. In the United States, while such commitment is central, it is predicated on and based on the larger commitment to the values of the Constitution, whereas in Australia the commitment to the civilian government is not transcended by a further commitment to a higher value system.

Australian society shares to a large extent many of the same fundamental values as American society. Like American society, Australian society is democratic and has a strong tradition of valuing individual political freedoms such as freedom of speech and freedom of political assembly. However, because Australia was originally a colony of the United Kingdom the Australian military was for a long time considered duty-bound to serve the national interests of the United Kingdom. As a result, the Australian military has traditionally played a greater support role to allied forces than the American military. Lieutenant Colonel M. L. Phelps argues that in the past the Australian Army viewed itself as an expeditionary force, 'structured and equipped to form part of larger allied forces deployed outside Australia'.[71] This is borne out by the participation of Australian forces in numerous wars defending the interests of Australia's allies, even when Australian interests were not directly threatened.[72] This view of the role of the Australian military has changed only recently. The shift towards homeland defence began in the 1970s with the publication of the White Paper, *The Defence of Australia*.[73] While Australian forces still play an important expeditionary role, as seen in the second Gulf War, the modern Australian army is more focused on the defence and protection of the Australian homeland and Australian interests than was the case in earlier wars in which Australian troops participated.

The influence of this historical role on the character of Australian military personnel is minor. Perhaps all that needs to be said is that Australian military personnel were originally loyal and patriotic to Australia as a British colony, rather than as an independent country. However, that has changed over the last century and modern military personnel are patriotic to Australia as an independent nation with its own set of national values.

One such value that seems to be unique to the Australian military is mateship, exemplified by the Anzac mythology. Mateship is a term that is used widely and not always clearly in Australian discourse. Within the military, mateship usually refers to the trait of standing by and helping one's fellow combatants. The importance of mateship has even been emphasized in official documents. In 1996 the Australian Army's value statement stated that 'The Army's ethos is based on a traditional set of shared values, embodied in the concept of Mateship.'[74] General Baker defined mateship in an address he gave at the memorial service for soldiers who died in a training accident: 'What you have here this morning is a demonstration of an Australian characteristic, an instinct – no matter what your station, no matter what your creed, no matter what you do – in times of crisis to hold out your hand to a mate.'[75] Mateship in the Australian military is therefore probably best defined as loyalty to one's comrades regardless of rank and class background.

In summary, the values common to both the American and Australian societies and therefore the values that Australian and American military forces are dedicated to protecting, are a commitment to individual freedoms (political, religious, etc.) and the value of democracy. While I have not explicitly discussed the United Kingdom, given that the UK is a liberal democracy its military forces are likely to be dedicated to similar values. In the case of the Australian military, the value of mateship – the virtue of standing by and protecting one's mates – is also a core military characteristic.

For the protection of these social values the good American or Australian combatant should develop the character traits of mateship, self-sacrifice, and selflessness.

The laws of war

The laws of war do not so much determine the character of the good combatant as delineate appropriate behaviour in warfare. These laws are usually divided into two areas, corresponding to the two areas of just war theory; *jus ad bellum* and *jus in bello*. As already defined, *jus ad bellum* determines when a declaration of war is justified and *jus in bello* determines what actions are permissible when fighting a war.[76] These laws act as side-constraints on the permissible uses of military force and on the behaviour of military personnel in war. They govern the kinds of force military personnel are permitted to use, how and when force should be used, and against whom force may be directed. The most famous documents outlining the laws of warfare are the Geneva Conventions. First written in 1929, the Geneva Conventions originally focused on the treatment of prisoners of war.[77] There have since been four further Geneva Conventions (from 1949) and in 1977 protocols were also added. The 1949 convention and the 1977 protocols deal with issues relating to the treatment of civilian populations in wartime, appropriate targets, permissible weapons, and permissible treatment of a defeated nation.[78]

The principles behind treaties such as the Geneva Conventions, the International Criminal Court, and the 1980 Certain Conventional Weapons Treaty (prohibiting the use of weapons such as mines and booby-traps) are largely humanitarian, governed by a conception of universal human rights that sets limits on how civilians and combatants may be treated during and after war. The United States and Australia are signatories to these treaties (although it should be noted that the United States has not yet ratified the 1977 protocols of the Geneva Conventions, has not ratified two out of the four protocols that were attached to the Certain Conventional Weapons Convention, and has not supported the International Criminal Court),[79] and the fact that they are willing to support (and legally bind themselves to) these documents indicates a support for the moral principles that underlie these treaties. Australia and the United States, by choosing to sign and ratify the Geneva Conventions, are indicating their support for the concept of universal human rights and signalling a rejection (in theory at least) of a purely utilitarian attitude towards warfare – an 'end justifies the means' attitude. The doctrine of human rights sets limits on what may be done for the sake of good consequences in warfare or for the sake of military efficiency. This emphasis on protecting certain basic human rights means that military personnel must develop a respect for and an understanding of the concept of human rights and the humanity of enemy combatants and civilians. In order to follow faithfully the limitations set by the laws of war they must understand the moral principles underlying those laws.

It is an interesting question whether the military forces of countries that have not signed these treaties should be bound by the moral principles underlying them, but it is a question that I cannot explore at any length here. If one accepts the doctrine of universal human rights then the fact that a country is not *legally* bound to observe the limitations on warfare set by those rights is not a reason to think that they are not *morally* bound to observe such limitations.[80] One of the main criticisms of America's use of Guantanamo Bay as a detention centre for suspected terrorists was the attempt by the US to side-step the legal constraints imposed by the Geneva Conventions on the treatment of prisoners of war. By calling terrorism suspects 'enemy combatants', the US attempted to claim that these suspects were not prisoners of war and so were not protected by the Geneva Conventions.[81] Given that the US military is bound by the moral principles underlying the Geneva Conventions, even if the prisoners at Guantanamo Bay were not prisoners of war, the military still had a moral and a professional duty to respect their rights. However, if a nation's civilian authority does not uphold the values of the Geneva Conventions it is not obvious that the military forces of that nation should be bound by those values, given that the military profession's primary duty is the security of the nation-state. As discussed previously, the military profession is essentially nationalistic and duty-bound to follow the orders of the civilian authority, regardless of the moral or even military value of those orders.

In summary, the functional requirements of the role, the values of the wider society, and the laws of war determine the character traits most suited to serving the ends of the military profession. A good combatant must be able to fulfil the functional requirements of his or her role, uphold and protect the values of the nation, and respect the laws of war. A good combatant must be a person of great moral integrity, a person of honour, loyalty, obedience, discipline, and selflessness. They must be a person of exceptional moral standards.

The regulative ideal of the military, encompassing the virtues of the good combatant, also gives rise to a conception of professional integrity that, as we shall see, provides grounds for a combatant's refusal to participate in a military action.

Professional integrity in the military

In Chapter 2 I explained that the regulative ideal of a profession gives rise to a conception of professional integrity that sets boundaries on appropriate professional behaviour and indicates when professionals should refuse to provide their professional services. In relation to the military this concept of professional integrity will be important for establishing when military personnel might justifiably refuse to fight altogether or refuse to carry out specific orders. First, it is important to distinguish between conscientious objection in the military and refusal of service on professional grounds.

Conscientious objection (which became highly topical during the Vietnam War) is probably the most common grounds for refusal of service. In the military, conscientious objection is a refusal to fight on the grounds that to do so would violate deeply held personal (usually religious) beliefs. Conscientious objection is most commonly an objection to serving in the military at all, rather than an objection to a particular order or military task, although such selective conscientious objection is not unknown.[82]

Indeed, given the importance of obedience in the military, it is highly unusual to encounter a refusal (on the basis of personal religious or secular moral ideals) to perform a *specific* military task, as opposed to a refusal to enlist in the military at all. Michael Walzer describes the limitations on the right to conscientious objection: 'the legal right of conscientious objection ... makes it possible for individuals with religious scruples against fighting or killing to avoid military service. The exemption does not extend to those who oppose some particular piece of fighting and killing, whether for religious or any other reasons.'[83]

Walzer is referring here to the *legal* right to conscientious objection. There may of course be cases of morally justified conscientious objection that are not legally permissible. Whether or not it is legally permissible, conscientious objection is usually considered justified only if two conditions are met.

In the United States conscientious objection must be on religious grounds, although in 1965 the United States Supreme Court ruled that an individual's moral belief could count as religious if it ' "fills the same place" in the life of the individual who holds it as belief in God fills in the life of an orthodox Christian, Jew, and so on'.[84] In Australia the right to conscientious objection is granted to conscripts during wartime and to volunteer personnel during peacetime, but such conscientious objection must be based on fundamental long-standing moral values regardless of whether or not those values are religious.[85]

Clearly not just *any* personal reason will justify conscientious objection. The objector needs to be objecting on the basis of principled reasons – reasons arising from deeply held moral and/or religious values, rather than from merely personal or self-interested reasons. This coincides with commonly held intuitions about justified conscientious objection on the part of doctors. We would be unlikely to think that a doctor who refused to perform abortions because he found them distasteful or thought that performing them would negatively affect his reputation was justified in refusing his services. His reasons are too self-interested and unprincipled to count as a legitimate form of conscientious objection. However, if he refused on the grounds that he was a devout Catholic and performing abortions was against his deeply held religious beliefs then his refusal would seem justified.

In Australia volunteer military personnel do not currently have the legal right to conscientious objection once they have joined the military. American military personnel can conscientiously object to participating in specific wars by requesting assignment to administrative or other non-combat duties.[86] While there are times when military personnel are in fact obligated to refuse to carry out certain orders (these will be discussed

in Chapter 4), such refusal is justified in the military only on very limited grounds and these would not include the combatant's personal
moral convictions.

There is no theoretical reason why the right to conscientious objection could not be extended to military personnel in relation to specific
orders and so justify a refusal to participate in particular military actions
on the grounds that to do so would violate personal moral considerations. The fact that this has never been a legal right does not mean it
should not be a moral right. Several instances of British and US military
personnel refusing to return to Iraq on the grounds that they believed
that the war violated international law indicates that some members of the
military believe that the moral right to conscientious objection should
extend to particular military missions.[87] However, the fact that these combatants were all court-martialled indicates that the military as an institution does not recognize the existence of such a right.

As I argued in Chapter 2, there is an important distinction between
conscientious objection and refusal of service on professional grounds.
Conscientious objection, while a widely recognized legitimate refusal of
service, is not connected to the military's regulative ideal. In the military,
refusal of service on professional grounds could take place at an individual
or an institutional level. On an individual level, when are military personnel justified in disobeying their superior's orders? On an institutional
level, when would the military as an institution be justified in refusing
to obey the orders of the civilian authority?

Institutional disobedience

Earlier I argued that there was a distinction between the nation and the
state and that this distinction could result in a conflict between the military's loyalty to the nation and its loyalty to the state. The military is the
agent of the civilian authority of the nation – the agent of the state.
However, the aim of the military is not just to obey the state, but also to
protect and defend the nation. While subordination to the civilian authority is vital, such subordination could plausibly be overridden if the state
ordered the military to engage in actions that seriously endangered the
physical or political life of the nation. This conflict is most obvious in
the American military, where officers swear to uphold the Constitution
as well as obey the President of the United States, but even in Australia it
is possible to imagine a government whose military policies were harmful to the nation. It is possible for the state's interests to be distinct from,
and in some cases counter to, the nation's interests. This would most
obviously occur in the case of an illegal coup, but it is also possible that a

particular government policy (when the government itself is legitimate) might run counter to what could be construed as the best interests of the nation. The United States government's Vietnam War policies could be an example of this. In such a case, where should the loyalty of the military lie?

In the United States and Australia the government is elected democratically and can be considered both legitimate and representative (to a degree) of the nation's interests. The military forces of these countries, and those of any nation with a legitimate state, can plausibly be said to serve the state first in the belief that by doing so they are also serving the nation. If, however, the state is no longer serving the interests of the nation then loyalty could become divided. It is useful at this point to consider actual cases of military disobedience to civilian rule.

The most obvious and striking cases are military coups, where the military not only disobeys but overthrows the civilian leadership and assumes control of the nation. In such cases the military often justifies its actions by claiming that the civilian leadership was failing to protect the nation's interests.[88] This is not to say that the military is in fact justified in taking power and the subsequent behaviour of military dictatorships indicates that the military itself is not to be relied upon to protect the interests of the nation (at least not when in power).

Military dictatorships often arise out of the military's belief that they could protect the national interests better than the current civilian government. As such, military coups seem to be based on an extreme version of the belief that the primary, most fundamental, duty of the military is to the wellbeing of the nation, not the state. However, the military's adoption of ultimate power is a clear case of the formation of an illegitimate state; one formed without the consent of the governed, and so such coups cannot be considered justified instances of military disobedience. Nor can military coups be justified by reference to the military's regulative ideal. The military's regulative ideal does not allow room for the military to interpret what is in the nation's interests independent of the civilian state. To do so would be analogous to the legal profession refusing to carry out the laws set by the state and deciding that in fact, *they* know best what is in the interests of justice and which laws should be made and enforced.

It is possible to find a middle ground between the military blindly obeying the state no matter what and the military taking over the state. As a profession the military is not a mere tool of the government but should be reflective about how its professional expertise is utilized. Therefore the military might be justified in disobeying an order from a legitimate state if that order would require the military to seriously violate the principles underlying the military's regulative ideal. The Australian and American military are sworn to uphold the principles of democracy and the attendant political freedoms and to protect the physical safety of the nation. If the Australian or American governments ordered the military to participate in military actions that would undermine or seriously violate these principles, harm the nation's interests, and needlessly endanger the lives of military personnel, then the military could legitimately refuse to participate on the grounds that to do so would violate the military profession's regulative ideal. Such selective refusal is the mean between blindly obeying the state's orders and completely overriding the state's authority.

There is one recent example of a nation's military forces refusing to obey the civilian authority. During 1989 the Romanian military, after having previously obeyed orders to fire on protestors in several regions, refused outright to obey Nicolae Ceausescu's orders and went on to play a central role in his downfall.[89] However, this example is the exception. In countries with democratically elected governments such disobedience and subsequent political manoeuvring by the military is almost unknown. There are however several notable cases of individuals objecting to and/or refusing to participate in certain military actions.

Individual disobedience

In the military, individual disobedience on professional grounds would be justified on the same grounds as institutional disobedience. Military personnel could (and should) refuse to obey orders if those orders seriously violate military professional ideals. While rare, there are several notable cases of such disobedience. The US and British military personnel mentioned previously are a case in point. While their refusal was also a form of conscientious objection, these combatants refused to continue fighting in the war against Iraq on the grounds that the war was immoral and illegal. Such a refusal, while not appealing to national security, clearly appeals to the values found in the Geneva Conventions, to which the United Kingdom and the United States are signatories. In the past some leading military professionals have objected strenuously to certain defence policies formulated by the civilian authority. In the United States, General Douglas MacArthur's beliefs about the actions necessary for national security during the Korean War brought him into strong conflict with his civilian superiors and he was eventually removed from his command because his objections endangered the principle of civilian control of the military.[90] Similarly, General Harold K. Johnson had serious misgivings about the military and political wisdom of the military strategy governing the American Vietnam War policy, but failed to act on his misgivings at the time.[91] In both these cases, however, the principle of civilian authority was never seriously threatened and the military did not cease to carry out the contentious policies. Indeed the dismissal of General MacArthur served to strengthen the belief that the military's role is to be strictly subordinate to civilian authority.[92]

In short, the military's regulative ideal clearly sets limits on appropriate professional behaviour and gives rise to a conception of military professional integrity that in some cases requires institutional and/or individual disobedience of orders. By claiming to be a profession the military is binding itself to a set of professional ideals that limit when and how its professional expertise should be used. Yet in the United States and Australia disobedience on an institutional level is unheard of and disobedience on an individual level is very rare and is most usually punished by the military itself or followed by the dismissal or resignation of the individual in question. Despite the fact that the military's regulative ideal provides clear grounds for justified disobedience of orders, there appears to be a conflict between the level of disobedience justified by the military's professional status and how and when such disobedience occurs in reality. There seems to be a discrepancy between military rhetoric and military reality.

Conclusion

The military arguably constitutes a profession. As such it is governed by a set of professional ethical standards that restrict how and when military force can be used. The military's regulative ideal is formed from the functional requirements of military action, the constraints imposed by the laws of war, important broad-based moral values, and the character traits that promote the ends of the military profession. As a profession the military must abide by strict moral standards and must strive to minimize the harms of war. The military's special moral permissions are very great and so every member of the military must strive to uphold the military's high professional standards, not only in terms of professional expertise but of moral character as well. The ideal combatant's character involves traits such as honesty, integrity, courage, discipline, and obedience. Indeed, institutional and individual obedience is one of the most important military virtues, one that seems to be essential for excellent military functioning. Yet professional integrity in the military also requires disobedience in certain cases. How are we to reconcile the need for obedience with the possibility of justified disobedience? What does military obedience actually entail? Perhaps the appearance of a discrepancy between rhetoric and reality is just that: an appearance. Clarifying the limits of military obedience on both an institutional and individual is of crucial importance.

4
Obedience in the Military

In Chapter 3, the list of virtues derived from the military's regulative ideal included honour, courage, integrity, obedience, patriotism, self-sacrifice and loyalty. This list is not exhaustive – there may be other military virtues – however these virtues would constitute the core of any plausible list of military virtues. Of these obedience is often claimed to be one of the most important. Obedience, it is argued, is not only necessary for swift and efficient military action but is also a character trait that demonstrates trust in one's superiors and in the legitimacy of military demands. Military personnel need to cultivate the habit of obedience so that they do not hesitate when ordered to act. Yet obedience to authority is notoriously problematic.

Crimes of obedience

Defining the appropriate limits to obedience to authority is crucial because of the problem of 'crimes of obedience' – atrocities that occur when 'authorities give orders that exceed the bounds of morality or law'.[1] There are, unfortunately, many examples of such crimes. The Holocaust, the massacre at My Lai during the Vietnam War, and the genocides in the former Yugoslavia are all notorious cases of gross violations of human rights under the guise of following orders. Stanley Milgram's experiments (which are discussed in detail in Chapter 6) also demonstrated the destructive nature of blind obedience to authority. Systematic torture is another example of a practice committed under orders that violates both moral and legal constraints. Blind unthinking obedience can and does lead to horrific acts.

It was partly in response to the recognition of this problem and the horrific crimes committed during World War II that the defence of 'just following orders' was largely rejected by international treaties and courts. Blind obedience is no longer believed to be the ideal military trait. If military obedience as a habitual trait is to be considered virtuous, therefore, we must look more closely at what this claim involves. Cultivating a trait that is connected to crimes of obedience needs a very strong justification. In this chapter I establish the limits of virtuous military obedience – is ideal military obedience habitual obedience or obedience restricted to legal and moral orders? Can obedience even be called a virtue or is it simply a militarily expedient trait justified by consequentialist considerations?

The virtue of obedience

As defined in Chapter 1, a virtue is a trait that both promotes and partly defines human flourishing. As such the virtues are both instrumentally valuable and valuable in their own right. Most importantly the virtues are more than emotional dispositions; they are a manifestation of rational choice and practical wisdom. Natural dispositions such as compassion or generosity can be useful and can form a good starting point for virtuous action, but they are not virtuous unless they are governed wisely. Children and animals cannot be virtuous because they lack the capacity for such wisdom. Being virtuous requires the exercise of (and the capacity for) reflective moral agency.

Obedience is essential for the fulfilment of military goals. Given this, it seems quite plausible to claim that obedience is part of excellent military functioning. If it is a professional virtue then it must be valuable in its own right, independent of the consequences of being obedient. This claim seems highly counter-intuitive. How can obedience *per se* be valuable regardless of the consequences of being obedient or the moral worth of one's orders? There are many situations where being obedient would seem to be thoroughly evil. There does not seem to be any value in obeying an order to torture and kill innocent civilians or bomb a hospital. If this is so, how can military obedience retain a value that is distinct from the consequences of obedience to evil orders? If obedience derives its value solely from the moral worth of one's orders, then it appears to have instrumental rather than intrinsic worth. If this is not the case and obedience is valuable in its own right, independent from the consequences of being obedient and independent from the moral value of one's orders, then where does the value of military obedience lie?

However, perhaps we can evade this problem. Military obedience is a professional virtue, not an ordinary virtue. As such, given Oakley and Cocking's account of professional virtues described in Chapter 2, it need not be a virtue in ordinary life as well, although it cannot be a vice. According to Oakley and Cocking's view, as long as the military profession serves a good that is linked to human flourishing and obedience genuinely helps achieve good military functioning, then it is a candidate for a professional virtue even if it is not an ordinary virtue. Obedience need not be constitutive of good human flourishing for it to be constitutive of good military functioning. That said, it still must fulfil the main criteria of a virtue: it must be a manifestation of choice and practical wisdom.

Claiming that obedience governed by moral judgement counts as a professional virtue may appear unproblematic, but this conclusion is not as straightforward as it seems. The nature of obedience makes it quite different from other military virtues and makes the requirement that obedience be paired with moral judgement highly problematic. The problem is this: being obedient requires the *suspension* of moral judgement and the substitution of another's judgement for one's own. As such, the concept of obedience *governed* by one's moral judgement seems to be a contradiction in terms. Is it conceptually possible for obedience to be governed by moral judgement?

Can suspending moral judgement be virtuous?

In Chapter 1 I explained that both Kant and Aristotle agreed that rational judgement was essential for virtuous action. Given the connection between rational judgement and virtue, is it possible to act virtuously if I suspend my capacity for reflective reasoning? By definition, being virtuous requires not only having certain emotional dispositions; it requires the exercise of practical wisdom. If obedience by definition involves suspending one's moral judgement and substituting another's judgement for one's own, then it is hard to see how being obedient could ever be virtuous. It is worth noting that Aristotle did in fact consider obedience to be a virtue, but only for slaves and women and precisely because he believed that they lacked the requisite reasoning skills to govern their actions by practical wisdom.[2] Obedience has also been considered an appropriate trait for children, again mainly because of their reduced capacity for reasoning. Obedience has rarely been considered a virtue in adults who have the capacity for moral judgement and practical reasoning. While many of us would be happy to be praised for being just, courageous, honest, and benevolent, few of us would desire to be praised for being obedient.

This characteristic of obedience is precisely why it is problematic to claim that it could be a virtuous character trait, professionally or otherwise. To claim that there is moral value in a character trait that suspends the very faculty needed to judge the moral value of orders seems highly counter-intuitive. Why is there value in *refraining* from making a reflective moral judgement? Where does such value lie?

Perhaps, though, submitting to another's judgement need not involve an undermining of moral judgement or be a failure of rationality. After all, there are times when accepting someone else's judgement in place of one's own might be the most rational thing to do. Co-operation and trust, for example, are essential for a flourishing human life. Sometimes we simply have to take another's judgement for granted when we do not have the information or the time to make the reflective judgement that we would make under ideal circumstances. If I am crossing the road and someone yells at me to 'Run!' I do it – I obey – without thinking. To hesitate could be disastrous. Similarly in school, in the family, at work, and in friendship we often allow ourselves to be persuaded by others' judgements. To take another's judgement as sufficient reason to act need not be a sign of faulty moral agency or a lack of moral autonomy.

There is one case in particular where the suspension of one's moral judgement is arguably not only rational but is in fact crucially important for the maintenance of important human goods such as interpersonal and societal relationships: trust in another's moral knowledge.

Obedience and trust

Sometimes we choose to act on another's advice or judgement because we have reason to believe that they know best or have our interests at heart. In her discussion of moral trust, Karen Jones presents a convincing case for the value of a different way of trusting – trusting another's judgement about the relevant moral issues or the application of moral principles in a given situation. As an example of when this kind of trust might be warranted, Jones has us imagine Peter, a young man who lives in a group house and is strongly committed to feminist principles. During the selection of a new housemate two women in the house decide against a particular applicant because they believe he showed a sexist attitude towards them during the interview. Peter, however, did not perceive the applicant's behaviour to be sexist. He felt he could not accept the women's judgement and decided to leave the house. Jones argues that in this case Peter would have been wiser to trust the women's judgement – to accept their claim that the applicant was sexist.[3] What would such trust involve?

This kind of trust requires us to accept that we might not know all the moral 'facts' of a situation and that we might not have had the kinds of experiences that would enable us to recognize the relevant moral issues.[4] Peter, while sharing the women's feminist principles, should have accepted that his housemates were likely to have experienced sexism and that those experiences would make them better judges of whether or not someone's attitude was sexist. He should have accepted that, because of their different experiences, he may not have been the best judge of whether his moral principles applied in that situation.

Jones argues that this kind of moral trust should not be given lightly. Given that our own and other's moral thinking is subject to 'distortion, due to, for example, wish fulfilment and self-interest',[5] we have good reason to be careful about trusting others' moral knowledge, particularly as the consequences of misplaced trust can be very serious. As she points out: 'If your source is wrong about the relative importance of a good, or wrong about which principles or ends to adopt, *and* you take her word for it, your error is going to surface not just in one place but in many.'[6]

Because of the possible consequences of trusting too easily, we should adopt a default stance of distrust regarding the acceptance of moral testimony. Yet there will still be occasions where trust is warranted, once we: 'have good evidence about the person's character, about possible hidden agendas, and about whether she has the sort of experiences that contribute to the kind of competence we counting are on her to have'.[7]

Under Jones' account trusting another's moral judgement is not a sign of irrationality or loss of autonomy. It is simply a fact that due to our own lack of morally relevant experiences (of racism or sexism or the value of freedom for example), we cannot always rely on our own judgement to tell us which principles are worth adopting or when certain principles apply. We are therefore justified (indeed it might even be taken as a sign of moral maturity) in trusting (wisely, of course) the moral testimony of others whose experiences differ from our own. Such trust has positive benefits for ourselves and for others: accepting the testimony of others can lead to a greater understanding of moral issues, greater self-awareness about such issues, and can enable us to attempt to revise the gaps in our own moral knowledge.[8] Trusting the moral testimony of others, far from being a sign of laziness or moral apathy, requires significant reflection and judgement: 'We must subject judgements about whom to trust on these matters to rational scrutiny, and we can be called on to revise our assessments of who is trustworthy. Accepting moral testimony is shown not to be in conflict with the value of autonomy, properly understood.'[9]

This is a convincing argument for why accepting others' moral judgements in place of our own is not irrational and does not indicate a lack of autonomy. When it is given carefully, such trust can be considered a virtue because of the importance of self-knowledge in the Socratic sense – that is, knowing the limits of our own knowledge. In addition, deferring to others' moral experiences can result in increased sensitivity and greater understanding. Accepting that we might not know all there is to know about morality can be the first necessary step to becoming a mature and reflective moral agent.

If moral trust – accepting another's moral judgements in place of our own – is not irrational, then perhaps obedience can be considered in the same light. Obedience could be seen as involving a kind of trust in another's judgement, a trust that leads to accepting their judgement as a sufficient reason to act. As we have seen in Chapter 3, good officers must be trustworthy because their subordinates' lives are in their hands – the consequences of loss of trust can be momentous. Officers must be able to command their subordinates' loyalty and faith. Military personnel must be able to trust each other absolutely. Perhaps, then, obedience can be seen as an expression of complete trust in the order-giver; a recognition of their greater professional expertise and their authority to make demands. If so, then we have solved the apparent contradiction between obedience and the exercise of moral judgement. Obedience can be understood as a kind of wise trusting and as such it involves no irrationality or undermining of moral agency

However, trust and obedience are conceptually quite different. First, obedience implies an *unequal* and *non-reciprocal* relationship between two parties: trust does not, although it does not exclude such a relationship. Obedience requires a hierarchical relationship of authority that need not have anything to do with trust. This is borne out by the Oxford English Dictionary definition of obedience: 'the action or practice of obeying; the fact of being obedient; submission to another's rule or authority; compliance with a law, command, etc.'[10] Trust can be reciprocal but obedience is one-way. Trust can occur between equals, obedience cannot. So even though obedience might be based on trust, it is significantly different from trust. Even officers who do not have their subordinates' trust might command their obedience.

Second, wise trusting requires us to have access to information about the character and experiences of those whom we trust and to exercise significant rational judgement about the standards of trust. My reasons for trusting another's moral testimony are based on judgement and reflection – I do not blindly trust just anyone. Trust in moral testimony, like any trait, must be wisely governed. In the case of obedience, however, I might not have any information about the order-giver's experiences or character. I don't withhold my obedience until I have reflected on whether the order-giver is someone whose judgement I can trust. Instead, obedience requires a *substitution* of their judgement for my own simply because they say so and they have authority over me. It implies an act of submission to their will rather than a reflective acceptance of their judgement. While it is possible to describe my obedience in such a way that trust forms one of my reasons for action (maybe I trust that the action ordered is necessary and that the justification is sound), obedience requires that I acquiesce even if I do not have access to that information. I might be obedient out of fear or ignorance. I might not trust the order-giver at all; I just might be afraid of them and of the consequences of disobedience.

My reasons for trusting someone's moral judgement are based on significant reflection on and judgement of their character and experiences. My reason for obeying someone is because I am subject to their authority. So long as I judge that they have legitimate authority over me their order is a *prima facie* reason to act. Obedience implies a *demand* – not a request, suggestion, or piece of advice. Advice, suggestions, orders, and requests play quite different roles in an agent's reasons for action. David Owens explains these differences. Using the example of attempting to persuade a colleague to teach a course, Owens argues that: 'There are two quite different ways in which one can try to get a colleague to give a course ... one can request that she do it, or advise her to do it, or threaten her with reprisals if she doesn't do it. These methods all involve giving her, or drawing her attention to, some reason to put on the course which will, one hopes, feed into her practical reflection on whether she ought to give the course and tip the balance in favour of her giving it.'[11]

Owens points out that a request, a piece of advice and a threat all influence the subject by adding a reason into the subject's practical reflection. They are added into the agent's reasoning for and against performing an action and may or may not tip the balance in favour of performing it. However, an order is quite different from these. An order does not add one more reason into the balancing of reasons for and against an act – it overrides the process of reason-weighing altogether. If I *order* my colleague to give the course: 'it indicates that I wish to take matters out of her hands. It is no longer up to her whether she should give the course, it is up to me. In requiring her to give the course, I am not attempting to address or influence her view of the merits of this action, I am not highlighting pros and cons for her consideration: rather I am taking control of what she does myself. I am seeking to substitute my practical judgement for hers.'[12]

An order supersedes the agent's own reasoning process about the desirability of the action in question and renders her reasoning irrelevant as to whether she should perform the action. The order-giver has already made the decision and in giving an order is telling the subordinate that no reflection is required.

The above discussion clearly illustrates the important differences between accepting someone's moral judgement out of trust (in their character, expertise, or for some other reason), and carrying out an order. The reasons for obeying an order may have nothing to do with trust. A combatant might obey her superior officers not just because she trusts them but because she recognizes that they have the authority to make demands and that she is subject to that authority. Her superior officers' authority is partly the authority to make judgements about what it is best to do and to order her to act in accordance with those judgements. The officer does so in the expectation that the combatant will obey, not because she agrees with the judgement or because she has reflected on the issue herself, but because it is an order.

This difference between trust and obedience has important consequences for the discussion about obedience as a military virtue. If military obedience does not necessarily involve or require trust, and in fact overrides the moral reasoning process necessary for wise trusting, this means that we must be careful about claiming that obedience is a military virtue. We have not as yet solved the apparent paradox of reflective obedience. Is there another way to understand military obedience so that it is virtuous?

Captain Christopher P. Yalanis offers one suggestion: 'Obedience is a moral bridge. It allows the individual to move from a position of ignorance to one of moral certainty – to bridge the moral gap when making decisions. It allows the subordinate to remain ignorant of the objectively correct decision, and to transfer varying degrees of his responsibility for making an autonomous moral decision to his superior.'[13]

Yalanis explains that there is an important distinction between *performing* an order and *obeying* an order. Upon being given an order a combatant might decide to obey after assessing the order's justification and deciding that it is, upon reflection, the right thing to do. Another combatant might perform the action without knowing whether it is in fact the right thing to do, but simply because it was ordered.[14] In the first case, as Yalanis points out, the combatant is not acting solely out of obedience because 'The fact that the desired action is the right thing to do is justification itself to perform the act without its having been ordered at all.'[15] While the fact that the action was ordered might prompt the combatant to consider it and might weigh as an extra reason for performing it, he has reason to perform the desired act anyway. The fact that the action was ordered does not constitute his (primary) reason for action. He performs the order rather than obeys it. Of course, it would be very strange for a combatant, even one who believed an ordered action to be justified, to carry out the action (say, 'take that village') *without* being ordered to, completely off his own bat. To do that would be to override the chain of command and overstep his authority, which would be extremely damaging to the military infrastructure.[16] Yalanis is not implying that military personnel should decide and execute military strategy by themselves. Instead, his point is that a combatant who performs orders does not obey without question. The fact that the ordered action accords with his own military judgement provides one reason for obeying it and the fact that it is an order gives him a further and perhaps very persuasive reason to carry it out. His obedience is governed by reflective judgement about the wisdom of the orders he receives and about the value of obedience.

On the other hand, the combatant who simply obeys an order suspends entirely his moral assessment about the justification of that order. The fact that it is an order tells him that no moral assessment is required. For him the reason to act is simply that the action was ordered. Obedience is what helps him move from the position of ignorance regarding the suitability of the action to a state of certainty.[17]

Does the military wish military personnel to obey or perform orders? Which of the two combatants described above does the military want? Military rhetoric seems to favour the first kind: military personnel who are capable of reflective moral reasoning and whose obedience (though still a default stance) is tempered by sound moral character and integrity. Such military personnel obey their officers for the same reasons they might trust their officers – because they know through experience that their officers are of good moral character and can reliably be expected to issue only legal and moral orders. These personnel govern their obedience and their trust wisely. However, it remains to be seen if military training and accepted behaviour bear this out in practice.

The problem with the above account of obedience is this: obedience by definition requires a suspension of moral judgement and it is moral judgement that would indicate when obedience is misplaced. It is not clear whether wise obedience is a conceptual possibility. A trusting agent does not suspend her moral judgement when she decides to trust someone – it is through *exercising* her moral judgement that she decides whether or not trust is warranted. But, when obeying an order, an obedient combatant suspends her moral judgement and so loses the main faculty by which she could tell whether obedience is in fact justified.[18] In response to this problem someone might say that military personnel have good reason to obey their superiors because they can trust that their officers would not give them immoral or illegal orders. As we saw in Chapter 3, integrity and trustworthiness are central to the ideal officer's character. Military rhetoric tells us that the special circumstances in which military obedience operates – the chain of command with increasing professional expertise, the importance of the laws of war, etc. – mean that military personnel can rely on their officers not to give illegal orders. Just as it is not a sign of faulty moral agency to trust another's moral testimony, so it is not a sign of faulty moral agency to obey one's superior officer.

The problem with this response is straightforward. The prevalence of war crimes in past and present wars suggests that military personnel cannot rest assured that they will only be given moral and legal orders. Even accepting that their superiors have greater knowledge of strategy and other professional matters, ordinary military personnel do not have good reason to automatically assume that their orders will be legal or moral. As we shall see, this same problem has plagued other situations in which obedience has been considered a virtue. Appealing to the unique requirements of the military profession and officers' professional expertise does not solve the paradox of reflective obedience.

In response to this apparent paradox, one might accept the claim that obedience requires substituting another's moral judgement for one's own[19] and accept that it is not equivalent to trust. But, one might argue, there still are areas in which habitual obedience is virtuous because it does contribute to human flourishing and because it is wise obedience. Even if it is unlikely to be considered a virtue in everyday life, there are two arenas in which obedience has been thought to be a professional (or at least role-oriented) virtue: religion and nursing.

Obedience as a religious virtue

In a religious context obedience specifically refers to obedience to God's commands.[20] Such obedience has traditionally been considered an important Christian virtue. While the desired extent of such obedience and the correct interpretation of God's commands have been hotly debated, this debate is not of central importance to this discussion. For present purposes there is only one point that needs to be made. The rationality of obeying God's commands and the claim that such obedience does not undermine autonomy relies on one crucial assumption – the assumption that God would not and could not impose obligations that were morally wrong. Since God is omnipotent, omniscient, and omnibenevolent, it would be impossible for him to give unjust or immoral orders: 'Being good, He will only impose obligations which it is good be imposed.'[21]

The obedient Christian can rest assured that she will not be obliged to obey an immoral or unjustified order. God would not and could not give such an order. This rather unusual situation therefore provides a perfectly rational reason for a devout Christian to obey God's commands. In the normal course of events we would expect a rational moral agent to assess the moral value of different courses of action, and come to an independent judgement about which course of action is best.[22] However, suspending this process is both justified and rational when the commands come from God, and cannot be considered a denial of autonomy. In fact, given that our own faculty of reflection can be flawed and incomplete, it would perhaps be irrational *not* to obey the orders of a perfectly rational and good God. As Joseph Shaw argues; 'Divine commands which encapsulate advice will, moreover, have weight far beyond the advice of our fellow creatures. The weight of advice depends on the trustworthiness of the adviser and the relative knowledge of the adviser and the advisee ... Since God is omniscient, perfectly rational, and perfectly good, any information He may provide about what we should do will be worth listening to.'[23]

Because of the unique nature of divine commands obedience can be considered a virtue in the context of religion, but only because there is no possibility of immoral or unjustified orders. Obedience in this context therefore derives its value from the rather unique nature of the order-giver. It is not obedience *per se* that is valuable here, but the perfectly good and perfectly rational nature of God's commands combined with God's undeniably legitimate authority to issue such commands. It is impossible therefore to draw a conclusion about the virtue of obedience in general from the religious case, as the rational basis for such obedience is limited to an entirely unique context.

Obedience in the nursing profession

The second arena in which obedience has traditionally been praised as a virtue is in the nursing profession. In the early days of the nursing profession (founded by Florence Nightingale in the 1850s), the ideal model of nursing was connected strongly with the military model of organization, which was unsurprising given that Nightingale worked in military hospitals for much of her early career.[24] Early nurses underwent 'military' training in which they learned 'to be prepared for the hardships of night duty, personal danger, weary walking, and so forth'.[25] A crucial component of the good nurse's character at this time was unquestioning obedience to higher-ranking medical personnel. The good nurse was supposed to be both loyal and obedient to the doctors she worked under even if she disagreed with the doctor's orders or thought him mistaken.[26] In the words of the first American book on nursing ethics: 'Apart from the fact that [the nurse] may be quite wrong in her opinions, her sole duty is to obey orders, and so long as she does this, she is not to be held responsible for untoward results.'[27]

This military model of nursing and the demand for unquestioning obedience that it required had its detractors from the start and by the 1930s nursing manuals and public discussions were revising the traditional ideas of the good nurse. The reason for this revision was simple: nurses were being asked to carry out procedures that they believed were harmful or at the very least not in the patient's best interests. Also, despite the reassurance of the nursing manual quoted above, nurses were often held responsible for the 'untoward results'.[28] Obedience as a professional virtue for nurses came under fire because of the impossibility of guaranteeing that doctors' orders would always be in their patients' best interests (to put it mildly). The military model was gradually rejected and replaced by alternative models of nursing for one main reason: the military model undermined nurses' autonomy and moral judgement by requiring them to substitute the doctor's judgement for their own, regardless of the moral worth (or medical value) of that judgement.[29]

Considering obedience as a virtue in the contexts of religion and nursing reveals an important point. In the case of religion obedience is justified only because it is impossible that God would give an immoral or unjustified order. In the case of nursing, obedience as a professional trait was rejected because of the impossibility of ensuring that doctors' orders were morally or even medically justified. Unquestioning obedience to doctors' orders implicated nurses in actions that were detrimental (and sometimes fatal) to patients, yet did not protect them from moral and legal responsibility for those consequences.

These two examples suggest that habitual obedience is only justified when there is very little possibility that an immoral or illegal order will be given. It is hard to see how obedience *per se* has value that is independent from the consequences of being obedient. It is of course true that there are occasional situations where obedience is necessary, just as there are situations where anger, aggression, and even violence are justified. But just as one does not deduce from this that violence, aggression and anger are virtues that contribute to human flourishing, so too one cannot claim that obedience as a cultivated character trait contributes to human flourishing. At best obedience is valuable only when constrained by judgement, only in the professional context, and *only* if the profession absolutely requires it. Obedience *per se* cannot be considered a virtue.

If we reject the possibility that obedience can be a virtue in ordinary life, perhaps we can accept the view that it is a virtue only in the limited professional context of the military. After all, the military is unique among the professions both in the scope of its regulative ideal and in what it demands from military personnel. Oakley and Cocking argue that applying the virtue ethics approach to professional roles is not simply a matter of applying the virtues of the good person to the good professional.[30] Rather, a list of distinct professional virtues can be derived from the regulative ideal of the profession. As we have seen, these dispositions might differ plausibly from those that the good virtuous agent should develop in an everyday context. Such discrepancies are justified only so far as those dispositions do in fact serve the regulative ideal of the profession, and only so far as the profession serves an important human need. Under this view it seems plausible to list obedience as a professional military virtue while admitting that outside the realm of the military profession obedience – while not a vice – does not contribute to a flourishing human life.[31]

However, obedience *must* be reflective obedience if it is to be a professional virtue and there is a tension in the concept of reflective obedience that is difficult to resolve. Even if one accepts the claim that military obedience can be virtuous, the nature of obedience in the military still remains troubling. The claim that obedience is a professional military virtue rests on two claims that have yet to be proven. These are first, the assumption that the military (as agent of the civilian government) will be used for morally legitimate purposes, and second, that making military personnel obedient is the best way to achieve military efficiency. These assumptions require far more investigation.

What is clear is that an agent who displays the military virtue of obedience must govern their obedience by practical rationality. Unthinking obedience to just any order or demand would not constitute a virtue. There are times where being obedient would be morally wrong, just as there are times where being trusting and loyal would be morally wrong. However, the virtuous agent has the reflective capacity and the practical rationality to know when obedience is justified. This means that only obedience governed by reflective judgement could count as virtuous obedience in the military. But the fact that obedience might be misused or misplaced does not necessarily imply that it is cannot be a professional virtue.

This means that for military obedience to be a professional virtue it must be a manifestation of rational choice: the result of rational deliberation. Blind obedience cannot plausibly be a military virtue.[32] The virtue of obedience in the military context cannot be the thoughtless Pavlovian following of orders. The good combatant must exercise significant judgement about what orders to give, how orders are to be carried out, and which orders should be carried out. The importance of judgement is borne out not only in the writings of military ethicists but in the literature and publications of the military forces.

The limits of military obedience

Most military writers agree that military obedience should not be blind obedience. General George C. Marshall, for example, argued that the military should be trained in 'intelligent rather than blind obedience'.[33] The belief that military personnel should be trained to blindly follow orders because military success and indeed lives might hang on instant obedience does not reflect reality. Michael Wheeler argues that it is only very rarely that instant obedience is a matter of life and death. In most cases military personnel have time to reflect on the meaning of an order before it must be carried out. The fact that obedience is sometimes a matter of life or death cannot be used to support the claim that military personnel should be constantly trained in the habit of blind obedience.[34]

It is clear that ideal military obedience is governed by judgement and experience; it is not mindless obedience. Military academies such as the Royal Military College Duntroon in Australia, and the United States West Point Academy stress the importance of responsibility and moral judgement in the character of the good officer.[35] Good military personnel are *expected* to disobey illegal or immoral orders.[36] This belief is reinforced during the training of officer cadets. Officer Cadets at the Australian Defence Force Academy, for example, are instructed in the laws of war in Military Law classes and Character Guidance and Development workshops taught by Chaplains.[37] In these classes students are taught the requirements of the Geneva Conventions and explore justifications for disobedience. The classes 'subtly reinforce the view that military behaviour should "reflect the legal and moral standards and values of society ... and the standards of the *Geneva Conventions*" '.[38] Despite this emphasis on the importance of disobeying illegal orders, military personnel are still expected to assume their orders are lawful – military personnel who disobey orders do so 'at [their] peril'.[39] Obedience is the default response to orders but only as long as those orders are legal and do not obviously violate important moral constraints. Military rhetoric is clear: military personnel of all ranks have a clear obligation to disobey illegal and immoral orders.[40]

The military law of many countries supports this view. In many countries the claim that one was 'just following orders' is no longer accepted as a legitimate defence in cases where illegal or immoral orders have been carried out.[41] For example, the United States' Department of the Army

Field Manual (FM) 27-10, *The Law of Land Warfare*, states that if a combatant is being court-martialled for a war crime: 'an order of a superior officer, whether military or civil, does not deprive the act in question of its character of a war crime, nor does it constitute a defence in the trial of an accused individual.'[42]

Military personnel are 'bound to obey only lawful orders'.[43] While it is true that disobedience of orders is a punishable offence in most military forces, this usually only holds if the order was legal.[44] Yet while military rhetoric and military law support the view that military personnel are only required to obey legal orders, in practice there is a great deal of variety in the level of legal responsibility that military personnel bear when they have carried out illegal or grossly immoral orders. If a combatant is charged with commission of a war crime, the fact that he was obeying orders can be considered anything from an exculpatory fact that significantly mitigates his responsibility for the crime, to a merely explanatory fact that may or may not affect decisions about his moral and legal responsibility, depending on extenuating circumstances.

Mark Osiel explains that the most stringent approach holds that the fact that the criminal action was ordered is simply one admissible fact that might explain why the combatant acted as he did. It may not mitigate his responsibility: 'The soldier claims that having received orders to perform his wrongful actions contributed (along with other things perhaps) to his mistaken belief [that the order was lawful].'[45] Under this approach the onus of proof is on the combatant's defence lawyers to show evidence that supports the claim that the combatant made a reasonable mistake.

Some military codes hold that a combatant's belief that his orders were lawful excuses his obedience only if his belief was not only honest but reasonable. If an ordinary person would have realized that the orders were illegal, the combatant's belief to the contrary does not count as a reasonable belief.[46] This is the approach taken by current US law. According to the US *Manual for Court-Martial* 11–109 (1995): 'It is a defense to any offense that the accused was acting pursuant to orders unless the accused knew the orders to be unlawful or a person of ordinary sense and understanding would have known the orders to be unlawful.'[47]

Under this view, the circumstances in which the order was given are relevant in determining whether or not the combatant's belief that his orders were legal was a reasonable belief.[48] The order itself need not be blatantly illegal or immoral. This is a relatively stringent approach in that it requires the combatant to show that his belief in the order's legality is a belief that *any* reasonable person might have *in those circumstances*. However, in practice the cases of obedience to illegal orders that are actually prosecuted in the US only tend to be cases where the wording of the order itself was obviously illegal (for example, 'shoot that prisoner'). Also, in these cases the courts have held that the combatant was not responsible if the order itself was not illegal and no further consideration need be given to the particular circumstances in which the order was given.[49] In practice, therefore, the US approach is closer to the far more lenient approach that holds that if a combatant obeys what turns out to be an illegal order; 'the law will presume – conclusively in some countries, rebuttably in others – that he reasonably believed his orders to be lawful. It will excuse him on that account.'[50] Under this view, if a combatant obeys an order that is not blatantly illegal, then the fact that the act was ordered is not simply an explanatory fact for his behaviour but a defence in its own right.[51]

There are many positions between these legal approaches, but the military law of most countries requires that military personnel presume that their orders are legal. It is the scope for rebutting this presumption that varies.[52] In most Western courts, the standard legal approach is usually called 'manifest illegality'.

Manifest illegality

The doctrine of manifest illegality holds that the only circumstances in which the defence of superior orders is unavailable to the obedient combatant is if the order was manifestly illegal or grossly immoral – when there is no possibility that the combatant could have mistakenly believed that his orders were legal.[53] This doctrine is found in the military codes of Britain, Canada, France, and West Germany, among others.[54] As noted above, while this may not be the official US approach it tends to be the approach that is adopted in practice.

This doctrine is quite lenient on military personnel who obey illegal orders because it: 'presumes that the soldier obeys unlawful orders because he mistakenly believes, honestly and reasonably, in their lawfulness. The presumption is rebutted only when the acts ordered were so egregious as to carry their wrongfulness on their face.'[55]

It is not immediately clear what it means for orders to 'carry their wrongfulness on their face'. The most common interpretation involves an appeal to the 'ordinary' person's moral understanding. An order is manifestly illegal if it is such that the man on the street, with no knowledge of military law, would know that it was illegal. As the Supreme Court of Canada stated in a recent war crimes case: 'Military orders can and must be obeyed unless they are manifestly unlawful. When is an order from a superior manifestly unlawful? It must be one that offends the conscience of every reasonable, right-thinking person; it must be an order which is obviously and flagrantly wrong. The order cannot be in a grey area or be merely questionable; rather it must be patently and obviously wrong.'[56]

If a combatant is unsure about an order's legality, or if an order is of doubtful but not manifest illegality, then the order must be obeyed. Under this doctrine military personnel are expected and encouraged to assume that their orders are legal unless they are obviously illegal or immoral. They are encouraged to resolve their doubts in favour of obedience rather than disobedience. This approach discourages military personnel from pursuing clarification if the legality of their orders is unclear.

It is worth commenting on just how lenient this doctrine is, given that one can imagine many situations where a reasonable member of the military, particularly a junior officer, might recognize that his orders were unlawful once he evaluated them in light of particular circumstances, including the likely consequences of obeying the order. For example, suppose an artillery battery is ordered to fire on coordinates where an enemy field hospital is known to be located. A junior officer questions these coordinates, but is told that the hospital has been moved. However, he has very recent air reconnaissance photos showing the hospital still in place. The order to fire on the coordinates is arguably legal, but in these circumstances we might think that the officer should assess the legality of obeying the order.[57] But this kind of assessment is precisely what the manifest illegality rule deliberately discourages him from doing. By definition, situational judgement is unnecessary when an order is illegal 'on its face'.[58]

It is also worth noting that this view supposes that military personnel cannot be expected to know more about the laws of war than ordinary civilians. As Osiel states, it 'abandons the civilian fiction that everyone knows his legal duties'.[59] The manifest illegality approach only requires that military personnel have the moral understanding of 'every reasonable, right-thinking person'. Under this approach military personnel are not required to have any special understanding of the moral complexities that can arise during warfare and are not expected to exercise any extra moral deliberation about the legality and morality of their orders. This is extremely strange given that the military claims professional status and claims that military personnel are professionals, which implies that they have a greater level of expertise than the ordinary person. As explained in Chapter 1, professionals have special permission to do acts which are normally morally impermissible partly because they have expertise that non-professionals do not. If military personnel are professionals then part of the reason they have permission to engage in military activity is because they have the expertise needed for such activity. Given the importance of the laws of war, we can reasonably expect that professional military personnel should have more than the 'ordinary person's' understanding of those laws. They are the experts: they should know the law governing their field of expertise. It is inconsistent to claim that military personnel are professionals and then claim that they cannot be expected to have a deeper knowledge of the laws of war then the ordinary person. Furthermore, the military's claim to be a profession is justified only so long as the military minimizes the harms of war as much as possible – and obeying the laws of war is one of the most important ways of accomplishing this. Expecting military personnel to have only the 'ordinary man's' understanding of the laws of war is certainly not going to help minimize war crimes.

This inconsistency between military rhetoric about the limits of obedience and the common use of the manifest illegality approach is deeply troubling given that many crimes of obedience occur not in response to manifestly illegal orders, but in response to accepted interpretations of orders that are legal on the face of it.[60] An inquiry into the massacre at My Lai during the Vietnam War reported that: 'While there is some conflict in the testimony as to whether LTC Barker ordered the destruction of houses, dwellings, livestock, and other foodstuffs in the Song My areas, the preponderance of evidence indicates that such destruction was implied, if not specifically directed, by his orders of 15 March.'[61]

It is quite possible that military personnel could find themselves in situations where even a shallow knowledge of the laws of war would prevent atrocities occurring. Discouraging moral reflection about the legality of orders will certainly not prevent the occurrence of war crimes, especially if there is no onus on military personnel to acquaint themselves with the details of the laws of war.

Leaving aside the question of legal responsibility for the moment, military personnel who receive ambiguous orders or orders of doubtful legality should at the very least assume that their superior officer intended the *legal* interpretation of the order to be carried out, and carry it out accordingly. Given the serious consequences that can result from carrying out an order that turns out to be immoral or illegal, the good combatant (if he truly embodies the military virtues) would attempt to establish the meaning and legality of any questionable orders he might receive. This approach not only makes the education of military personnel of *all* ranks (not just the officer class) vitally important but also acknowledges their capacities as moral agents to interpret and investigate the serious moral issues arising from military action.[62] As I argued earlier, it is those capacities that are needed for obedience to be virtuous. Unless it is governed by moral judgement, obedience is not a virtue.

There seems to be a discrepancy between the reflective, virtuous obedience extolled by military rhetoric and the kind of obedience fostered through the common legal approach to crimes of obedience. How well does the current legal approach reflect ideal military obedience?[63]

Ideal military obedience

Despite clear discrepancies between theory and practice it is clear from both military rhetoric and military law that military obedience is intended to be reflective obedience. Furthermore, only reflective obedience is consistent with the military's claim to be a profession and only reflective obedience can be a professional virtue. From the analysis of ideal military obedience it is clear that the manifest illegality approach does not reflect the kind of obedience supported by military rhetoric. Military rhetoric emphasizes the need for military personnel to be reflective moral agents; to have moral integrity and courage. As Anthony Hartle explains, 'Obedience and responsibility in the military today requires considerable maturity, good judgement, and reflective preparation for challenging situations.'[64] It clear from statements such as this that that the role of good military personnel is (among other things) to protect and uphold the laws of war and the values underlying those laws. For military personnel to be able to do this – to be able to identify the relevant laws, apply them, and know what actions violate them – requires a level of knowledge inconsistent with the level of awareness encouraged and assumed by the manifest illegality approach. Given that the manifest illegality approach encourages military personnel *not* to reflect about the legality of their orders unless their orders are so blatantly illegal that anyone would realize it, this approach is unlikely to reduce the occurrence of crimes of obedience. Indeed, if past and current wars are anything to go by, it has failed dismally to minimize the occurrence of war crimes. Current military law should not therefore be taken as reflecting the most appropriate or morally justifiable version of ideal military obedience.

The military's public statements and legal requirements support quite a rigorous view of the limits of military obedience and of the responsibility of military personnel to disobey illegal orders. Even under the manifest illegality approach military obedience is not blind obedience. Under the manifest illegality view, obedience should be governed by the moral constraints imposed (at the very least) by a moral understanding similar to that of an everyday reasonable person. Given that the military considers itself to be a profession and military personnel to be professionals, there are strong grounds for thinking that the constraints imposed by the manifest illegality approach are far too lenient. Ideal military obedience is obedience governed not only by ordinary moral constraints but by the laws of war. Only when it is governed in this way can it plausibly be considered a professional military virtue.

Conclusion

Obedience is claimed to be a military virtue because of the need for an efficient, disciplined force that can respond instantly to military demands. In the military, obedience is demanded not just when there is no time for reflection (indeed, such cases are very few and far between in the day to day running of the military profession), but as a default position in regard to *all* legitimate orders. The military also claims that it wants military personnel to be reflectively obedient – to disobey illegal or immoral orders. But despite the clear limits of military obedience and the requirement that military personnel understand those limits, crimes of obedience still occur. If the military is genuinely committed to developing the moral judgement and reflective obedience it claims to hold most valuable we must wonder why it fails so badly.

The importance of military obedience cannot be underestimated, and nor can the importance of the question of what military obedience is obedience *to*. The military requires military personnel who can kill efficiently and without hesitation when ordered to do so. The fact that such obedience by definition involves a suspension of combatants' moral judgement is very troubling. We want to be very sure about the permissible nature of killing in warfare before we want military personnel to suspend their moral judgement about such killing. There appears to be a tension between the kind of obedience expected in the military and the kind of obedience that is commensurate with the moral integrity and moral judgement that are also desired and that are consistent with the military's claim to professional status.

The previous three chapters have established the criteria of a profession and the nature of special professional permissions, and it is clear that there is a strong case for the professional status of the military. Adopting the virtue ethics approach provided a way of allowing some distance between professional norms and those of broad-based morality, and provided a comprehensive way of establishing the roles and character traits that best promote the ends of the military profession. From the discussion of the military's regulative ideal in Chapter 3, we have seen that the military personality is quite distinct: the military requires its personnel to be nationalistic, loyal, obedient, disciplined, honest, and selfless.

Yet because of its role as the agent of the civilian authority the military may be required to carry out policies that are neither morally nor militarily justified. The military's special professional permissions are therefore strictly limited by the laws of war and by the broad-based moral principles underlying those laws. These principles and the role they play in the military's regulative ideal provide a foundation for justified disobedience on both an individual and an institutional level. Such disobedience is, in theory, encouraged by the military – the military virtue of obedience must, as I have argued, be reflective obedience.

Yet despite the military's own claims about the limits of military obedience, military personnel are obeying illegal orders and committing crimes of obedience. There is evidence that the US military has systematically used torture during the interrogation of terrorism suspects in Afghanistan, Iraq, and Guantanamo Bay – torture authorized by high-ranking military officials.[65] Furthermore, military dictatorships in South and Latin America, Greece, Burma, and elsewhere also systematically used torture against perceived enemies. Why are military personnel violating not only important broad-based moral values but the values of their own profession? Why are military personnel becoming torturers?

The following three chapters turn from the theoretical side of military professionalism to the reality of military behaviour. Using the case study of torture, I argue that the use of torture is aided by the dispositions generated through military training and through the use of the discourse of professionalism. The discrepancy already apparent between military rhetoric and military reality is indicative of a widespread fundamental inconsistency between the dispositions generated by military training and the dispositions needed for virtuous military action. Furthermore, it will become apparent that there is a strong connection between the dispositions created through military training and the dispositions linked to crimes of obedience.

To understand the nature of military torture, we must be clear about the definition of torture. We must establish whether the interrogation techniques used at Guantanamo Bay and elsewhere really do constitute torture and if so, whether the use of such torture could be justified by reference to the ends of the military profession.

5
Military Torture

'Make no mistake: every regime that tortures does so in the name
of salvation, some superior goal, some promise of paradise. Call
it communism, call it the free market, call it the free world, call
it the national interest, call it fascism, call it the leader, call it
civilisation, call it the service of God, call it the need for information, call it what you will.'

Ariel Dorfman[1]

Chapter 4 established that obedience can only be a virtue if it is reflective
obedience – obedience governed by rational judgement. In the context
of the military this means that good military personnel are constrained
to obey only moral and legal orders. An officer who had internalized the
military's regulative ideal would obey orders subject to the caveat that
those orders did not violate the values of the military profession, the
laws of war or important broad-based moral values. In theory the military virtues of integrity, honesty, and moral courage should provide a
solid basis for military personnel to become strong and reflective moral
agents with the judgement and courage to disobey illegal orders. We would
expect such virtues to be more than mere window-dressing, but actually
reinforced in combat training and during combat itself, when the stress
of war might tempt some to abandon the hard work of maintaining
integrity. After all, it is often said that it is in times of great hardship that
one's true colours are shown. In theory good military personnel should
never commit crimes of obedience.

It seems obvious that torture is morally wrong. Even a 'man of ordinary
sense and understanding' would recognize that. It seems equally obvious
that the character traits of good military personnel are incompatible with
those of torturers. Most of today's military forces officially condemn the

use of torture. The Australian and American governments are signatories to conventions banning torture and have condemned torture in numerous public statements. President George W. Bush said in 2003; 'I call on all governments to join with the United States and the community of law-abiding nations in prohibiting, investigating, and prosecuting all acts of torture ... and we are leading this fight by example.'[2]

Yet despite the illegality and immorality of torture and despite the fact that modern military personnel are required to refuse an order to perform torture, the vast majority of systematic torture takes place in a military environment and is performed by trained military personnel.[3] Historically, the use of systematic torture is closely associated with military dictatorships. Currently, there is evidence that torture is being used by military juntas such as that of Myanmar, in countries including Jordan, Syria, Pakistan, and, by US military forces in Guantanamo Bay, Iraq, and elsewhere. This use of torture involves military personnel of all ranks. Attempts are made to justify the use of torture by appeals to the role of the military as protector of national security. Implicit in these kinds of justifications is the belief that the military has an exceptional special moral permission to use torture in circumstances when the normal laws of war cannot apply.

In order to evaluate these justifications for the use of torture we must establish whether the interrogation techniques used in Guantanamo Bay and elsewhere constitute torture and, if so, whether the use of torture can be justified by appeals to the military's professional role as protector of national security. Does the war on terrorism plausibly give rise to an exceptional special moral permission to use torture? If torture is illegal and immoral and the justifications for the use of torture fail, why are military personnel obeying orders to torture?

In this chapter I show that interrogation techniques currently used in Guantanamo Bay and elsewhere clearly constitute torture, and that the arguments supporting this use of torture fail. The use of torture is not only illegal and immoral but violates the military's own professional standards. Military personnel have a clear moral duty (and a clear professional duty) to refuse orders to torture. Given this, how do we explain the involvement of military personnel in torture?

The reason for the widespread involvement of military personnel in torture cannot be explained by reference to the horrors of war or individual failures to live up to the professional standards of the military. Using a real-life case study of a virtuous officer I show that there is an inconsistency between military rhetoric about ideal military obedience and the military's attitudes towards military personnel who embody that ideal. Furthermore, it is far from clear that such an inconsistency is accidental.

Psychological and physical torture

It is not always clear what 'torture' refers to and how it is to be differentiated from the techniques of coercion and persuasion that are likely to be part of any interrogation. In the United Nations 1984 *Convention against Torture and Other Cruel, Inhuman, or Degrading treatment or Punishment* torture is defined as: 'any act by which severe pain and suffering, whether physical or mental, is intentionally inflicted on a person for such purposes as obtaining from him or a third person information or a confession, punishing him for an act he or a third person has committed or is suspected of having committed, or intimidating or coercing him or a third person, or for any reason based on discrimination of any kind, when such pain or suffering is inflicted by or at the instigation of or with the consent or acquiescence of a public official or other person acting in an official capacity'.[4]

Traditionally, the word 'torture' brings to mind images of severe *physical* tortures – beatings, electric shocks, branding, and other atrocities. However, the definition of torture in international treaties and conventions also refers to actions that cause severe *psychological* suffering. This more inclusive definition arose because the twentieth century witnessed the development of torture techniques that left few physical marks on the victim but were just as (if not more) effective in terrorizing and tormenting. These techniques include what are known as 'stress and duress' or 'torture lite' techniques, such as sleep deprivation, hooding, noise bombardment, poor food, solitary confinement, forced standing (making the prisoner stand in uncomfortable positions for long periods of time), and mock executions.[5] It is sometimes claimed that these techniques should not be considered torture because of the lack of physical injury – hence the phrase 'torture lite'. Mark Bowden, for example, argues that: 'A method that produces life-saving information without doing lasting [physical] harm to anyone is not just preferable; it appears to be morally sound. Hereafter I will use "torture" to mean the more severe traditional outrages, and "coercion" to refer to torture lite, or moderate physical pressure.'[6]

During the war against terrorism the US Government defined torture extremely narrowly so as to exclude everything but extreme physical abuse from the definition. For example, a 2001 Justice Department memo written for the CIA defined torture so narrowly that the Agency was permitted to use a wide range of techniques including sleep deprivation, 'stress factors', and the use of phobias during interrogations of Al Qaeda suspects.[7]

The claim that psychological techniques do not count as forms of torture relies on two related assumptions. The first is that these techniques do not cause any lasting harm, simply because they do not cause lasting *physical* harm. The second assumption is that the impermissibility of torture must rest to some degree on the assessment of long-term effects and not just on the immediate suffering and harm caused to the victim. The first of these assumptions can be effectively rebutted by a survey of the impact of torture 'lite' on victims, and the second by a survey of the moral arguments against the use of torture.

The victims of torture

In Belfast in 1971 14 Irish men were detained for nine days by the British forces. During the time of their detention they were subjected to what was known as the 'five techniques' – food deprivation, sleep deprivation, hooding, noise bombardment, and forced standing.[8] These techniques fall under the definition of 'torture lite' because they do not involve extreme or severe physical injury. However, far from not causing long-lasting harm to the victims, the experience at the time of interrogation and afterwards was extremely traumatic. During the course of the interrogations these techniques 'induce a state of psychosis, a temporary madness with long-lasting after-effects'.[9] Some of the men hallucinated; one saw his own funeral casket and heard hymns, another man's tongue became so swollen that he could not swallow, and another lost the ability to spell his own name.[10] Some of the immediate after-effects of the treatment were horrific. One man lost the use of his hands, another lost his memory, and yet another could not stop crying and suffered from blackouts, intense headaches, insomnia, and nightmares.[11] After this incident, the British Government denied that any brutality had taken place and vigorously denied the accusation of torture.[12] The Irish government complained to the European Commission on Human Rights with the result that a hearing into the allegations took place. After hearing testimony from psychiatrists and psychologists[13] on the effects of the treatment on the victims and after considering 16 cases carefully the committee, in a unanimous decision, ruled that: 'the use of the five techniques amounted to torture and inhuman and degrading treatment'.[14]

The long-term effects of this kind of torture (indeed of *any* kind of torture) vary considerably and are hard to quantify. There is a great deal of variety in both the kinds of torture used and in related factors such as the length of imprisonment and the environment in which torture occurs.

Other factors such as the victim's level of education, the level of stress experienced, and access to support networks after release will also affect a torture victim's capacity to recover.[15] Despite this variability, studies have shown that there are commonalities among the symptoms experienced by torture victims even many years after the torture. One study of 24 torture victims revealed that headaches, memory impairment, fear and anxiety, vertigo, loss of social interaction, and nightmares were common symptoms.[16] Ex-American and English prisoners of war often report similar symptoms, even many years after the events. One study concluded that 'some effects are "essentially permanent" '.[17]

Studies on former political prisoners in East Germany confirm these claims. These prisoners were not physically beaten or injured, but they were: 'exposed without warning to the following extreme stressors: frequent, repressive, and long interrogations; isolation and no contact with other people apart from the prison service and the interrogators; systematic sleep deprivation with the lights switched on and the person being called every 10 minutes; degrading treatment and discrimination; and complete uncertainty regarding their own and other family members' future'.[18]

Some of these prisoners continue to suffer from long-term effects which would 'qualify for a diagnosis of PTSD [Post Traumatic Stress Disorder]'.[19] Similarly, a study of Turkish torture survivors reported that many of them suffered from PTSD symptoms such as 'nightmares, flashbacks, distress when reminded of the trauma, avoidance of trauma-related thoughts, activities, or situations, and physiological reactivity to reminders of torture'.[20] A study of Bhutanese refugees who had been tortured found similar results: 'We found that 5 of every 6 refugees had a lifetime disorder, and we noted a high rate of PTSD among tortured refugees.'[21]

It is clear that all forms of torture cause immediate severe harm and distress, and are likely to have very serious long-term effects. As for the purported difference between the long-term effects of torture and torture 'lite', there are some torture 'lite' techniques that seem to cause more severe long-term psychological harm than the supposedly more serious physical tortures. For example, a Danish study found that 83 per cent of victims who had experienced mock executions (a common torture 'lite' technique) developed psychiatric symptoms, 20 per cent more than those who had not experienced that particular torture.[22] It is therefore completely untenable to conclude that psychological torture techniques such as mock executions, hooding, noise bombardment, sleep deprivation, and forced standing do not constitute 'real' torture just because they do not involve much immediate or long term *physical* damage. The term 'torture lite' is a gross misrepresentation of and disregard for the extreme suffering that such torture causes.

It is because of the evidence that psychological torture techniques produce extreme distress, suffering, and long-term psychological harm that international law makes no distinction between psychological and physical harm in the definition of torture used by treaties and conventions. Torture is the infliction of severe pain, *whether or not* it is physical or psychological.

The second assumption underlying Bowden's remark is that the moral impermissibility of torture lies at least partly in its long-term effects. It is true that a consideration of the long-term effects does add to the moral assessment of torture, but it is hardly the sole reason why torture is generally condemned. If some torture victims recovered completely after severe physical or psychological torture this would not reduce the moral wrong that was committed.[23] There are victims of rape who manage to recover and avoid long-lasting psychological or physical harm, yet this is not a reason to consider rape (or their rape) as less morally wrong. Rape (and torture) can be condemned as a deep violation of the victim's sense of self – of their physical and mental integrity.[24] As such it is a gross moral wrong regardless of how well a particular victim recovers. Some survivors of crime might be fortunate enough to have excellent support from family and friends, good quality counselling and readily available medical treatment. None of these factors mitigate the wrong that was done. An act of rape, torture, or assault does not rely for its final moral status on how quickly the victim recovers. We do not withhold our moral judgement about rape until we see how well the victim gets over it. Rape and assault are wrong *at the time they were committed* – their moral status does not solely rely on an assessment of actual or foreseen consequences.[25] Similarly, many of the arguments against torture do not rely on a consideration of long-term consequences; they argue that torture is a wrong at the time it is used, not because of what the long-term impact on the victim might be.

Arguments for and against the use of torture

It might be considered redundant to consider why torture is commonly believed to be morally wrong. Most people will agree (and international law agrees) that deliberately inflicting pain and suffering on another human being against their will is wrong. Indeed, most arguments in favour of the use of torture do not deny that torture is bad; they just argue that in some cases it is necessary. It is beyond the scope of this book to discuss in depth the various arguments regarding the moral status of torture. I will therefore summarize the various ethical positions on the use of torture to outline the reasons why it is considered to be a moral wrong, and why it is now prohibited.

Arguments for the use of torture

Before discussing the philosophical positions for and against the use of torture, it is worth considering how the use of torture has been justified by military forces in the past.

Military justifications for the use of torture

Military forces in many countries (and in many times) have used torture systematically against perceived enemies. In South America, where there were military dictatorships in Brazil, Argentina, Chile, and Uruguay during the 1960s, 70s, and early 80s, torture (along with disappearances, extra-judicial executions, and political imprisonment) was used extensively against the perceived enemies of the regimes.[26]

Most commonly, military authorities justify the use of torture by appealing to perceived threats to national security – the permission to use torture is claimed to be an exceptional special moral permission justified by the military's professional status and its duty to protect national security. When the threat to national security is extreme, the argument runs, the military must regrettably resort to normally impermissible actions. Interviews with military officers who served in the South American regimes and who held ranks up to that of admiral provide an insight into this attitude towards the use of torture.[27] By far the most common justifications refer to the threat to internal stability posed by enemies such as guerrilla groups (in Argentina), communist and left-wing political (largely non-violent) groups, and more generally by 'sedition' and 'subversion'.[28] In some accounts, immediate danger to comrades also appears as a motive. As General Hugo Medina, former head of the Uruguayan army, explained: 'in many instances, the life of one of our comrades was in danger, and it was necessary to get information quickly. That was what made it necessary to compel them.'[29] The belief that military torture, while usually impermissible, is justified under certain kinds of threats to national security is illustrated by the remarks of US officials interviewed by the *Washington Post* in 2002: ' "If you don't violate someone's human rights some of the time, you probably aren't doing your job," said one official who has supervised the capture and transfer of accused terrorists. "I don't think we want to be promoting a view of zero tolerance on this [the torture of prisoners]." '[30]

The claim that terrorism poses such an extreme threat that the prohibition against torture cannot be maintained is nothing new. Herbert Kelman points out that 'In democratic societies it [torture] is most likely to occur in the context of counter-terrorism activities.'[31] This is borne out by recent indications that the acceptance of the torture (in theory at least) of terrorist suspects is gaining popular support – in a 2003 online poll, 65 per cent of respondents approved of the use of torture interrogation for terrorist suspects, and 49 per cent of those approved of the use of torture in *all* interrogations.[32]

Officers from South America compared their fight against terrorism with the fight against terrorism in Western Europe, implying that 'the methods used in their cases were primarily or exclusively a response to the magnitude of the threat encountered'.[33] The extremity of the threat posed by an ineffectual civilian government, active opposition forces, left-wing groups, and trade unions was seen to create a situation where the 'normal' laws could no longer be applied and would no longer maintain order.[34] As the Brazilian Colonel Brilhante Ustra explained: 'Our accusers complain about our interrogations. They allege that innocent prisoners were being held for hours under tension, without sleep while they are interrogated ... Thus, it is necessary to explain that one does not combat terrorism by using ordinary laws for an ordinary citizen. The terrorists were not ordinary citizens.'[35]

Here it is implied that the war against terrorism cannot be fought under the same rules that govern 'ordinary' warfare. The covert nature of terrorism means that new rules must come into force. This belief has become prominent in recent times, particularly after the 11 September 2001 terrorist attack in New York. For example, the former head of the US Counterterrorism Centre stated that: 'There was a before 9/11, and there was an after 9/11 ... After 9/11 the gloves come off.'[36]

There is strong evidence that the US has been using torture against prisoners suspected of terrorism since 11 September 2001. This became graphically evident in the photos from the Iraqi prison Abu Ghraib, but organizations such as the International Committee of the Red Cross, Amnesty International and Human Rights Watch have also documented evidence of the use of torture in Guantanamo Bay and in prisons in Afghanistan and Iraq. The US administration has justified the use of torture by exactly the kind of rationalizations referred to above. In a 2002 memo to George Bush, the White House legal counsel Alberto Gonzales stated that: 'the war against terrorism is a new kind of war ... The nature of the new war places a high premium on other factors, such as the ability to quickly obtain information from captured terrorists and their sponsors in order to avoid further atrocities against American civilians ... In my judgement, this new paradigm renders obsolete Geneva's [the Geneva Conventions] strict limitations on questioning of enemy prisoners and renders quaint some of its provisions.'[37]

The above justifications do not deny that torture is normally impermissible. Instead, they claim that due to special circumstances (terrorism, civil strife, etc.) the normal rules of war do not apply. Under this view the military's commitment to the laws of war is superseded by its commitment to the protection of national security. If the threat to the nation is severe enough the laws of war can be ignored. This view clearly puts the military's primary loyalty to the nation above and beyond its commitment to the laws of war and the principles underlying those laws. The military profession is given permission to perform acts of extreme violence when carrying out its duties; torture is one such act – an act that is normally morally wrong but that is justified under certain extreme circumstances. Under this view the military's special moral permissions come to include even acts that violate the laws of war. Because torture is claimed to be necessary if threats to national security are to be countered, the use of torture becomes part of the military's professional jurisdiction. Torture, if it is required, must be performed by professionals.

While this justification for the use of torture is clearly misused in many instances, for example during the South American dictatorships, such misuse is not enough to render the justification a bad one. Can a case be made for the use of torture in the circumstances described above?

Arguments in favour of torture

While many military forces would deny that *systematic* torture (such as that used by the South American dictatorships) is justified, there are still common arguments put forward to support the claim that torture in very specific one-off circumstances might be justified. Normally, it is argued, the consequences of inflicting severe pain on another person against their wishes will not outweigh the possible benefits to be gained from the information they might be forced to reveal. Torture is indeed an awful act that causes great suffering, but, the argument runs, in some situations the potential death of thousands of innocent civilians outweighs the suffering of the victim and outweighs the risk that the information will not be forthcoming even under torture.[38] These cases are often known as 'ticking bomb' scenarios. A classic example of a 'ticking bomb' scenario is the following: 'Suppose a fanatic, perfectly willing to die rather than collaborate in the thwarting of his own scheme, has set a hidden nuclear device to explode in the heart of Paris. There is no time to evacuate the innocent people or even the movable art treasures – the only hope of preventing tragedy is to torture the perpetrator, find the device, and deactivate it.'[39]

However, as several authors have noted, such utilitarian justifications fail to take into account the other serious consequences of permitting torture even in such apparently limited circumstances. For example, Major William D. Casebeer argues that: 'most consequentialist justifications for the permissibility of torture neglect to consider the institutional and character-based harm that we do to ourselves when we actually attempt to build a system for torture interrogation that the utilitarian would find praiseworthy. Perversely, consequential justifications for torture interrogation require well-trained torturers who know where and when to apply pain, but establishing the institutions required in order to sustain such well-honed practice is fraught with perils that the utilitarian would condemn, all things considered.'[40]

The classic utilitarian thought experiments used to justify isolated cases of torture are highly implausible because they fail to take into consideration what would actually be involved in making even such rare cases of torture possible. Consider, for a moment, the difficulty of meeting even the epistemological requirements of the 'ticking bomb' scenario. Christopher Tindale notes, for instance, that the 'ticking bomb' scenario rests for its plausibility on a series of far from plausible epistemological claims: 'We know for certain that we have the right person. We also know that he has the information we require, and we know exactly what that is. We are further sure (although it is not explained how) that the bomb does exist, that it will explode, and of the human cost that will result.'[41]

Social psychologist Jean Maria Arrigo details just how complex these epistemological requirements are and how many institutional procedures already need to be place in order to meet them. For example, to have identified the key terrorist, to be sure that he has the information we need, and to know how and where to capture him, we must already have a very well established intelligence network involving 'informants, electronic surveillance networks, and undercover agents'.[42] We must also be sure both that we cannot find out the information we need through these (already formidable) intelligence resources, and that torture is the best way to force the terrorist to reveal the information we require.

Furthermore, there could be no infliction of pain after the desired information has been revealed, so we must have ways of testing the truth of the information that the terrorist reveals.[43] This is highly problematic given the likelihood that a fanatical terrorist will either withstand the torture (he might even be trained to withstand torture, just as US Special Forces are trained to withstand torture), or give misleading information.[44]

Tindale also notes that we must be sure that the foreseen human cost of not torturing will in fact result – we cannot, he argues, 'justify a practice against which we have a natural prohibition by using ideal cases that are successful only in retrospect'.[45]

Already it is clear that meeting the requirements of the 'ticking bomb' scenario is far more complex than is usually recognized. There are further considerations that Arrigo explores in detail, considerations that are rarely mentioned by supporters of the 'ticking bomb' argument. For example, the torture must be purely interrogational: 'Its goal is to extract information and its victims are therefore restricted to those who hold or are believed to hold the desired information.'[46] Torture for other purposes, such as to punish or dehumanize the victim, to deter other individuals, or to force another person to confess, is impermissible.[47] Indeed very few if any supporters of the use of torture in the 'ticking bomb' case argue that torture should be permitted for these kinds of purposes.

To make sure that the torture is both efficient and not excessively cruel the torturer would have to use the most effective techniques available in order to achieve the goal of the torture in the shortest possible time.[48] At first glance these limitations on the use of torture might seem relatively unproblematic. Closer analysis reveals that these requirements would in fact entail highly problematic long-term institutional arrangements: 'physician assistance; cutting edge, secret biomedical research for torture techniques unknown to the terrorist organization and tailored to the individual captive for swift effect; well trained torturers, quickly accessible at major locations; pre-arranged permission from the courts because of the urgency; rejection of independent monitoring due to security issues; and so on'.[49]

While these claims might seem far-fetched, a little consideration shows that they are not. Take, for example, the need for the most effective torture techniques tailored to the psychology of the captive. Fulfilling this requirement would require biomedical research involving medical personnel, pharmaceutical companies, research scientists, and tests on human subjects – how else could we discover which techniques were the most effective?[50] These factors, when combined with the necessity of providing torturers with torture equipment and the potential psychological damage to the torturers themselves,[51] are all considerations that might well weigh against the traditional utilitarian justification for torture in the 'ticking bomb' scenario.

It is conceivable that a consequentialist might claim that the above side-effects are permissible if the entire infrastructure – the involvement of the medical, legal, intelligence, and scientific communities; the torture research, the training of torturers – is governed by strict standards and controlled by military and governmental organizations, thus containing the impact of permitting torture. Perhaps the threat of terrorism is so great as to outweigh the uncertainty about the effectiveness of torture, the huge institutional changes required, and the possibility that torturers and torture techniques will be used for illegitimate purposes.

In response to this objection it is important to consider what has occurred in the past when torture has been used (justified, as we have seen, by exactly the same kinds of arguments as those put forward by the US government). If there is strong evidence that permitting torture has frequently led to serious and widespread consequences, then there is good reason to be suspicious of claims that such consequences would not occur now.

Throughout history when torture has been used there has been illegal and immoral involvement of the medical profession (in Uruguay, for example, doctors regularly supervised torture sessions),[52] and there has been international involvement in the training and provision of torturers. The use of torture has almost never been restricted to one-off emergency situations. Instead, torture and torture training have become international enterprises.

Amnesty International, for example, found that the US had provided military training to the police and military forces of six countries, and over 24 countries (including Angola, Bolivia, Bosnia, Colombia, Ghana, Haiti, and Uganda)[53] had received military training from private US security companies. The groups receiving this training were often implicated in torture, killings, and other human rights abuses. For example, US Special Operations Forces trained military personnel in the Philippines in 'unconventional' warfare tactics, intelligence gathering, and interrogation skills. These same forces were involved in rapes, torture and executions, undertaken in the process of 'counter-insurgency' operations – the very operations for which they were trained.[54] The former School of the Americas (now called the Western Hemisphere Institute for Security Cooperation) in Fort Benning (whose mission is to 'develop and conduct resident training for Latin American military personnel')[55] trained many officers who were later involved in atrocities committed in South America.[56] The US has also handed prisoners of war and terrorism suspects to the military and intelligence forces of countries with less than salubrious human rights records: 'Since Sept. 11, the CIA has arranged for 230 suspects in 40 countries around the globe to be jailed and questioned. One notable aspect of putting possible terrorists in the hands of foreign security services is that [those] states ... use interrogation methods that include torture and threats to family members.'[57]

The testimony of former torturers from countries such as El Salvador confirms that at least some of their training in torture techniques came from American military instructors. One member of a death squad had an American trainer 'who emphasised "psychological techniques" ... the American also advised on the use of torture, stressing the importance of being choosy ... He favoured selective torture.'[58]

Arrigo also notes that torture techniques have been part of a world-wide trade in both training and equipment: American instructors taught South American torturers and Brazilian torturers taught the Chileans.[59] This testimony is supported by accounts from the military themselves. For example, General Ramon Campos, former Chief of Police of Buenos Aires province, stated that: 'In Argentina, we were influenced first by the French and then by the United States. We used their methods separately at first and then together, until the United States' ideas finally predominated. France and the United States were our main sources of counter-insurgency training. They organized centers for teaching counterinsurgency techniques (especially in the U.S.) and sent out instructors, observers, and an enormous amount of literature.'[60]

Australian forces have also been involved in the training of foreign military forces implicated in torture and other human rights abuses. Australia's Special Air Services trained with and taught Kopassus, Indonesia's notorious Special Forces, who have been implicated in numerous human rights abuses. Indeed, training links were severed in 1999 precisely because of Kopassus' atrocious human rights record. However, renewed training activities began in 2003, to widespread protest.[61]

It is clear that both the use of torture and the kinds of torture techniques used by military forces do not remain isolated within a country. Instead, the torture techniques used by military torturers are often the most up-to-date and effective methods, honed by training with the professional military forces of other countries such as the United States.

Another consistent consequence of permitting torture is the expansion of the pool of torture victims. In the Roman Empire torture was initially only permitted to be used on slaves, but over time came to be used on both freemen and slaves who were merely suspected of involvement in a crime or of possessing guilty knowledge.[62] In most of Europe from 1250 to the eighteenth century torture was part of ordinary criminal procedure. Those who were initially exempt from torture (such as children or pregnant women) were, by the fifteenth century, legitimate victims.[63] Similarly, in the South American military dictatorships the use of torture was limited at first to accused terrorists, but again gradually spread to include associates and bystanders.[64] David Luban describes this process of escalation in the 'Dirty War' in Argentina, where at first military officers were reluctant to use torture but towards the end of the military dictatorship: 'hardened young officers were placing bets on who could kidnap the prettiest girl to rape and torture ... Escalation, is the rule, not the aberration.'[65] Arrigo's analysis similarly concludes that, historically, dragnet interrogations are the norm.[66]

Like the South American dictatorships, the United States has not restricted the use of torture to terrorist suspects who pose an immediate threat or whose knowledge would prevent an immediate attack. Instead, the US has imprisoned and interrogated a wide range of prisoners – including 80-year-old prisoners suffering from dementia[67] – over several years. As far back as 2002, a CIA analyst sent to Guantanamo Bay interviewed over 30 prisoners and 'became convinced that we [the United States] were committing war crimes'.[68] A Red Cross report from June 2004 found that the US military were using psychological torture techniques on prisoners and that medical personnel were implicated in interrogation sessions.[69] There is also substantial evidence that this use of torture is not new; not just a 'last resort' in the new fight against terrorism. The US military used torture in Vietnam,[70] and in 1997 reporters unearthed the infamous Kubark Manual, the manual of interrogation and torture techniques developed by the CIA in 1963 and echoed in numerous subsequent Army manuals on interrogation.[71] When military torture is used, it is almost always used in ways that would never fit the stringent requirements of the 'ticking bomb' example. Far from being limited to one-off extreme emergencies, military torture is nearly always systematic, long-term, and widespread.

Given these precedents and the widespread arrangements that need to be in place before the hypothetical 'ticking-bomb' interrogation can take place, combined with the serious problem of monitoring and controlling such arrangements, we cannot assume – and we have no basis from which to assume – that a similar expansion of victims and the involvement of the medical, legal, and intelligence communities would not occur now.[72] Nearly every real-life case of military torture has involved a background of institutional changes and has resulted in the expansion of the pool of permissible victims. This suggests that, in reality, interrogational torture may not even be possible without such changes. Certainly there are few if any cases of such torture taking place without this institutional background. This is then a further reason to be suspicious of 'ticking bomb' justifications for the use of torture.

At this point an objector might claim that, despite this empirical evidence, there is no necessary connection between the use of torture and the consequences listed above. Theoretically there could still be an instance of torture that did not require all the problematic arrangements discussed above and that fulfilled all the necessary criteria (and problematic epistemological requirements) of the 'ticking bomb' scenario. It is perhaps possible to imagine a situation where the threat was sufficiently great that there was absolutely no alternative but to resort to torture, very little likelihood that torture would become more generally used, no infliction of excessive pain, little or no likelihood of long-term or widespread institutional changes, no moral damage to the torturer, and no problematic involvement of the medical and legal institutions. In such a situation torture might be the morally correct thing to do. Indeed, in such a situation, some non-consequentialists might also allow the use of torture. We could easily imagine someone who believed torture to be wrong *pro tanto* accepting that in such a case torture should be permitted. Under this view (let's call it the view of common-sense morality), torture would still be a moral wrong (and the torturer would still get moral 'dirty hands') and the victim still cannot be compensated, but the alternative would be far worse.

There are two responses to this objection. First, I am not interested in the permissibility of torture in any possible world or hypothetical example. I am concerned with the permissibility and justification of torture *in this world*. I am interested in the *actual* arrangements that are needed for even isolated instances of torture to occur. What is at stake here is the permissibility of torture *in this world*, and so moral arguments must take into consideration what permitting torture involves in reality, not just in a purely hypothetical example. That torture might be justified in a hypothetical example in a hypothetical world gives us no reason to think that it can be justified (or should be legalized) in *this* world. Henry Shue makes the same point: 'Does the possibility that torture might be justifiable in some of the rarefied situations which can be imagined provide any reason to consider relaxing the legal prohibitions against it? Absolutely not. The distance between the situations which much be concocted in order to have a plausible case of morally permissible torture and the situations which actually occur is, if anything, further reason why the existing prohibitions against torture should remain.'[73]

Consequentialists are very fond of accusing non-consequentialists of using extreme hypothetical examples to attack consequentialism. They should therefore be prepared to accept the same response here: a consequentialist argument for the use of torture cannot appeal to purely hypothetical cases; it must be concerned with the real consequences of permitting torture in this world. Given the likely consequences (supported by strong evidence from past and present cases) it is extremely difficult to create a strong consequentialist argument in favour of even limited cases of torture that would also justify the institutional arrangements needed to create torturers, torture techniques, and torture equipment.[74] In this world it is almost impossible that an isolated use of torture could fit the limitations noted above and not also involve on-going and wide-scale institutionalization of torture research and training, which would necessarily involve the legal system and medical practitioners. The military's claim that torture is justified because of threats to national security is false. The military cannot claim a special moral permission to use torture.

Arguments against torture

Rights-based arguments are by far the most common arguments against the permissibility of torture in *any* circumstances. Without entering into the debate about the nature and basis for the ascription of rights (and familiar debates about what should happen in situations where rights conflict), it is sufficient to note that most rights-based theories will generally denounce all torture as a violation of basic human rights. Casebeer argues that a Kantian approach can give a solid foundation for this view. Torture is a clear example of using another simply as a means, something that is expressly forbidden under Kant's view because it violates the second version of the categorical imperative – it denies the other the respect that their humanity and moral agency demands. Even if a rights-based theory is based on an account of consent rather than on Kantian theory, there is no possible way torture can be construed so as to involve tacit or explicit consent on the part of the victim.[75]

While virtue ethics is not widely discussed in the literature on the morality of torture, virtue ethics can also be used to provide an argument against torture. It is certainly difficult to imagine that the character traits of the good torturer could constitute virtues under any version of virtue ethics. Casebeer points out that: 'Virtuous people are probably not involved in the intentional and coerced causation of pain and suffering in other human beings.'[76] Nor could the role of torturer conceivably form part of a flourishing human society – the establishment of a 'professional torture force' and the consequent pain and suffering caused (and the kinds of traits developed in the torturers) would not contribute to human well-being or serve a necessary human need.[77]

In summary, all moral theories can provide strong arguments against the use of torture. It is very difficult to create an adequate argument in favour of even limited uses of torture that does not rely on assuming an added justification for the institutional arrangements needed to create torturers, torture techniques, and torture equipment. Such justifications are rarely, if ever, spelled out and so the burden of proof remains with those who believe that torture might still be justified. The overwhelming condemnation of torture from the rights-based perspective has probably had the most influence on the legal status of torture.

The legal status of torture

Military law is governed by treaties and conventions at several different levels. On an international level, the UN's *Universal Declaration of Human Rights* (1948), *International Covenant on Civil and Political Rights* (1966), *Convention against Torture and other Cruel, Inhuman, or Degrading Treatment or Punishment* (1984), and the Geneva Conventions all expressly prohibit torture: 'Torture and ill-treatment are prohibited under international human rights law, under the laws of war (international humanitarian law) and under general international law. In addition, individual acts of torture or ill-treatment are proscribed as crimes under international law if committed as war crimes, as crimes against humanity or as genocide. International human rights standards also prescribe measures which governments should take to prevent torture and ill-treatment, to investigate alleged cases, to bring to justice those responsible and to afford reparation to victims.'[78]

Torture is also banned under the legal and military codes of many specific regions. There is, for example, *The Inter-American Convention to Prevent and Punish Torture* 'which provides for universal jurisdiction over torture among states parties in the Americas region and sets out other measures regarding prevention, investigation, bringing those responsible to justice and affording reparation', and *The European Convention for the Prevention of Torture and Inhuman or Degrading Treatment or Punishment*.[79]

Both general international law and customary law also forbid the use of torture: 'The UN Human Rights Committee has stated that the obligation not to subject people to torture or ill-treatment is a rule of customary international law and that the prohibition of torture is a peremptory norm. These points can be considered to be firmly established: they have never been seriously challenged, and they are supported by important judicial decisions.'[80]

It is clear then that torture, as defined previously, is absolutely forbidden under both international and local laws. There are *no* exceptions in any of these treaties and conventions, and because torture is banned according to customary law, prohibitions against the use of torture are binding on states that are not signatories to specific conventions. Torture is absolutely legally impermissible.

Given that torture is both legally impermissible and cannot be justified by arguments appealing to the military's role as protector of national security, then the military's regulative ideal cannot allow a special moral permission to torture. The military's special moral permissions are justified only if they contribute to the ends of the profession and only if they do not violate important broad-based moral constraints and the laws of war. Torture violates both the laws of war and broad-based moral standards. The military's primary role is to protect national security; how they may fulfil that role is subject to strict constraints – constraints that the military has willingly accepted by claiming professional status. If the military believes that the laws of war may be violated in the name of national security then it cannot claim professional status and the special moral permissions that follow from that status. Just as doctors cannot experiment on unwilling patients in the name of advancing their profession, neither can military personnel use torture in the name of national security.

Military obedience and torture

In Chapter 4, I explained the legal obligations of military personnel regarding orders that violate international or local military law. Given that an order to torture violates numerous laws of war and would be recognizably illegal by a person of 'ordinary understanding',[81] such an order would count as illegal and immoral and should therefore be disobeyed. Disobedience of an order to torture is therefore not only justified but required. A combatant who obeys an order to torture does more than violate ordinary moral standards; she violates important professional ideals as well.

However, perhaps it will not always be obvious to military personnel what actions constitute torture. The definition of torture in the laws of war and other conventions covers a wide range of actions. For example, it might be difficult for a combatant to know whether an order to put a hood over a prisoner's face counts as torture or whether holding a prisoner in solitary confinement violates the laws of war. While it is true that the moral and legal status of particular acts might be unclear, there are two points to make about such cases. First, as explained in Chapter 4, if a combatant is unclear about the legal and moral status of her order then she has an obligation to clarify the legality of the order before she obeys it. If she is unable to do so then she should at least interpret it in its best light, legally and morally speaking.

Second, there is no denying that there are cases that fall in the grey area between torture and legitimate treatment of prisoners. In such cases the duty of military personnel might be unclear. However the existence of such cases does not mean that there is *no* clear distinction between torture and legitimate treatment and does not mean that military personnel cannot be expected to know the difference. An order that requires the causing of severe mental or physical suffering is an order to perform torture. Note too that the existence of grey areas does not alter the obligation of military personnel to refuse to obey an order that *does* clearly constitute torture (for example, an order that demanded not only solitary confinement, but noise bombardment and hooding). The solution to the problem of grey areas is not to let military personnel off the hook, but to both strengthen their understanding of the legal definition of torture and cultivate the dispositions of reflective obedience. If military personnel have a clear understanding of their duty to disobey illegal and immoral orders and a clear understanding of the effects of torture on the victims, they will be in a far better position to recognize when torture occurs and to refuse to take part in it. Indeed, such understanding should be part of the professional expertise of military personnel. Many military personnel will be in situations where they might have to guard prisoners and interrogate them. Understanding what is and is not permitted in such cases is clearly a part of their professional expertise. It is inconsistent to claim that military personnel are professionals but deny that they could have the time or understanding to know when their orders are illegal and immoral. Professional status (and professional special moral permissions) is granted on the assumption that professionals have expertise in their area.

Having established that the arguments for the use of torture fail and that military personnel have a clear legal and professional obligation to disobey orders to torture, we must wonder why so many military personnel are implicated in the use of torture. Why aren't the personnel at Guantanamo Bay refusing their orders? Why is there such a discrepancy between military rhetoric and the behaviour of real military personnel?

The problem: real fighters versus ideal fighters

That there is a discrepancy between military rhetoric and the behaviour of actual military personnel is nothing new. There are, unfortunately, numerous examples of actions that are in direct opposition to military values – not just the use of torture, but other atrocities such as massacres and rapes. Ordinary military personnel of all ranks have committed and are still committing atrocities. The abuse and torture of prisoners in Iraq was perpetrated by ordinary Army reservists.[82] During the Vietnam War both American and Australian troops were involved in incidents of torture, rape, and massacre. These crimes were not committed by renegade individuals but by regular platoons often with the tacit consent of their commanding officers. In fact some of these crimes were committed *by* the officers of the companies.[83] Furthermore these atrocities were not even roundly condemned by the military hierarchy. On the whole the military hierarchy either ignored or even supported such atrocities. For example, Drill Sergeant Kenneth Hodges said of the soldiers of Charlie Company who committed the massacre at My Lai in March 1968: 'They turned out to be very good soldiers. The fact that they were able to go into My Lai and carry out the orders they had been given, I think this is a direct result of the good training they had.'[84]

Similarly the guards at Abu Ghraib, far from being disciplined by their superiors in the prison, felt safe enough to take photos of their activities and distribute them throughout the battalion. The guards' activities were given active support by Military Intelligence and CIA officers who told the soldiers involved in the abuse: '"Great job", they were now getting positive results and information.'[85]

Perhaps then the prevalence of torture is just symptomatic of a larger problem with the gap between military ideals and real military behaviour. This discrepancy between rhetoric and reality may not point to anything more controversial than human weakness. Indeed, there have been attempts (by philosophers and by others) to explain the existence of this discrepancy in terms of either the problematic nature of the military's role, a failure of adequate training in ethics or the result of the unique stresses that men and women at war are subject to.

One common approach has been to appeal to the unique environment of war and the horrors that military personnel experience. For example, one explanation offered for the particularly bloody nature of the Vietnam War was that it was a war where the line between civilians and enemies became blurred, making it hard for military personnel to tell the innocent from the guilty.[86]

There are two problems with this explanation. First, the Vietnam War is hardly unique. Crimes of obedience are still occurring, as witnessed in Iraq and Afghanistan. Second, since we can reliably expect wars to be horrific, stressful and gruesome, we must wonder why the military profession does not train its personnel to maintain the military's own standards under those conditions. By claiming to be a profession, the military claims to have professional expertise in warfare. This professional expertise should surely cover the conditions of war and the kinds of situations that military personnel are likely to encounter during military operations.

It is inconsistent to explain the failure of military personnel to uphold the laws of war and to maintain the military's own professional standards in its stated field of expertise by referring to the horrible nature of warfare. Dealing with the horrible nature of warfare is part of the military's professional jurisdiction. That it is difficult to maintain strong ethical standards in the face of extreme horror and stress is hardly surprising. The laws of war were developed because war is a unique environment involving unique moral dilemmas so clear guidelines need to be in place. The laws of war only come into play when the conditions of war hold as that is when ethical guidance is most needed. They are in place precisely to guide behaviour when conditions are confusing, horrific, and the 'fog of war' has taken hold.[87]

This discrepancy between rhetoric and reality has also been recognized by philosophers. Hilliard Aronovitch argues that there is a paradox in training military personnel to obey orders 'almost automatically', so that the success of military missions is not endangered, and yet also requiring them to reflect on the legality of their orders.[88] To find a balance between the constraints imposed by military ideals and the laws of war on the one hand, and the need for effective war-fighting and effective killing on the other seems fraught with problems. A Colonel in the US Special Forces described the dilemma thus: 'Our guys have got to be confident in their ability to use lethal force. But they've got to be principled enough to know when not to use it. We're not training pirates.'[89] There seems to be a tension at the heart of the military profession between the need for obedient effective killers and the equally important need for moral reflection and moral courage, both of which are crucial if the costs of war are to be minimized. Aronovitch explains the paradox neatly: 'How can we take people who aren't and shouldn't be disposed to kill, and who anyway are inept at means of violence, and train them to become ready and effective fighters without transforming them into morally desensitised beings? Is wanting one without the other, actually and because of the tendencies involved and the means of inculcating them, contradictory?'[90]

Aronovitch claims that the way to solve this paradox is to adopt a virtue ethics approach to military ethics training, as this will provide the moral guidance needed to resolve this dilemma – virtue ethics will enable military personnel to abide by the deontological constraints imposed by the laws of war and broad-based morality.[91] He supports this claim by arguing that the essential character traits needed for military personnel to be effective are in fact the same traits needed for military personnel to be ethical. By carefully cultivating the virtues of truthfulness, courage, good judgement and temperance (self-control), he argues, military training can produce personnel who will not obey or give unethical orders.[92] Therefore, according to his view, the prevalence of atrocity in warfare is not indicative of anything fundamentally wrong with the role of combatant or with the military virtues. Instead, such problems result from a 'morally distorted version' of military professionalism.[93]

It is certainly true that the virtues on Aronovitch's list are necessary for effective military functioning. They appear regularly in the writings of military ethicists. Claiming that military personnel must be trained in such a way as to cultivate these traits is also uncontroversial. However Aronovitch misses an essential point. He fails to mention what is *also* regularly described as a crucial military virtue: obedience. As a result he fails to address both the limits of such obedience and the possibility that there might be an irreconcilable conflict between training military personnel to be obedient and requiring them to develop the moral judgement they need to be able to embody the military virtues. After all, the need for obedience runs right through military training and military practice. His choice of military virtues is far too selective and is in fact incompatible with the military's own needs.

By avoiding the issue of obedience Aronovitch fails to consider two issues. He fails to clarify which kind of obedience is consistent with military ideals and he fails to ascertain if this is the kind of obedience that is actually promoted during military training. He is right in claiming that military training should develop traits such as honesty, integrity, and courage – the military itself admits as much – but lessons in character development represent only a tiny proportion of military training. Military personnel must also be trained to obey any legitimate order – including orders to kill enemy combatants and destroy enemy cities. The necessity of creating obedient military personnel is not simply neutralized by also training them to be truthful and courageous. We do not know yet whether military personnel are trained in the reflective obedience consistent with the military's professional status or whether they are trained in the habits of blind obedience. Until we know the answer to this question we cannot know why military personnel are committing crimes of obedience. Claiming, as Aronovitch does, that the prevalence of war crimes represents simply a 'morally distorted professionalism' fails to address the question of why such a distortion is so widespread and persistent, particularly since the virtues he discusses are ones that have long been accepted as essential military virtues by writers in military ethics.

Aronovitch's argument relies on the assumption that a combatant's failure to disobey illegal and immoral orders is a failure of the individual's character and of misguided ideas about military professionalism, rather than indicating anything problematic about the military ideal itself. His argument implies that the problem of crimes of obedience could be fixed by giving military personnel extra ethics training or by teaching the military to recognize that good military personnel need to be trustworthy, honest, courageous, and have integrity. This is a hopelessly naïve view because it fails to address the fact that the military also requires good military personnel to be obedient. Aronovitch's argument fails to solve the paradox of training military personnel to be both obedient and reflective moral agents.

The prevalence of war crimes cannot be attributed to the 'fog of war' or to a 'morally distorted professionalism'. If the military is genuinely committed to developing the character traits and moral judgement it claims to hold most valuable, and is genuinely committed to upholding its own professional ideals, then we must wonder why the behaviour of real military personnel falls so far short of the ideal. We must establish if the military is genuinely committed to promoting reflective obedience. Considering a real-life example of a soldier who was reflectively obedient will enable us to do this. There are military personnel who *do* uphold military virtues as best they can. Looking at their experiences can provide an indication of the military's attitude towards personnel who do embody the military ideal of obedience.

Obedience versus integrity: Captain Rockwood in Haiti

In 1994 Captain Lawrence Rockwood was stationed in Haiti as part of a mission (Operation Uphold Democracy) to depose the dictator Cedras and restore the democratically elected Jean-Bertrand Aristide.[94] Rockwood believed that preventing human rights abuses was also a central part of their mission, given that President Clinton had stated that a main objective of the operation was to 'stop the brutal atrocities'.[95]

Once in Haiti, Rockwood received intelligence reports indicating that torture and other crimes were being committed in the National Penitentiary, yet his superior officers forbade any interference or inspections of the prisons. Rockwood, believing that 'Rescuing the helpless and opposing the tyrannous is precisely what a military is for',[96] tried unsuccessfully to convince his superiors to order an inspection. They refused on the grounds that to do so would 'endanger fragile relations with the peacefully departing Cedras Regime'.[97] He then took matters into his own hands. After lodging a complaint with the Inspector General and receiving no assistance, he armed himself and went to inspect the jails on his own. He was later arrested and court-martialled in the United States where he was found guilty of four violations of the Uniform Code of Military Justice.[98]

There are several points of note about this case. First, Rockwood tried many different legitimate ways to persuade his superior officers to order a search of the prisons. It was only after exhausting these avenues that he intentionally disobeyed orders. His decision was not impetuous and thoughtless, but was taken after significant reflection about the morality and legality of his orders. Second, Rockwood was a dedicated officer who sincerely believed in the military values and who took seriously the importance of maintaining moral integrity and upholding the moral principles espoused in treaties such as the Geneva Conventions.[99] Yet not only did his actions result in a court-martial, but *none* of the many people he approached (the Inspector-General, the division's chief legal officer, the command's chaplain, and his commanding officer, amongst others) considered such an inspection to be their duty. The commanding officer stated that the main goal of the mission was not to protect Haitian civilians but to protect the US forces.[100] Despite Clinton's statement to the contrary, the prevention of human rights abuses was not considered important enough to warrant the potential endangerment of US forces.

Looking at this case in light of the military virtues outlined in Chapters 3 and 4 and in light of military rhetoric about the importance of humanitarian concerns gives rise to a curious conclusion. Rockwood clearly thought that, as the agent of the civilian authority (personified by Clinton at that time), it was the military's duty to carry out that authority's stated aims, in this case, to 'stop the brutal atrocities'. To do otherwise would be to undermine the basis of military legitimacy: subservience to the civilian authority. Rockwood also believed that obedience to orders, while highly important, was conditional upon the legal and moral standing of those orders. His decision to disobey was taken only after he had tried all other avenues. Finally, he decided that the orders to not intervene were immoral because they were in direct contradiction of the supposed mission in Haiti, and because obeying them would result in grave violations of human rights the protection of which the military had claimed to be one of its main missions. In fact, his defence at his court-martial was that the orders were not only immoral but were also illegal. He argued that the US forces had a duty under international law to intervene in known human rights abuses, particularly when they could do so without serious endangerment to themselves.[101]

It therefore seems at first glance that it is the disobedient Captain Rockwood, not the many others involved, who was actually trying to embody the military virtues in this situation. Rockwood clearly thought that given the circumstances the duty to prevent gross human rights violations was more important than the duty to obey orders. His disobedience was not a case of selective conscientious objection – he was not disobeying because his orders violated his deeply held personal beliefs. Instead his disobedience was based on a concept of professional integrity. He refused to obey because he thought that to do so would violate important *professional* values. This belief is supported by the military's emphasis on the virtue of moral integrity and on the moral principles espoused in international treaties. The concept of military loyalty and obedience is not meant to be limited solely to loyalty and obedience to one's superior officers. Instead, as one senior military officer argued, loyalty 'must involve not only loyalty to superiors, but loyalty to subordinates, the profession, and fundamentally to the Constitution found in the Oath of Office.'[102]

This is consistent with my argument in Chapter 4 that the military virtue of obedience is and has to be *reflective* obedience, which is precisely the kind of obedience that Rockwood displayed. The military clearly and openly states that unreflective obedience is *not* what it desires. Furthermore, unreflective obedience is inconsistent with the military's claim to be a profession. The military virtue of obedience and the military law of many countries support justified disobedience, particularly when all other avenues have been tried. Given these facts it can be argued that Rockwood was right to act as he did. He disobeyed only after trying other avenues and only after serious reflection on the consequences of disobeying. He even attempted to find the relevant legal information – only to discover that the only material available on Haiti was a 1954 Army field manual.[103] Yet he was court-martialled (and found guilty) *because* he had disobeyed orders. Furthermore, his case is now taught in ethics courses in various military academies throughout the United States and almost without exception his actions are criticized – one of the questions discussed is how he might have handled the situation differently.[104] The assumption is that he should have obeyed orders and found a different way of dealing with the situation. Being obedient is assumed to be more important than protecting human rights.

It might be objected that Captain Rockwood was not justified in his disobedience because the orders he received (to not enter the jails) were not obviously illegal or immoral. Given that military personnel have a duty to presume that their orders are lawful unless it is very clear that they are not, it could seem that Captain Rockwood overstepped the mark here.

The case of Captain Rockwood is not a straightforward example of an officer disobeying a manifestly illegal or immoral order. Perhaps the situation is better construed as a failure of omission on the part of his superiors, since it could be argued that they should have intervened and should have ordered an inspection of the jails. The order 'Do not enter the jails' is neither manifestly illegal nor immoral according to the broad-based standards used by the manifest illegality approach. This order would not offend the conscience of a 'man of ordinary sense and understanding.'[105] It does not seem to be an example of an order that should, on the face of it, be disobeyed. Disobedience to such an order is not justified under the manifest illegality approach. It can be argued that the military would never have court-martialled Rockwood had his orders been manifestly illegal. In theory the military fully supports disobedience when an outright atrocity is ordered in no uncertain terms, and pays lip service to the prosecution of military personnel who obey such orders (although, as noted in Chapter 4, there are very few such prosecutions). It is only because Rockwood overstepped his duty that he was charged. Not only did he think he knew the right course of action when he was not in a position to order or even fully assess such a course of action, but he also took it upon himself to disobey a clear order.

There are two responses I will make to this objection. First, the doctrine of manifest illegality is a *legal* doctrine that sets out the grounds for the defence and prosecution of a crime committed under orders. It does not therefore follow that it *should* be the approach taken to this issue or even that it is the most appropriate or the most faithful legal interpretation of the military's professional ideals. As I argued in Chapter 4 the manifest illegality approach is very lenient on military personnel and only requires them to check that their orders are not *prima facie* illegal (requiring no more understanding of the laws of war than an ordinary person) and it is far from clear that this approach fits best with the military's stated values and objectives. Indeed the manifest illegality approach seems particularly inappropriate for officers, given their greater responsibility and their (presumably) greater professional expertise. All members of the military profession lay claim to special moral permissions that flow from the military's professional status, and expertise is a crucial criterion of a profession. Officers bear greater responsibility, exercise greater autonomy, and are indisputably professionals. Therefore they should possess even greater professional expertise than lower-ranking military personnel, expertise that includes a thorough knowledge of the laws of war particularly as they apply to specific missions such as the Haiti operation.

Second, the manifest illegality approach does not reflect the high standards of professional excellence supposedly desired in military personnel of all ranks. Captain Rockwood disobeyed an order that he believed to be illegal not just because it violated broad-based moral principles but also because he believed it violated deeply-held *professional* principles. If the military truly wants personnel who uphold the professional values of the military – who are professionals, in other words – then we would expect the military to support personnel who disobey orders if they have good grounds for doing so.[106]

There is of course disagreement about whether Rockwood's orders were illegal but the point is that Rockwood had good reason to believe that they were illegal, particularly given President Clinton's statement about the goal of the mission in Haiti. He did not disobey on a whim or out of ignorance. Instead he attempted to clarify his orders. He spoke to several superior officers, considered how the orders cohered with the military's professional values and decided to disobey. He displayed the ideal kind of military obedience. But the military flatly condemned Rockwood's behaviour and argued that regardless of the strength of his reasons for disobeying he should have obeyed orders. If the military was serious about the importance of reflective obedience, Rockwood's case should have warranted at least an investigation into the legality and morality of his orders. Instead of supporting Rockwood and other personnel in similar situations the military automatically condemned him for disobeying orders. Given the consequences of obeying illegal orders (for the victims and for the military itself)[107] surely it is preferable to have personnel who, like Rockwood, err on the side of disobedience when there is serious doubt as to the morality and legality of their orders, than it is to have personnel who take the opposite path.[108] As a profession claiming special moral permissions the military should not wish to create personnel who will obey illegal orders without question. In fact, even if Captain Rockwood's orders were legal, this does not necessarily mean that he did not have good grounds for disobedience. Anthony Hartle, for one, has argued that if obeying a legal order will cause or fail to prevent the commission of human rights abuses, then a good combatant should disobey. For example, obeying an order not to return fire unless fired upon might mean a soldier will not intervene to save civilians from a massacre by enemy militia.[109]

Just war theory and common-sense morality tell us that the harms of war (the deaths, destruction of property, disenfranchisement of populations etc.) must be minimized as much as possible; that war, if it is to be a just war, must be fought within strict constraints. If the military is to be a justified profession it must aim to minimize the costs of waging war and must aim to train military personnel to uphold the laws of war and to develop the dispositions of reflective, not destructive, obedience. We should therefore expect the military to encourage military personnel to develop their understanding of the laws of war and to exercise reflective obedience.

The manifest illegality approach is not the best legal interpretation of the military rhetoric and is not consistent with the military's claims to professional status. Military personnel, particularly officers, should be required to have more than the 'ordinary man's' understanding of the laws of war, at the very least. It seems plausible to argue that military personnel, when given an order of doubtful legality, must consider not only the *prima facie* legal status of the order but also the consequences of carrying out the order. This belief is apparent in some of the more stringent laws regarding responsibility for obedience to illegal orders discussed in Chapter 4. If the legality of an order is unclear and the consequences of carrying it out are unclear then good military personnel should at least carry out only the *legal* interpretation of the order, to the best of their knowledge.

The ability to make that kind of judgement does not require detailed analysis but merely a decent knowledge of the laws of war and an understanding of the possible interpretations of such laws. Such split-second decisions are part and parcel of being in the military. Australian pilots in Iraq, for example, aborted many missions 'when they saw the target and decided there was not a valid military reason to drop their bombs ... it seems that it was often to avoid killing civilians unnecessarily.'[110] They had to make a split-second decision whether to drop their bombs and they chose to err on the side of caution: 'If we were not 100 per cent sure we were taking out a valid military target in accordance with our specifications, we just did not drop.'[111] Clearly, having to make decisions under pressure does not compromise one's capacity for judging the legal and moral status of one's decision. Such a capacity does not require an in-depth understanding of the laws of war: all it requires is that military personnel have a good understanding of the laws of war *as they apply to their mission* (the Rules of Engagement) and are able to assess the likely consequences of their actions. Neither of these requirements is likely to radically reduce response times in the relatively few cases in which a split-second decision is required. So the common claim that there would not be time for military personnel to judge the legality of their orders does not hold up under examination. Indeed, the more practice they have in exercising such reflection the more likely it is that it will become second nature even when split-second decisions have to be made.

Conclusion

The treatment of Captain Rockwood reveals an inconsistency in the military's attitude towards obedience. The Rockwood case is an example of the military failing to reward or even acknowledge the kind of obedience it supposedly holds most valuable. Contrary to the claims of military rhetoric, the reaction to the Rockwood case indicates that obedience is taken to be overriding even when military personnel are given orders of doubtful legality. Why does this inconsistency arise? Is the Captain Rockwood case a one-off example or is it indicative of a more widespread problem? After all, the Australian pilots referred to earlier seemed to display the kind of reflective obedience consistent with military professionalism and they were not punished for it. The Captain Rockwood case is an example of the problems with the manifest illegality approach towards military obedience but it unclear as yet if the discrepancy between rhetoric and reality is indicative of more serious problems within the military. Understanding more about the kind of obedience instilled during military training will enable us to clarify this issue.

6
Military Training and Moral Agency

In Chapter 5 I argued that the military profession cannot claim a special permission to use torture even in cases of emergency. Torture is both illegal and immoral and the military cannot appeal to professional goals to justify its use. Yet military personnel are still obeying orders to torture. Why? The Captain Rockwood case suggested that there is an inconsistency in the military's attitude towards obedience. Despite the legal and professional duty of military personnel to disobey illegal and immoral orders, such disobedience rarely occurs and when it does it is punished rather than encouraged. But this inconsistency could just be indicative of problems with the manifest illegality approach without reflecting any more fundamental problems within the military profession itself. Maybe all that is needed to address the problem of crimes of obedience is more stringent laws that better reflect the military's professional ideals and the limits of military obedience. To decide whether this is the case we need to know more about the kind of obedience instilled in military personnel during their basic military training.

As I will demonstrate in this chapter, the inconsistency revealed in the military's attitude towards Captain Rockwood is far from being an anomaly. The problem lies not only in the legal interpretation of the limits of military obedience but also in the kind of obedience cultivated during basic military training. The discrepancy between military rhetoric and the behaviour of real military personnel is not accidental, and nor does it arise from an irresolvable tension between training military personnel to be obedient and training them to be reflective. There is no tension between distinct and competing aims of military training because currently military personnel are not trained to be reflective moral agents. As we shall see, the primary aim of actual military training is to cultivate the habits of unreflective obedience. Military training not only makes moral reflection harder for military personnel, it aims to remove the capacity for such reflection altogether. The combination of modern military combat training methods and the military environment corrupts the moral agency of military personnel. The psychological dispositions created by military training are fundamentally in conflict with the traits needed for military personnel to be reflective moral agents.

The second part of this chapter shows how military training succeeds in instilling unreflective obedience. The training works by deliberately reinforcing pre-existing dispositions towards unreflective obedience. Using the work of psychologist Stanley Milgram and sociologists Herbert Kelman and V. Lee Hamilton I show that military training enhances the traits that are characteristic of unreflective obedience – traits that many of us have already – and simultaneously aims to eradicate the moral and emotional distress associated with obedience to destructive authority. This process does far more than alter combatants' emotional and affective dispositions; it perverts the decision-making process itself and thereby undermines combatants' reflective moral agency.

A comparison of the traits characteristic of obedience to authority and the traits developed through military training shows that the habits of unreflective obedience are not merely expressed more openly in the military; they are deliberately enhanced by military training techniques.

Military training and moral agency

The military personality is developed not just through overt training and education, but through the very nature of the military's function and needs. From the discussion in Chapter 3 it seemed that the functional requirements of the military institution required military personnel to develop admirable character traits such as self-discipline and honesty. A closer look reveals that there is a less salutary side to this aspect of the military institution.

The military mindset

The military is the servant of the state. It is a loyal and dedicated organization that must be able to respond rapidly to the demands of the civilian government. As a result of these unique requirements military personnel are likely to develop a set of values and beliefs that are at odds with those that govern the wider society. In both Australia and America the military is a totalitarian, authoritarian, anti-individualistic, hierarchical, and conservative organization. Yet American and Australian societies value individualism, freedom of speech, freedom of religion, freedom of political assembly and democracy. An American military officer explained this conflict: 'Vital to combat operations and therefore a necessary part of traditional military professionalism is a set of values which are to some extent contrary to those held by liberal civilian society. Military organization is hierarchical, not egalitarian, and is oriented to the group rather than the individual; it stresses discipline and obedience, not freedom of expression; it depends on confidence and trust, not *caveat emptor*. It requires immediate decision and prompt action, not thorough analysis and extensive debate; it relies on training, simplification and predictable behaviour, not education, sophistication, and empiricism.'[1]

The nature of the military's role generates traits and attitudes that can become the very antithesis of those that are valued most by the wider society. The military personality is also likely to develop a bleak view of human nature. Samuel Huntington argues that the military mind 'emphasises the permanence, irrationality, weakness in human nature. It stresses the supremacy of society over the individual and the importance of order, hierarchy, and division of function. It accepts the nation-state as the highest form of political organisation, and recognises the continuing likelihood of wars among nations-states ... It exalts obedience as the highest virtue of military men.'[2]

The military personality encourages the development of traits that could be highly problematic in everyday life. Strong nationalism, authoritarianism, obedience to authority, pessimism and conservatism[3] are traits that are in tension with the values of tolerance, individualism, and open dialogue that are the hallmarks of a liberal democracy. The fact that the military is a legitimate organization does not necessarily provide a *prima facie* reason to consider the development of these traits within the military as desirable. All that can be said is that, in theory at least, these traits are governed in the military by strict standards and so do not threaten the wider society. However such a defence is problematic for two reasons. One, there are many examples of military coups, so it is unclear whether the military is really strictly 'under control'. Two, there might be reasons to distrust the development of these traits in and of themselves – after all, many military personnel (particularly reservists) are not career combatants and will be part of the civilian community. We might question the development of a morally problematic mindset in individuals who will take it back with them into civilian life.

The need for these traits arises because the military is the agent of the civilian government. The importance of maintaining this subservience to civilian authority cannot be denied. To serve the government rapidly and without dissent requires that military personnel cultivate loyalty, patriotism, and obedience. All personnel, and particularly higher-ranking officers, *must* be politically conservative.[4] The military cannot allow political disagreement and debate within its ranks. The military is a political tool of the government but in and of itself it is not a political organization. The duty of the military is to follow the government's orders regardless of the political party currently in power. It therefore cannot take a political stance itself and cannot permit political debate to divide its members. However, because of the military's duties and deference to the civilian authority, the military as an organization is strongly politically conservative rather than simply politically neutral.

Military personnel are likely to be politically conservative because they must sustain a belief in the necessity and importance of military action, a belief that is likely to involve a degree of pessimism about the prospects of peaceful solutions to conflict, and an expectation that war and political violence are inevitable. Lance Betros claims that military officers might develop 'a hint of paranoia in their thinking. They focus on enemy capabilities instead of intent, prepare themselves constantly for battle, and search for every possible military advantage ... They view man as inherently flawed, motivated by power and self-interest, and predisposed to war.'[5]

The belief that war is an inevitable feature of human society and that military action will always be necessary implies a belief that humans will eventually resort to aggression to solve conflicts. It also implies a belief that injustice and the oppression of the weak by the strong are inevitable features of human society and that force will be needed to settle these cases. It is far from clear whether the military could operate without such a set of beliefs although it is interesting to imagine what such a military would be like.

It seems clear from the above discussion that the nature of the military's role and objectives gives rise to distinctive character traits that are different from (and in some cases opposed to) the traits and values held by most democratic societies. The new recruit must develop a character and a set of beliefs that are conservative, authoritarian and hierarchical – group-centred anti-individual traits that could be inappropriate or even harmful in everyday life. But perhaps this need not pose a problem for the concept of the military virtues. As noted previously the virtue ethics account of professional roles allows for the possibility that a professional might need to develop traits that are not everyday virtues and might need to cultivate some virtues at the expense of others. This might be justified as long as those traits are governed wisely, promote the ends of the profession, and do not result in violations of important side-constraints.[6] Perhaps

military personnel, after reflection, recognize that they must be prepared to sacrifice some of their rights and their more optimistic beliefs
for the protection of the nation. They must bear the burden of pessimism so that the rest of us can afford to be optimistic. To do otherwise
would mean that the military could not perform its function and that
could result in tragedy.

Before accepting this justification we should consider more closely the
manner in which the military personality is created. It is one thing to
accept that the military personality must be of a certain (perhaps regret-
table) type. It is another to consider what is lost in the creation of that
personality. How are the military virtues developed in new recruits?
What is the effect of this development on their moral psychology? To
answer these questions we need to look at the modern military training
process.

Group bonding

The first and perhaps the most formative experience for the new recruit is
immersion in the enclosed, group-oriented training environment. Modern
military training is an intense, all-encompassing process. Cadets live,
work, and socialize almost exclusively within the military world. The new
cadet is removed almost entirely from the civilian world and finds herself in an environment where everything she does is observed by her
superiors and her peers. The military profession, unlike any other profession, requires that new members identify completely with their new
role as members of the military profession. There is no 'taking the soldier's hat off'. Either the new combatant commits fully to her role or she
fails to be a good combatant. Even the lowest-ranking military personnel and unwilling conscripts in wartime are *constantly* in the military
world. The effects of such immersion and 'professional socialisation'[7] on
the character and independence of new recruits cannot be underestimated. Military training must not only develop recruits' technical skills,
it must also develop the dispositions necessary for living and working in
a specialized hierarchical group-oriented environment. As I shall
explain, this is done partly through the strict discipline of the training
regime with its emphasis on duty, obedience, and loyalty, and partly
through unofficial bonding processes.

Loyalty and trust are crucial to mission survival and for maintaining
respect and obedience between ranks. The effectiveness of military action
is severely impaired and lives can be endangered if military personnel do
not trust each other or their commanding officers. Adhesion to the group
is an essential part of military training and an essential way of cementing

obedience. Military personnel must come to identify so strongly with their unit and the military organization that they would be willing to die for it. One Canadian soldier explained the importance of loyalty as follows, 'A little private out there in the trenches doesn't know beans about why he is there, except that he is there with his buddies and they will die for one another. It's as simple as that.'[8] Disobedience undermines this group-bonding and is usually interpreted as showing disloyalty to and lack of trust in both the commanding officer and one's fellow combatants.

Trust and loyalty play a crucial role in encouraging obedience and aiding successful military action. Military training must therefore instil unwavering loyalty in new recruits. A report on the military culture in Canada argued that: 'As a result of its distinctive mandate and the need to instil organisational loyalty and obedience, most military organisations develop a culture unto themselves, distinguished by an emphasis on hierarchy, tradition, rituals and customs, and distinctive dress and insignia.'[9]

The importance of drill and ceremonial rituals in cultivating new recruits' loyalty to and identification with their units and the military institution as a whole is also evident in the number of hours dedicated to these aspects of basic training. For example, Army, Navy, and Air Force cadets at the Australian Defence Force Academy have certain basic training units in common. The number of hours dedicated to the different units of this training is indicative of their relative importance. It is therefore highly telling that over three years cadets undertake 205 hours of drill and ceremonial training compared to only 44 hours of character development and 24 hours of military law.[10]

Given the importance of group loyalty and trust in the military environment the cost of not 'fitting in' can be very high. Aside from the official drill and ceremonial rituals, loyalty to the unit is often instilled through unofficial initiation rituals intended to bond the new cadet firmly with the other members of her unit. These initiation rituals can involve very brutal and humiliating treatment – the very severity of which can further bond the group together. In a study of a Canadian Airborne Regiment Dr Donna Winslow argued that 'an initiate who endures severe hazing [bullying] is likely to find membership in the group all the more appealing. In these rituals, soldiers are proving their readiness to participate in the group regardless of the personal cost, thus gaining peer acceptance. As one soldier put it: "I am proud to have done it, it proves to myself and others that as a member of the Canadian Airborne Regiment, I will face and overpass any challenge to or tasking given to me."'[11]

The experience of the following cadets reveals just how severe these kinds of bonding rituals can be. A cadet at the Australian Army's infantry training school in NSW committed suicide after suffering from anxiety and depression and after being told that he was 'worthless to the army'.[12] Another cadet (a 15-year-old girl) hanged herself after being bullied by other cadets.[13] At least 30 paratroopers in the Royal Australian Regiment in Queensland were victims of illegal beatings and punishments in 1997 and 1998.[14] In Canada, an Airborne Regiment commando unit was disbanded after the publication of videos showing hazing rituals including one showing a black cadet in a humiliating position with the words 'I Love KKK' written on his back.[15]

The continued prevalence of these practices despite many attempts to outlaw them is indicative of a widespread culture of unofficial and very brutal group-bonding rites. Although such practices are not part of official training techniques their prevalence indicates that they cannot be lightly dismissed when looking at the psychological traits developed during military training. Such brutalization not only desensitizes new cadets to their own suffering but also desensitizes them to inflicting suffering upon others. The cadets accused of bullying the young girl mentioned above no doubt experienced much the same kind of bullying themselves.

Empathy and sympathy are eroded, as is tolerance of dissent and disobedience within the group.

Such unofficial bonding rituals serve to enforce conformity and obedience, partly through fear and partly through a belief in the necessity of conformity for military success. This pressure to conform is extremely strong and arguably reduces the likelihood that cadets will 'blow the whistle' on comrades or superiors who misbehave. As I noted earlier, questioning the behaviour of others or questioning orders would be easily construed as a form of disloyalty to the unit; a disloyalty that could endanger lives. Winslow points out that this problem with group-bonding was noted as early as 1946: '[sociologists] Brotz and Wilson ... noted that, in the army, bonding was so strong that "covering up for, defence of and devotion to one's buddy was expected" '.[16] The result of Winslow's inquiry into the behaviour of Canadian regiments in Somalia and Yugoslavia demonstrates that this belief is still prominent.[17] She found that: 'Information that may tarnish the reputation of the Regiment may be hidden ... It is not well accepted to denounce wrongdoing to outsiders, particularly civilians. "There are some things you just don't talk about ... Being a stool pigeon is worse than being a homosexual. There's a climate of fear. It's better not to talk about certain things, for your own security" ' (Canadian soldier).[18]

This soldier 'still did not want to hurt the good name of the Airborne Regiment and was reluctant to criticise his former unit'[19] even though he was depicted in a video undergoing an extremely brutal and humili-ating initiation. When questioned, other members of this unit claimed they couldn't remember the details of the initiation.[20]

Of course group cohesion and trust between military personnel is crucial for military effectiveness and we would expect such trust to be reinforced during basic military training. It is vital for the protection and survival of the whole group. However, loyalty to the military as an institution and to the combatant's own unit should not be blind loyalty. Like blind obedience, blind loyalty is inconsistent with military professionalism. The military claims that it wants personnel who will uphold profes-sional ideals. Such personnel will not be loyal to their units regardless of the behaviour of those units. Professional military personnel would not cover up other combatants' illegal activities, would not participate in illegal and degrading hazing rituals, and would not put group conformity above the military's own values. Unfortunately the kind of conformity and loyalty encouraged through official rhetoric (as seen, for example, in the almost mythological status of 'mateship' in the Australian military) and rituals, and reinforced by unofficial group-bonding rituals, encourages blind obedience. These kinds of initiation rituals reinforce the belief that blind – not reflective – obedience is the cornerstone of effective military functioning by making disobedience seem like betrayal of the unit and a mark of disloyalty.[21] This blind obedience is further encouraged through combat training methods.

Creating obedient killers

Alongside the unofficial bonding processes discussed above are the day-to-day aspects of basic military training. While military training involves many different aspects there is a one feature of the military pro-fession that is crucial to military success: the ability to kill. New recruits must become obedient killers.

As killing is an unavoidable part of war, training military personnel to deal with killing is essential for the achievement of military goals. After all, war is 'essentially the business of killing'.[22] Even if one objects to the par-ticulars of modern training, the fact still remains that military personnel *must* learn to kill. It is during the basic training process that new recruits learn the less tangible skills and psychological dispositions required to deal with inflicting the violence that war requires. The training process must therefore develop character traits that will enable military personnel to kill on command and to order others to kill, and that will minimize the psychological impact of killing. These training techniques work by making killing into a routine action, divorced from its moral context.

Training to kill

Making killing a routine action is no easy task. Training military personnel to be obedient killers has always posed problems for the military institution. The likelihood that military personnel will be killed has always been accepted as one of the risks of going to war but it is only recently that the psychological impact of killing has become recognized as a significant cost of war. As Richard Gabriel explains: 'in every war in which American soldiers have fought in this century, the chances of becoming a psychiatric casualty – of being debilitated for some period of time as a consequence of the stresses of military life – were greater than the chances of being killed by enemy fire'.[23]

In the past factors such as fear, fatigue and stress were blamed for the high rate of psychological disturbances in military personnel.[24] However, comparative studies involving sailors, civilian victims of bombings, and prisoners of war revealed that exposure to fear and stress did not routinely result in psychiatric disturbances. These factors alone could not account for the high rates of psychiatric disorders in military personnel who participated in face-to-face combat.[25] The crucial difference between military personnel and the other groups in the above studies is that only military personnel (particularly soldiers) deliberately kill others at close range.[26] There is evidence linking participation in killing to psychiatric symptoms similar to those characteristic of Post-Traumatic Stress Disorder (PTSD). There is also some evidence of similar symptoms in military personnel who did not kill at close quarters but participated in long-range killing such as bombing runs.[27] The prevalence of PTSD symptoms connected with killing has produced a new term: 'Perpetration-Induced Traumatic Stress'.[28]

It is clear that one reason for the high level of psychiatric illness among military personnel is that many personnel find the deliberate killing of another human being extremely traumatic, so much so that in past wars there is evidence that a significant number of military personnel either did not fire their weapons or deliberately missed.[29] In fact, the issue of so-called 'non-firers' was a recognized problem during the first and second world wars.[30] Studies undertaken during the Second World War suggested that many military personnel tried hard to avoid killing.[31] The truth seems to be that the majority of military personnel are not 'natural' killers.

In response to these findings, and the implication that traditional training methods were unable to overcome many combatants' resistance to face-to-face killing, new training methods were developed prior to the Vietnam War that specifically aimed at overcoming the psychological resistance to killing.[32] While retaining the use of traditional repetitive drills, the new methods attempted to recreate the experience of killing a real human being as closely as possible in order to make the act of killing a routine, conditioned response.[33] These training methods worked by utilizing a combination of desensitization, dehumanization, and behavioural conditioning, unlike previous training methods that had primarily used bulls-eye targets and firing ranges.[34] These methods were so successful that during the Vietnam War firing rates were claimed to be between 85–95 per cent.[35]

Desensitization and dehumanization: making killing routine

The training process desensitizes military personnel in different ways. Through the intense physical training military personnel become desensitized to their own physical suffering. Through the 'hazing' and bullying rituals described earlier they become desensitized to the infliction and endurance of pain and humiliation.[36] The first step in desensitizing military personnel to the act of killing is to familiarize them with the *idea* of killing. Slang and chants make the idea of killing the enemy part of the everyday barracks atmosphere and training environment. By referring to the enemy by derogatory nicknames such 'towel-heads', 'gooks', and 'nips' and by depicting them as morally, racially, or physically inferior these slang and barracks chants dehumanize and demonize the enemy.[37] Through this constant desensitization and dehumanization military personnel rapidly become used to the idea of killing enemy combatants and come to see the enemy as contemptible. The success of such methods is clearly apparent in the attitudes of the American soldiers at Abu Ghraib who referred to the prisoners they tortured as 'animals'. The attitude of these soldiers also demonstrates how normal such dehumanization can become. Seymour Hersh describes how 'The 372nd's [the Military Police Company involved in the abuse] abuse of prisoners seemed almost routine – a fact of Army life that the soldiers felt no need to hide.'[38]

Dehumanization plays a very important role in the process of making killing easier. Put simply, having contempt for people makes it easier to kill them. As Jonathon Glover points out; 'Atrocities are easier to commit if respect for the victims is neutralised.'[39] Desensitization to the idea of killing works by altering the way military personnel perceive the act of killing the enemy, a process achieved partly through the use of dehumanization. Combining a casual attitude towards killing with dehumanization of the enemy encourages an almost light-hearted view of killing. Military personnel cease to see killing as a morally serious act and instead see it as a more realistic form of target practice, a view encouraged by the use of language that makes no reference to the damage done to human bodies by military actions: actions that involve killing are referred to by terms such as 'mopping-up operations', 'surgical strikes', and 'dealing with a target'.[40] One American soldier described this process: 'I yelled "kill, kill" 'til I was hoarse. We yelled it as we engaged in bayonet and hand-to-hand combat drills. And then we sang about it as we marched. "I want to be an airborne ranger ... I want to kill the Viet Cong"... in 1969 I was drafted and very uncertain about the war. I had nothing against the Viet Cong. But by the end of basic training I was ready to kill them.'[41]

Desensitization to killing is further reinforced by the use of human-shaped targets that the trainee 'engages' (a euphemism for 'kills') on a mock-up of an actual battlefield. Some training grounds even use devices such as balloon-filled uniforms and fake blood to make the conditioning even more effective.[42] One trainer for an anti-terrorist course described his favourite method as follows: 'I changed the standard firing targets to full-size, anatomically correct figures because no Syrian runs around with a big white square on his chest with numbers on it. I put clothes on these targets and polyurethane heads. I cut up a cabbage and poured catsup into it and put it back together. I said, "When you look through that scope, I want you to see a head blowing up." '[43]

This process of desensitization and dehumanization is combined with the use of the Operant Conditioning techniques developed by B. F. Skinner in his experiments on rats. Operant Conditioning works by combining constant repetition of the act of killing with the use of positive reinforcements to reward correct behaviour. Like Skinner's rats, military personnel eventually learn to respond instantly to the appropriate stimulus – to fire upon the enemy when ordered to do so.[44] The purpose of this training is summarized succinctly by David Grossman: 'What is being taught in this environment is the ability to shoot reflexively and instantly and a precise mimicry of the act of killing on the modern battlefield. In behavioural terms, the man shape popping up in the soldier's field of fire is the "conditioned stimulus", the immediate engaging of the target is the "target behaviour". "Positive reinforcement" is given in the form of immediate feedback when the target drops if it is hit. In the form of "token economy" these hits are then exchanged for marksmanship badges that usually have some form of privilege or reward (praise, public recognition, three-day passes, and so on) associated with them.'[45]

The last stage of this training process involves the development of what Grossman calls 'denial defence mechanisms'.[46] These function both to protect military personnel from the psychological trauma of killing itself and from the trauma of being trained to kill. The most effective defence mechanism is the nature of the training itself. The trainee practises the act of killing so often that the distinction between a practice kill on a man-shaped target and a 'real' kill is diminished. As a result the first *real* kill doesn't seem 'real' at all and therefore it is easier for the combatant to deny that he has killed a real person as opposed to just 'engaged' another 'target'. Ideally the end result of this training is military personnel who will shoot to kill instantaneously when the appropriate stimuli are present; when the target is seen and the orders are given.

The effectiveness of this training process in turning the experience of killing into a form of conditioned target practice can best be described in the words of military personnel themselves. One high-ranking American officer told a visiting lecturer: 'We do not call it "Killing the enemy". We call it "Servicing the target".'[47] A British soldier told a researcher that 'he thought of the enemy as nothing more or less than Figure II [man-shaped] targets',[48] and a Green Beret sergeant major said of his experience of killing: 'all I felt was the recoil [of the gun]'.[49] Another soldier described his first experience of killing as follows: 'Two shots. Bam-Bam. Just like we had been trained in "Quick-Shoot". When I killed, I did it just like that. Just like I'd been trained. Without even thinking.'[50]

Not only does this training create very effective killers on the battlefield, it also develops the capacity to kill in all those who undergo it, even if they never see action. The training introduces military personnel to their own capacity for killing by teaching them to imagine and practise doing the unthinkable over and over again, regardless of whether a war is imminent. Through this process they develop the attitude and ability of a killer which, as Grossman explains, makes it 'possible to share the guilt of killing without ever actually having killed'.[51]

The aim of this training is straightforward. The processes of desensitization, dehumanization, conditioning, and denial defence mechanisms are intended to produce military personnel who will shoot to kill when ordered to do so without hesitation and without doubt. But what kind of psychological dispositions does this training instil?

The 'bullet-proof mind'

David Grossman refers to the psychological state cultivated by this training as the 'bullet-proof mind'.[52] Military personnel are trained to be able to withstand not only the physical hardship of warfare but also the immediate psychological trauma of killing and being witness to killing. As a result of this process the ideal modern combatant is more lethal than ever before and is less likely to suffer immediate psychological distress.[53] However the long-term effects of this training are a different matter, as I demonstrate below. But besides creating military personnel who are effective killers this training also develops a particular set of moral dispositions and a very specific attitude to the act of killing.

This attitude towards killing is evident in the experiences of the soldiers who fought in the 1993 Battle of Mogadishu in Somalia (the focus of the book and later the film *Black Hawk Down*). In this battle, fought between a few hundred American troops against several thousand Somalis (both fighting with the same kinds of weapons)[54], there were only 18 American casualties compared to 300–1,000 Somalian[55] – statistics that demonstrate the effectiveness of this training in creating efficient killers. The following quote is characteristic of the American soldiers' attitude toward killing: 'I just started picking them out as they were running across the intersection two blocks away, and it was weird because it was much easier than you would think. You hear all these stories about "the first time you kill somebody is very hard". And it was so much like basic training, they were just targets out there, and I don't know if it was the training that we had ingrained in us, but it seemed to me it was like a moving target range, and you could just hit the target and watch it fall and hit the target and watch it fall, and it wasn't real. They were far enough away so that you didn't see, or I didn't see, all the guts and the gore and things like that, but you would just see this target running across in your sight picture, you pull the trigger and the target would fall.'[56]

The attitude displayed by the above quotes is quite clear. Killing is experienced literally as a thoughtless action. Phrases like 'it was so much like basic training, they were just targets out there', 'all I felt was the recoil', and 'without even thinking', demonstrate the effectiveness of these training techniques in making killing a conditioned, knee-jerk response. This training therefore not only modifies combatants' emotional responses to killing – a process that is probably necessary if military personnel are to be efficient killers – but aims to remove the act of killing from the moral awareness of military personnel; to alter how military personnel *think* about killing. The above quotes clearly demonstrate the effectiveness of this training in undermining combatants' awareness of the moral dimension of killing. Killing the enemy is described as if it were an act divorced from not just a broader moral context but from *any* moral context. Killing is discussed as if it were a non-issue, morally speaking – as if it were something not significantly different from shooting targets during basic training and something that is done 'without even thinking'.

Furthermore, at the time the soldiers quoted above saw the people they killed not as fellow human beings but as 'just targets out there'. This dehumanization of the enemy contributes to the sense that killing them is not a moral issue. If reflection on the morality of killing does occur, it occurs after the event. As one military officer argued: 'Modern combat training conditions soldiers to act reflexively to stimuli – such as fire commands, enemy contact, or the sudden appearance of a "target" – and maximises soldiers' lethality, but it does so by bypassing their moral autonomy. Soldiers are conditioned to act without considering the moral repercussions of their actions; they are enabled to kill without making the conscious decision to do so.'[57]

The training methods work by altering combatants' moral consciousness about killing the enemy so that, at the time of killing, the act of killing ceases to be thought of as a moral issue. For the soldiers quoted above the enemy is completely and literally de-humanized. These soldiers are perfect examples of the success of these methods in making killing under orders a conditioned, reflexive response.

However, this improved killing ability comes at a high price. While this training makes killing *during* war psychologically easier, that very fact can lead to greater psychological problems post-combat. The problem is succinctly put by Captain Pete Kilner: 'soldiers who kill *reflexively* in combat will likely one day reconsider their actions reflectively'.[58] Military personnel can find themselves only considering the moral implications of their actions after it is too late, sometimes many years after their combat experience.[59] The impact of this delayed response to killing (amongst other factors) is plausibly linked to the scale and number of psychological causalities experienced by veterans of Vietnam and recent wars such as the First Gulf War.[60] For some military personnel it was the fact that they had been such efficient, unreflective killers – that killing was so easy – that became the most traumatic issue. One of the soldiers from the Black Hawk Down incident said: '[I just] reali[zed] that he was another human being, just like I am. And so that's hard to deal with, but that day it was too easy. *That upsets me more than anything else, how easy it was to pull the trigger over and over again.*'[61]

The Black Hawk Down incident had such an impact on the soldiers who participated in it that as of 2000 only six out of the original task force of 130 were still in service.[62]

Rhetoric vs reality

The combat training described above results in a moral psychology directly at odds with the moral psychology consistent with the military ideal. According to the military virtues described in Chapter 3, good military personnel should be people of moral integrity with a strong capacity for moral reflection. Indeed integrity was considered to be one of the most essential military virtues. Note too that the military virtue of obedience has to be governed by moral reflection if it is to count as a virtue at all. As Rosalind Hursthouse argues, the conditions on virtuous action rule out acting in comprehending, but blind, knee-jerk obedience to an order (see p. 32). As Anscombe rightly remarks, ' "Because he told me to" can gives one's reason for doing something ... But it can also give no more than a "mental cause".'[63]

Yet the training described above produces a moral psychology that not only makes reflective obedience difficult, but in fact aims at by-passing such reflection altogether. It seems that the military wants military personnel to develop the 'mental cause' type of obedience referred to by Anscombe instead of reflective obedience. The soldiers quoted earlier all describe the act of killing as an automatic, reflexive response – as an act of unthinking obedience, reinforced by the intense group-bonding rituals and by the conservative military personality.

There is therefore a direct contradiction between the kind of obedience claimed to be a military virtue and the kind of obedience trained into military personnel and cemented by unofficial group-bonding rituals. In theory good military personnel should be able to distinguish justified orders from immoral or illegal orders and should be able to reflect on the moral issues that emerge during war. However such judgement requires the kind of moral reflection and integrity that are undermined by the military training described earlier. Perhaps it is simply not possible to be both a morally good and an effective combatant. There seems to be a double-bind for military personnel who strive to embody the military professional ideal. Personnel, who, like Captain Rockwood, take seriously the military's claim that obedience should be reflective and should be subservient to the laws of war are unlikely to be promoted and may in fact be punished if they act on their beliefs, as evidenced by the removal of General Baccus from Guantanamo Bay for being 'too soft' – he objected to the interrogation techniques being used in Guantanamo Bay and reminded prisoners of their rights under the Geneva Conventions.[64] Like Captain Rockwood, General Baccus was punished for taking the military's commitment to the laws of war seriously.

In order to truly embody the military virtues good military personnel need to do more than reflect on killing *after* the fact: they need to be capable of moral reflection *at the time* of killing. This does not entail that military personnel should therefore spend time considering the moral pros and cons of every order they receive. As explained in Chapter 4, military personnel are expected to take a default position of obedience unless there is significant doubt about the legitimacy of their orders. But such a position does not entail that the good military personnel should renounce moral reflection altogether. Instead, it requires good military personnel to develop the moral faculties to enable them to recognize illegal and immoral orders – something that can be done even when a split-second decision is needed, as seen in the behaviour of the Australian pilots described in Chapter 5. However, the military combat training described earlier does not encourage even such a selective development of moral reflection. Instead it aims to remove moral reflection wholesale and by doing so is likely to encourage the habits of unreflective obedience. Despite the fact that the military should not wish to create military personnel who commit crimes of obedience, this training increases the possibility that military personnel will both obey illegal orders and interpret ambiguous orders in an illegal manner.

Trained military personnel are not, however, the only groups or individuals who commit atrocities. Ordinary people have massacred, raped, tortured and committed numerous other atrocities without any specialist training and without being members of the military. One has only to consider the Rwandan genocide to realize that ordinary people can commit the most heinous of crimes.[65] The capacity to inflict violence on other human beings is not unique to trained military personnel. Is the reason why military personnel commit crimes of obedience *solely* because of military training, or is it also because many of us have innate tendencies towards unreflective obedience?

Human nature and military training

Killing, maiming, and torturing are not exclusively the province of trained military personnel. People can become perpetrators of horrendous violence in many different circumstances. However, the institutionalized systematic use of violence is different from the criminal violence and mob violence such as that shown in the Rwandan massacre.[66] Unlike acts of civilian violence, military atrocities are often crimes of obedience that take place in an institutionalized setting and are claimed to be justified by legitimate military concerns.[67] Maybe the transition from legitimate military obedience to unreflective destructive obedience happens because many of us already have the capacity for crimes of obedience and this capacity finds easy expression in the military profession because of the military environment and military training. If so, how does military training succeed in bringing out these capacities? To address this possibility we must know more about the pre-existing traits that military training builds on. Understanding the connection between ordinary people's capacity for atrocities and military crimes of obedience requires a deeper knowledge of the characteristic features of unreflective obedience. Stanley Milgram developed the most famous work on this issue.

Stanley Milgram's experiments

The participation of thousands of ordinary Germans in the bureaucracy and administration used to carry out the mass genocide of the Jews and other 'undesirables' motivated Milgram to study the issue of obedience to authority.[68] He conducted a total of 24 experiments but his most famous result, and the experiment that provided the basic model for all other variations, was the Voice-Feedback or Base-Line experiment.

In the Base-Line experiment the subject of the experiment is given the role of teacher. The teacher believes that he is participating in an experiment investigating the effects of punishment on learning. In another room is the learner, who the teacher believes to be a voluntary participant like himself. The roles of teacher and learner are assigned in such a way as to make the subject think that the choice is random. However the choice is rigged so that the subject always becomes the teacher – the learner is in fact an actor. In this version of the experiment the learner is audible but not visible. The teacher is instructed to ask the learner a series of questions and for each wrong answer is told to administer an electric shock by depressing a lever on a board. The voltages on the board are labelled from 15 volts to 450 volts with 30 switches (each indicating a 15 volt increment) labelled in groups of four, from *Slight Shock* to *Danger: Severe Shock*.[69] The learner gives verbal feedback throughout the experiment, beginning with mild protests and ending with a refusal to continue and a demand to be released from the experiment. This is not permitted and as the shocks continue there are screams and then finally silence. The experimenter gives a series of four set responses if and when the teacher questions the continuation of the experiment, according to the strength of the teacher's protest.[70] The experiment was designed to investigate the conditions under which the teacher would continue to administer shocks.

When he first devised this experiment Milgram believed that only a tiny percentage of subjects would continue obeying the experimenter once it became apparent that carrying out the experimenter's orders was causing the learner pain and distress. This expectation was shared by others – Yale University students and psychiatry professors predicted obedience rates of only 1.2 per cent and 0.125 per cent of subjects respectively.[71] The naivety of these assessments rapidly became apparent.

The results of these experiments are infamous. In the Voice-Feedback experiment 62.5 per cent of subjects were fully obedient. In other variations obedience dropped when the learner was visible as well as audible

(40 per cent of subjects were fully obedient) and dropped further when the teacher had to place the learner's hand on a metal plate to administer the shocks (30 per cent fully obedient).[72]

Milgram was greatly shocked by these results. He believed that the most salient lesson of the experimental findings was that: 'ordinary people, simply doing their jobs, and without any particular hostility on their part, can become agents in a terribly destructive process'.[73]

In his attempt to explain these findings Milgram identified several features (of the situation and of the individuals involved) that he believed contributed to the high levels of obedience displayed in the experiments. These features included the sequential nature of the experiment (making it hard for the subject to choose the 'right' moment to stop), the experimenter's supposed superior knowledge and authority as well as the status of the university in which the experiments were held,[74] and the conflict between the perceived obligation to the experimenter, the learner's demands, and the subject's own distress.[75]

From his studies of obedient and disobedient subjects Milgram claimed that when subjects are in a position of subordination to a legitimate authority they often enter into what he termed the *Agentic state*. However the meaning of this term should not be confused with the meaning of 'agency' as it is used in moral philosophy. According to Milgram, the Agentic state is defined as 'the condition a person is in when he sees himself as an agent for carrying out another person's wishes'.[76]

To avoid confusion I will replace the term 'Agentic state' with 'Operative state'. When in the Operative state the subject sees themselves as acting out the motives and desires of the authority figure (the experimenter).[77] They do not feel that the action they are performing originates in their own motives. Instead they see themselves as mere operatives (or agents, in Milgram's terminology) used by the experimenter to carry out a task. However, this is not to say that the obedient subjects happily obeyed the experimenter without any internal conflict. On the contrary, many obedient subjects were obviously very distressed by what was happening and what they were doing. As John Doris points out; 'It is badly mistaken to think that the obedient subjects generally found their job easy.'[78] Many subjects exhibited signs of great stress: hysterical laughter, sweating, trembling, stuttering, and groaning.[79] Yet despite these signs of conflict and anxiety the obedient subjects clearly felt unable or unwilling to act on their distress and end the experiment. Milgram describes one such subject: 'I observed a mature and initially poised businessman enter the laboratory smiling and confident. Within 20 minutes he was reduced to a twitching, stuttering wreck, who was rapidly approaching a point of nervous collapse. ... And yet he continued to respond to every word of the experimenter, and obeyed to the end.'[80]

Milgram argued that once subjects entered the Operative state they felt unable to stop because, as the motive for action was not *their* motive, they felt unable to control the course of events.[81] According to Milgram, there are three significant results of the Operative state: an abdication of responsibility, a narrowing of focus (allowing the subject to 'tune' their attention away from the distress of the victim and instead focus their attention on performing the task in front of them),[82] and devaluation of the victim.

Abdication of responsibility

In follow-up interviews obedient subjects tended to describe their actions as if they were not personally (and therefore morally) responsible for the consequence of those actions – the learner's suffering. This denial of personal responsibility is dramatically apparent in one subject's responses. When the learner (who is audible but not visible) fell silent and ceased responding to the questions after complaining of his heart condition and asking to be released from the experiment, the subject asked the experimenter if he should continue and expressed concern about the learner's welfare. The experimenter told him to continue and when asked stated that he would accept all responsibility. The subject then continued to administer the shocks to the highest voltage. When debriefed, this participant was asked if there was anything the learner could have said or done that would have made him stop administering the shocks. The subject seemed very confused by this question because in *his* mind he had stopped – it was the *experimenter* who had continued.[83]

This subject's response is a dramatic example of what was a common response on the part of obedient subjects when they were questioned about responsibility. When asked who they believed was responsible for continuing the shocks until the end they attributed the majority of responsibility to the experimenter. One subject said: 'I say your [the experimenter's] fault; for the simple reason that I was paid for doing this. I had to follow orders.'[84] Like many military personnel in the past this subject, and indeed most of the obedient subjects, appealed to a variation of the 'I was just following orders' excuse. This view rests on certain assumptions about how to divide blame and responsibility for an act that is the result of more than one person's actions. Douglas Lackey explains this belief: 'most people assume that the quantity of blame that is associated with an evil act is a finite quantity, that this quantity is proportional to the gravity of the act, and that, if several people are responsible for an act, this quantity must be divided among the perpetrators'.[85]

Obedient subjects adopted a variation of this belief and so assigned the majority of blame to the experimenter because he was directing the experiment and was the locus for the intention to shock the learner. As a result of this abdication of responsibility, obedient subjects tended to feel responsible for how well they performed their tasks but not responsible for the *intention* to carry them out.[86] As Milgram explained, 'The most far-reaching consequence of the agentic shift is that a man feels responsible *to* the authority directing him but feels no responsibility *for* the content of the actions that the authority prescribes.'[87]

The prevalence of this view among the obedient subjects indicates that many of them believed (or at least felt) that they had no control over the progress of the experiment; that the decision to continue (or discontinue) was not 'up to them'.[88] This feeling of helplessness contributed to the abdication of responsibility for the continuation of the experiment and the apparent harm to the learner. The experience of helplessness and the consequent denial of responsibility are evident in one subject's experience: 'My reactions were awfully peculiar ... my reactions were giggly, and trying to stifle laughter. This isn't the way I usually am. This was a sheer reaction to a totally impossible situation. And my reaction was to the situation of having to hurt somebody. And being totally helpless and caught up in a set of circumstances where I just couldn't deviate and I couldn't try to help.'[89]

The obedient subjects' description of their situation and their beliefs about the attribution of responsibility for harming the learner fit with a particular view about the nature of responsibility. It is as if they saw their situation as follows: there is a single action (shocking the learner) that is divided into two stages: the experimenter gives the order and then the obedient subject carries it out. What occurs here (or is felt to occur by the participants) is similar to what Elizabeth Wolgast calls 'fractured autonomy', where a normally single autonomous action involving an intention to act and the act itself is split between two separate agents.[90] As she explains: 'where an agent [an operative – someone acting for another] enters the picture, the paradigm [of autonomy] gets fractured. One person deliberates but doesn't confront the reality of acting; while another person confronts the circumstances and acts, but hasn't made the choice. Thus, the author who chose might have changed his mind, and the one carrying out the instructions might have chosen differently had he been permitted to.'[91]

Both individuals (the experimenter and the subject) are missing part of what Thomas Nagel calls the 'moral phenomenology' that would normally inform their moral assessment of the required action and influence their decision whether or not to carry it out.[92] The obedient subject had the phenomenological aspect – how it *felt* to shock the learner – but not the intention; the experimenter had (at least in the mind of the obedient subject) the intention but not the phenomenological aspect. This apparent division between intention and action contributed to the sense of helplessness experienced by subjects such as the subject quoted above, who felt that he had no control over the course of events; that he was a helpless tool of the experimenter.

The abdication of responsibility also served to maintain subjects' positive self-image. Remarks such as 'If it were up to me, I would not have administered shocks to the learner' were common.[93] In such a remark the subject is distinguishing between his own motives and intentions (which, had they been able to be acted on, would have been benign) and the experimenter's. In the post-experiment interviews, subjects often interpreted their distress and anxiety during the experiment as signs of their virtue: 'Within themselves, at least – they had been on the side of the angels.'[94]

From their statements obedient subjects seemed to believe (albeit not consciously) that when two or more individuals carry out a single action there is a *morally* relevant distinction between having the intention and carrying out the action. This belief lessened the strain of harming the learner and allowed the obedient subjects to retain a view of themselves as benign. Such a belief was by no means deliberately adopted or even articulated but it certainly seems to be implied in the way obedient subjects attributed responsibility to themselves and the experimenter. They appeared to adopt (unconsciously or at least not in these terms) Wolgast's concept of fractured autonomy as a means of evading a sense of personal moral responsibility and retaining an intact positive self-image.[95]

The obedient subjects' denial of responsibility for the learner's distress and their belief (and feeling) that they had no control over the continuation of the experiment does not necessarily tell us anything about their *actual* responsibility. There is no *prima facie* reason to hold them less morally responsible simply because they adopted a way (consciously or unconsciously) of viewing the situation that enabled them to *feel* less responsible. The point here is not to assess actual responsibility but to derive an understanding of the obedient subjects' moral psychology – to see what common features emerged from their explanations and justifications of their behaviour. As we have seen, a sense of helplessness and an abdication of responsibility were characteristic of the obedient subjects. Milgram also identified a process of narrowing of attention that he called 'tuning'.

Tuning

Obedient subjects focused primarily on accurately performing the task assigned to them instead of focusing on the impact of the shocks on the victim. Milgram described this alteration of focus as 'tuning'.[96] The obedient subjects tuned their attention and receptivity to the experimenter and his demands, and the demands of the victim became 'muted and psychologically remote'.[97] The subjects' attention narrowed to performing their duties and fulfilling the experimenter's orders adequately. Some subjects became inordinately focused on the technical aspects of the task, such as depressing the levers correctly.[98] One subject (who participated in the Remote condition, where the learner was not visible but banged on the wall at several points as the shocks became higher) described his experience as follows: 'It's funny how you really begin to forget that there's a guy out there, even though you can hear him. For a long time I just concentrated on pressing the switches and reading the words.'[99]

This narrowing of conscious (and moral) awareness meant that the subjects failed to be moved strongly by the victim's pain and distress because they were not 'tuned' to the larger implications of the act they were performing.[100] This focus on role performance seemed to develop in response to the stress caused by continuing obedience. Of course, such narrowing of focus can in other circumstances be a healthy form of self-control. For example, Jeanette Kennett describes how one can regain control over a desire that one doesn't wish to act on, such as a craving for chocolate cake, by deliberately limiting one's attention to a specific task such as the process of typing.[101] However, Milgram's obedient subjects used this technique not to control an unhealthy or unwanted desire but to avoid distress and manage anxiety – distress and anxiety that many of us might think should have signalled to the obedient subjects that they were engaged in morally problematic actions.[102]

When tuning is used as a healthy method of self-control it can help us act in ways consistent with our values. So by managing to control my desire for chocolate I am able to act in a way consistent with my belief in the importance of good health. But the use of tuning by Milgram's obedient subjects led them to act in ways that went *against* not only their desires but their moral values and their moral self-perception. The Milgram subjects felt unable to act in accordance with their value judgements – what they believed was the right thing to do. They exhibited a failure of what Kennett calls *orthonomous* self-control: they failed to act in accordance with their evaluative judgements. However, they did exhibit a form of *intentional* self-control because they were able to overcome internal or external impediments to intentional action (fear, distress, etc.) in order to do something that they believed to be wrong – continue obeying the experimenter's orders. This kind of self-control – self-control in order to do something against one's larger evaluative judgements – is what Alfred Mele calls *errant* self-control.[103] The Milgram subjects' probably unconscious use of tuning enabled this errant self-control by protecting them from the moral implications of what they were doing. It enabled the subjects to contain feelings of conflict or distress and to distance their self-image from the act they were performing ('If it were up *to me*, I would not have administered shocks to the learner').[104] As Milgram explains; 'A person's ego ideal can be an important source of internal inhibitory regulation. Tempted to perform harsh actions, he may assess its consequences for his self-image and refrain. But once the person has moved to the Agentic [Operative] state, this evaluative mechanism is wholly absent. The action, since it no longer stems from motives of his own, no longer reflects on his self-image and thus has no consequences for self-conception.'[105]

By psychologically 'tuning out' the victim's distress the subjects were able to continue obeying the experimenter's orders without being overwhelmed by anxiety and guilt. The consequences of the act for the victim largely disappeared from the subjects' attention.

In contrast to the attitudes of the fully obedient subjects, subjects who disobeyed expressed their dissent in several different ways. Some simply refused to continue, claiming that the choice was up to the learner and flatly denying the experimenter's claim that there was no choice but to continue.[106] Other disobedient subjects qualified their disobedience by referring to personal weakness. For example, one subject gave his reason for disobeying as follows: 'Well ... to me ... well, whether I'm a weakling or what, I just can't, Sir.'[107] A significant number of disobedient subjects felt wholly responsible for what they saw as their failure to fulfil their role correctly. Many who refused to continue the experiment felt guilty about 'letting down' the experimenter and abandoning their role. Milgram described this phenomenon: 'While the obedient subject shifts responsibility for shocking the learner onto the experimenter, those who disobey accept responsibility for the destruction of the experiment. In disobeying, the subject believes he has ruined the experiment, thwarted the purposes of the scientist, and *proved inadequate to the task assigned to him.*'[108]

A significant number of obedient *and* disobedient subjects focused primarily on their success or failure in meeting the role requirements. Many disobedient subjects saw their empathy with the victim as a failure on their part to live up to the required task rather than as evidence of the immorality of the experimenter's orders.

Devaluation of the victim

Obedient subjects also tended to excuse their behaviour by reference to the learner's failings. Milgram reported that remarks such as 'He was so stupid and stubborn he deserved to get shocked' were common.[109] Despite the fact that such devaluation was not encouraged by the experimenter before, during, or after the experiment, post-experiment devaluation was quite common among obedient subjects. As they saw it, it was the learner's fault that he received the shocks – after all, he was only shocked when he answered the questions incorrectly. As one subject explained: 'Well, we have more a less a stubborn person [the learner]. If he understood what this here was, he would'a went along without getting the punishment.'[110] The function of such unprompted devaluation seems relatively straightforward. It is much easier to inflict punishment on a victim, and to justify one's obedience to oneself, when the victim appears to deserve punishment because of stupidity, stubbornness or some other negative trait. Indeed, as we saw in Chapter 6 (p. 136), dehumanization of the enemy is a common part of military training for the same reason: it makes it much easier to harm the enemy.

In summary, the evidence of the experimental results and the self-reporting of the subjects reveal that a sense of role obligation (given legitimization by the experimenter's apparent authority) was a powerful psychological force that served to distance subjects from the moral implications of their actions. The tuning and role-orientation characteristic of the Operative state enabled subjects to feel less responsible because, as they saw it, the act of harming did not stem from their intentions or desires and did not reflect on their moral character: they were merely conduits for the experimenter's intentions. Given that they were not responsible for the *intention* to harm they were similarly not responsible for the *act* of harming. The post-experiment devaluation of the learner also served to minimize the sense of having committed a wrong – if the victim deserved it, then harming him could hardly be morally wrong.

Milgram identified three features characteristic of fully obedient subjects; tuning and role-orientation, dehumanization, and abdication of responsibility. These aided obedient subjects to rationalize their actions, manage the psychological stress caused by their situation, and maintain a view of themselves as morally good people with no intention to harm, thereby minimizing their sense of personal moral wrongdoing. These features, particularly the tuning and the focus on role performance, were also found by sociologists Herbert Kelman and V. Lee Hamilton in their study of attitudes towards obedience to authority.

Kelman and Hamilton: general attitudes towards obedience to authority

In *Crimes of Obedience: towards a Social Psychology of Authority and Responsibility* sociologists Kelman and Hamilton surveyed public attitudes about obedience to authority in general and in relation to war crimes in particular, focusing on attitudes towards the 1971 trial of Lieutenant William Calley for the Vietnam War massacre at My Lai.[111]

Unlike Milgram, Kelman and Hamilton were not testing people's actual rates of obedience to authority. Instead, their aim was to survey the general populations' attitudes about crimes of obedience. Kelman and Hamilton conducted a national survey of attitudes towards Lt Calley's trial, using questions that were designed to probe attitudes about responsibility for illegal or immoral acts committed under orders. Among other questions, subjects were asked whether Lt Calley had behaved correctly, if they themselves would have obeyed his orders and who they thought should bear responsibility for the massacre.[112] From the results of this survey and follow-on surveys Kelman and Hamilton identified three distinct attitudes that individuals might adopt towards social institutions: compliance, identification, and internalization.[113] These processes were connected to and reflected three distinct moral orientations towards obedience to legitimate authority and to the attribution of moral responsibility for actions taken under orders. Kelman and Hamilton termed these three orientations rule, role, and value orientations.[114] The features of these orientations are summarized as follows.

Rule, role, and value orientations

Rule-oriented people have a *compliant* attitudes toward the authority of the prevailing social structure. They follow society's rules in order to reap the rewards of being law-abiding and to avoid punishment but their attachment to the social structure is no deeper than that. In relation to obedience to authority, they are likely to obey authority because they fear punishment and/or feel powerless. While this means they will usually be very obedient, they will disobey if they think they will not be punished because their attachment to the authority system is not central to their personal identity or value system. In relation to the Lt Calley case, rule-oriented individuals tended to deny that Lt Calley should be held responsible for the massacre (because military personnel get punished if they disobey orders) and they tended to assign more responsibility to the higher authorities.

Role-oriented people have a strong orientation towards 'being a good citizen'. A role-oriented individual incorporates the values and requirements of roles such as that of citizen (or of other roles in society) into their self-definition and self-identity. Role-oriented individuals strongly desire to meet the expectations of the roles they occupy and so they are likely to obey if obedience is a role requirement. Role-oriented people also tend to believe that role duties and role obligations can at times take priority over broad-based or personal morality.

The role-oriented individual's incorporation of role performance into their self-image means that unlike the rule-oriented individual, the role-oriented individual is likely to be obedient even when not directly under surveillance. Unlike the rule-oriented person, they are also likely to consider obedience to be a virtue; having value independent from the rewards for being obedient. In relation to Lt Calley's trial, they tended to consider obedience to be the correct response on Lt Calley's part because obedience is a central part of the soldier's role. In their view a good solider cannot and should not be expected to question superior orders in warfare.[115] Thus they were much more likely to deny Lt Calley's responsibility for the massacre and place it on the higher authorities.

Value-oriented individuals internalize the moral values and ideals that their society (and the institutions of that society) claims to uphold. They incorporate the values that a legitimate authority espouses into their personal value system. In relation to Lt Calley's trial, they assigned most importance to the causal chain of events and so were likely to hold Lt Calley fully responsible for his actions at My Lai as he was causally responsible for the massacre. A value-oriented individual will obey orders only so far as those orders do not conflict with the values that the authority system espouses. This means that they are likely to *disobey* if they think the orders do not cohere with these values. Given that Lt Calley's orders were in clear violation of the values not only of the wider society but of the military itself, value-oriented individuals tended to believe that Lt Calley should have disobeyed.

These three orientations do not represent all-or-nothing states. Kelman and Hamilton do not claim that people can only have one orientation. Most people display aspects of each orientation in relation to the different areas of authority they come into contact with and their relationship with those authorities.[116] Kelman and Hamilton used these orientations to categorize their survey results and identify respondents who fitted clearly into distinct orientations, although the distinctions between role- and rule-orientations were not always clear, given the similarity of their responses to questions about responsibility.[117]

Kelman and Hamilton's survey results indicated that rule- and role-orientations were strongly linked with a tendency to deny individual responsibility for actions taken under orders and were also linked to a tendency to believe that orders should be obeyed if they are given by a perceived legitimate authority.[118] Value-orientation, on the other hand, was associated with a tendency to 'assert individual responsibility for crimes of obedience and to a disposition to disobey commands that violate the individual's own principles'.[119] How do these results compare with the moral psychology of the Milgram subjects?

Comparison with Milgram

Kelman and Hamilton's findings are consistent with the psychology of Milgram's obedient subjects. Kelman and Hamilton found that a focus on role performance – on being a 'good' subject – and a denial of personal responsibility was associated with obedience to authority, and this was also characteristic of Milgram's fully obedient subjects

From Milgram's results and Kelman and Hamilton's concepts of role- and rule-orientations, we can derive a basic understanding of the moral psychology of obedience to destructive authority and of the psychological dispositions and techniques that subjects use to protect themselves from the stress of such obedience. Milgram's experiment revealed that in order to minimize the stress of obedience and maintain a positive self-image, obedient subjects tended to tune their attention to the performance of the role, devalue the victim, and deny personal responsibility for the harm to the learner, all without prior coaching or training. Kelman and Hamilton's results similarly demonstrated that if obedience was a role requirement a focus on role performance was connected with a denial of responsibility for actions taken under orders and a willingness to obey orders even when not under surveillance.

The findings of Milgram and Kelman and Hamilton do not necessarily provide a complete understanding of the moral psychology of destructive obedience. Some commentators on Milgram have argued that the high level of obedience was perhaps not as closely linked to the Agentic [Operative] state as Milgram suggested. Moti Nissani, for instance, cites several experiments in belief transition in order to argue that one of the contributing reasons for the high level of obedience could be the subjects' difficulty in making the transition from believing the experimenter's intentions to be benevolent to believing them to be malevolent even when there was 'overwhelming evidence that suggests that this authority [the experimenter] is indeed malevolent. Hence the underlying cause for the subjects' striking conduct could well be conceptual.'[120]

Other commentators have argued that the experimenter's role as 'guide' also provides an explanation of the high rates of obedience. John Sabini and Maury Silver, for example, argue that the subjects' perception of the situation as involving a morally problematic act was thrown into doubt by the experimenter's cool and detached demeanour. The experimenter behaved as if the process of the experiment was entirely normal, and so the subjects lost their 'moral compass' in the face of the experimenter's calm behaviour.[121]

However Nissani and Sabini and Silver's explanations do not alter the fact that obedient subjects explained and justified their behaviour in certain consistent ways, as described earlier in this chapter. Regardless of the forces that might have contributed to obedience (such as the gradual nature of the experiment, the difficultly of belief transition, and the belief that the 'experimenter knows best'), subjects dealt with the stress of their obedience in consistent ways: by tuning, devaluing the victim, and by denying personal responsibility.

In relation to Kelman and Hamilton's conclusion that role- and rule-orientations were closely linked with an abdication of responsibility for crimes of obedience, it might be objected that their survey results cannot be used to infer anything about the moral psychology of obedience to authority because the subjects were asked questions about what they *think* they would do – this might of course be very different to what they would do in reality. As Milgram's studies demonstrated, and subsequent studies have confirmed,[122] predictions about one's own and others' levels of obedience are notoriously incorrect. In fact Milgram's study showed that we tend to greatly *underestimate* rather than overestimate levels of obedience. However, Kelman and Hamilton's survey was not intended to predict actual rates of obedience to authority. Instead, their study was intended to provide an outline of the moral framework that supports a compliant attitude towards obedience to destructive authority and supports the denial of responsibility characteristic of such obedience. Role-orientation in particular is strikingly similar to the moral psychology of Milgram's obedient subjects, in the use of the techniques of tuning and the denial of responsibility. These techniques seem consistently associated with the justification and performance of obedience to destructive authority.

Indeed, dehumanization and displacement of responsibility have also been strongly associated with what is known in psychology as 'moral disengagement'. Moral disengagement occurs when one's normal moral sanctions against harming others are 'disengaged' in order to enable one to carry out one's role. A study of US executioners found that the mechanisms of displacement of responsibility, dehumanization of the victim, and minimization of harmful consequences of one's actions were characteristic of the moral disengagement process that enabled executioners to carry out the killing of another person without being overcome by distress.[123] An International Committee of the Red Cross study on violations of International Humanitarian Law found similar processes in military personnel.[124]

Both Milgram's experiments and Kelman and Hamilton's work indicates that many of us are disposed to obey orders if those orders are given by a supposedly legitimate authority figure. Many of us seem capable of harming others if we are ordered to do so. Given this disposition, we must wonder if the training described in the first two sections of this chapter (pp. 128–40) is primarily to blame for combatants' habits of destructive obedience. In light of what we now know about military training and the moral psychology of obedience to authority we are in a position to see how military training interacts with the dispositions of destructive obedience.

Military training and the dispositions of destructive obedience

I argued above (pp. 140–2) that ordinary military combat training cultivates psychological dispositions that undermine the reflective judgement that military personnel need in order to maintain moral integrity and honour. Unreflective obedience is encouraged both by the training itself and by the kinds of behaviour that is rewarded and punished. Furthermore, the manifest illegality principle explained in Chapter 4 also encourages non-reflective obedience. Ordinary military personnel are desensitized to the infliction of violence, are encouraged to dehumanize the enemy and have been trained to kill unreflectively. Military personnel are also taught to see their role as a professional role governed by professional ideals. These training methods and the professional role-orientation are remarkably similar to the dispositions of destructive obedience identified by Milgram and Kelman and Hamilton.

The similarity between the military training techniques and the dispositions of destructive obedience is not merely coincidental. Military training does more than provide a fertile ground for the expression of these dispositions; it deliberately enhances them. Milgram's obedient subjects devalued the victim without prior coaching. Military personnel are deliberately taught to dehumanize the enemy. Milgram's obedient subjects were often greatly distressed by what they were doing. Military personnel are trained by behavioural conditioning techniques that aim to minimize the distress associated with killing. Many of Milgram's subjects used 'tuning' as way of avoiding anxiety and unease about their actions. Military personnel are trained to see killing as a non-moral issue – to 'tune' their moral awareness away from the act of killing and the humanity of the enemy. Milgram's subjects often tried not to reflect on the morality of their actions in order to deal with the stress of obedience. Military personnel are deliberately encouraged not to reflect on the morality of killing.[125]

This comparison clearly demonstrates that ordinary military training methods develop the dispositions of unreflective obedience so that military personnel will be able to perform their work unreflectively – will be able to kill the enemy without even thinking. The training of military personnel, therefore, aims to cultivate the very dispositions that Milgram's experiments and Kelman and Hamilton's survey demonstrated are linked with crimes of obedience. By undermining the moral agency and moral reflection of military personnel, military training undermines the very faculties that would prevent or at least lessen the likelihood of obedience to illegal orders. The nature of unreflective obedience is such that it is resistant to containment within the military hierarchy and the laws of war. Once combatants' moral reflection has been undermined, military obedience is more likely to become destructive because the moral capacities that would prevent destructive obedience are crippled. Cultivating the dispositions of unreflective obedience may make military personnel more effective killers (arguably a necessary goal of military training) but encourages the proliferation of crimes of obedience.

Military training in its current form instils highly problematic dispositions in military personnel. However military personnel need to be trained to overcome their resistance to killing if they are to be effective fighters. The training techniques described in this chapter are successful in achieving this aim. Can we reconcile the need for military personnel to become desensitized to killing with the problem of creating the dispositions of unreflective obedience, or is this training a grim necessity of modern warfare that demonstrates that military rhetoric is over-idealistic? Is it unrealistic to demand that military personnel be both effective killers and reflective moral agents?

Is military rhetoric too idealistic?

The virtue ethics approach to the military profession is idealistic. Living up to the ideals of the military profession is very difficult. Perhaps the difficulty in reconciling military ideals with real military behaviour indicates that military ideals should not be intended to be achievable. This is not to deny that there are good consequentialist reasons for having military ideals and military rhetoric. For instance, it is important to maintain the military's public image as an honourable profession because this image reassures the civilian population and makes them more likely to trust the military. Military rhetoric also helps attract new recruits and provides some moral constraints on military behaviour. Giving military personnel a moral ideal to aim for – even if it is unachievable – is likely to prevent at least some unethical behaviour. As we saw in Chapter 5, some military personnel take these ideals seriously and so having the ideals serves the important purpose of maintaining some degree of moral restraint. Maybe this is the main role that military professional ideals should play.

The training methods used by most Western military forces produces military personnel who can kill reflexively when ordered to so. These methods have succeeded in overcoming the natural resistance to killing that caused the problem of non-firers in previous wars. It is simply a fact of the nature of military profession that killing is an unavoidable part of war. Training military personnel to deal with killing is absolutely necessary for the achievement of military goals. The attitude to killing displayed by the military personnel quoted earlier has made the American military one of the most efficient and the most formidable in the world. Even if one objects to the particulars of modern training, the fact still remains that military personnel must learn to kill and must learn to deal with having killed. Unlike doctors and other professionals, military personnel need to become detached not just from the emotional distress that can arise from their professional activities – the sights and sounds of war – but also from moral qualms they might feel about their role. Military personnel need to be desensitized to the act of killing and some of this desensitization will have to be to the moral issues that might arise. If this desensitization is best produced through the training methods I have discussed then undermining the moral agency of military personnel could be seen as a necessary sacrifice justified by the need for an effective military force. However, for the reasons I mentioned above, if the military is justified in submitting military personnel to this training it should not advertise the fact. The 'dirty hands' that come from using training techniques that undermine the moral agency of military personnel must remain hidden from the public view.[126]

This response is tempting, if cynical. It allows us to accept that military professional ideals play an important, if deceptive, role; to accept that these dispositions are necessary, but also to acknowledge that they are unfortunate. However, this response is misguided. The claim that the military is justified in training military personnel in blind obedience because of the unique requirements of military action has two main flaws. First, this claim is only justified if there is a serious attempt to minimize the likelihood that military personnel will be given illegal and immoral orders – a serious attempt to ensure that the dispositions produced by the training will be controlled by the laws of war and the chain of command. An appeal to 'dirty hands' only works if sacrificing the moral agency of military personnel really does bring about the best outcome which in this case is effective *legitimate* military action. But this training does not merely enable military personnel to carry out their legitimate military duties more effectively – it cultivates dispositions that make destructive illegitimate obedience more likely. Given that there is no guarantee that military personnel will only be given legal and moral orders, and much evidence that they won't, we cannot accept the assumption that the best way to ensure good military behaviour is to instil unreflective obedience.

Second, this claim undermines the military's claim to professional status. The military claims special moral permission to perform acts of great destructiveness; to kill and to send military personnel to their deaths. The military can only claim these permissions if it is a profession and abides by the moral constraints that flow from that status. If the military can only succeed in carrying out its function by undermining the moral agency of military personnel and encouraging the habits of blind obedience and blind loyalty, then it can no longer claim the status of a profession and the special moral permissions that follow from that status. Arguing that professional status is just for public show implies that the military as an institution has no strong moral grounding – has no greater moral standing than a mercenary army. Furthermore, the prevalence of public statements, value statements and writings in military ethics that refer to the military as a profession, take seriously the moral ideals of the military and recognize the importance of the laws of war, demonstrates a genuine belief in the military's professional status. Unless there is an international conspiracy to perpetuate this belief, we should assume that it is genuine. We are justified in taking seriously the military's claim to professional status and the moral obligations and constraints that follow from that status.

The military cannot claim a 'dirty hands' justification for the training methods that I have described. These training methods enhance pre-existing dispositions towards obedience to authority and hone them so that the distress and moral unease associated with such obedience is minimized. Understanding how these methods work provides an insight into how and why atrocities such as the abuse of prisoners at

Abu Ghraib occur. But even with the discrepancy between military rhetoric and military reality and the process of military training, many military personnel do not abuse and torture prisoners.

Ordinary military personnel and torturers

There is a moral difference between ordinary military personnel and torturers. Even if military personnel are trained in the habits of unreflective obedience and thereby have reduced moral agency, the manifest illegality and immorality of the abuse of prisoners at Abu Ghraib should have been blindingly obvious. Indeed many military personnel were appalled by what they witnessed there – the abuse came to light because one of the soldiers sent a CD-ROM containing photos of the abuse to the Army's Criminal Investigation Unit.[127] Nor did the military support or condone the actions of the Abu Ghraib guards. There was no implicit or explicit appeal to a 'special permission' for such abuse and there was nothing about the situation at Abu Ghraib that even remotely fit the requirements of the 'ticking bomb' justification for the use of torture. Defenders of the use of torture would not defend what happened at Abu Ghraib. The Abu Ghraib guards were inefficient, sadistic, foolish and inadequately trained for the tasks that were assigned to them – many of them had originally been training for traffic duties before being assigned to Abu Ghraib.[128]

On the other hand, there has been relatively little outcry within the military about Guantanamo Bay. Unlike most of the abuse that took place at Abu Ghraib, the torture practised at Guantanamo Bay is part of a systematic exercise in intelligence gathering, and it is this kind of torture which the military claims a special permission for and which is authorized by senior military and government officials.[129] The torture at Guantanamo Bay is claimed to be part of a legitimate interrogation process, performed by trained military interrogators. This difference between the military's attitude to the torturers at Abu Ghraib and the torturers at Guantanamo Bay is clear from the decision to transfer the commander of Guantanamo Bay to Iraq to 'clean up' the prisons there.[130] The way torture is used at Guantanamo Bay is the way it should be done.

There is therefore a difference between the unprofessional Abu Ghraib guards who were so foolish that they took photos and the professional torturers who carry out the authorized torture of terrorism suspects. The justifications for the use of such torture imply a justification for training professional torturers. The reason why the military requires professional torturers rather than untrained ordinary military personnel is clear from this quote from a commander of a military police unit in Baghdad.

A Military Intelligence officer requested this commander to 'keep the detainees awake around the clock'. The commander refused because while the Military Intelligence officers had received training in interrogation: 'my soldiers don't know how to do it. And when you ask an eighteen-year-old kid to keep someone awake, and he doesn't know how to do it, he's going to get creative.'[131]

The military does not want military personnel to 'get creative' with prisoners. Ordinary military training does not account for the difference between untrained personnel who 'get creative' when ordered to 'soften' prisoners up or keep them awake and those who become the efficient, trained torturers needed for effective interrogations. Ordinary military training desensitizes military personnel to the infliction of suffering, dehumanizes the enemy, and reduces the moral sensitivity of military personnel. These processes partly explain why some military personnel, like the Abu Ghraib guards, treat prisoners like animals and indulge in grossly immoral behaviour, but it does not explain why some personnel would become the professional torturers needed for the 'authorized' torture of terrorism suspects.

Conclusion

Ordinary military training enhances the dispositions of unreflective obedience and aims to undermine the moral agency of military personnel. This training aims to make military personnel desensitized to suffering, encourages the dehumanization of the enemy and uses behavioural conditioning to make killing an automatic response. The aim of this training is to minimize the psychological distress associated with killing and encourage military personnel to see killing as an amoral issue. This training is often very successful and as a consequence some military personnel do treat the enemy as if they were less than human, do obey illegal orders and do become desensitized to the infliction of suffering. It is little wonder then that situations like Abu Ghraib arise. Ordinary military combat training lays the psychological framework for destructive obedience.

But the torture at Abu Ghraib is different from the torture that the military claims is justified by appeals to the protection of national security. Ordinary training does not by itself explain why military personnel would both accept such an illegitimate justification and choose to become torturers. To understand how military personnel become torturers requires a deeper understanding of the moral psychology of torture. How does the concept of military professional special moral permissions come to include the permission to use torture?

7
The Moral Psychology of Torture

In Chapter 5 I argued that the military cannot claim a special permission to torture. The role of torturer is not a legitimate professional military role. However, despite the immorality and illegality of torture, the military does train military personnel to become torturers. What kinds of military personnel accept this training? What is the difference between the military personnel at Abu Ghraib and those at Guantanamo Bay – between renegade, untrained torturers and 'real' torturers? How does military torture come to seen as a legitimate professional activity?

In this chapter I show that the use of torture is closely linked to elite military training. The training of elite military personnel builds on the dispositions generated during basic training, creates dispositions that make the performance of torture psychologically easier, and enables torturers to rationalize and justify their actions. This process is enhanced by the use of the discourse of professionalism. The discourse of professionalism allows torturers to restrict their moral vision to their professional activities: it helps instil a belief in their special moral permission to torture and a belief that torture is necessary for the protection of national security. The combination of elite military training and the discourse of professionalism further enhance the dispositions of destructive obedience identified by Milgram and Kelman and Hamilton and cultivated during basic military training. Basic military training and the training of torturers is on a continuum. Professional torturers are the most professional military personnel.[1]

The torturer

The revelations about Abu Ghraib and the findings of the subsequent Senate inquiry have shown that American military personnel are capable of blatantly immoral abuse, torture and killings – actions that cannot be justified by any appeal to national security. Are these the kinds of military personnel who are chosen to become professional torturers? Are military torturers the 'bad apples' of the military profession?

The individual torturer

Contrary to what we might like to believe, studies have shown that professional torturers are generally neither sadistic nor psychopathic. Instead they are usually military personnel chosen on the basis of their obedience and their commitment to the ideology of the ruling authority.[2] In other words, torturers are usually the most loyal, patriotic, and obedient personnel – traits that many military personnel would strive to attain.[3] They are not radically different from the vast majority of military personnel. It is true that not all committed and obedient military personnel are chosen to become torturers. Torturers are chosen by the authorities on the basis of certain characteristics – characteristics superficially similar to those of the ideal military combatant. But even allowing for self-selection and selection by authorities, several studies have revealed that there is no significant psychological difference between military personnel who become torturers and those who do not. Psychologists Mika Haritos-Fatouros and Janice Gibson conducted a study of Greek torturers and concluded that: 'there was no evidence of sadism, abusive, or authoritarian behaviour in the Greek torturers before they entered the army, that there was nothing in their family or personal histories to differentiate them from the rest of their nation's male population of their age at that time, and in the years after they stopped torturing, they lived what seemed to be normal lives'.[4]

Similar results were found in studies of American military personnel who engaged in atrocities during the Vietnam War, in Rorschach tests on high-ranking Nazis and in studies of men who participated in the Nazi regime's murder squads (the *Einsatzgruppen*).[5] In summary, there is no evidence that military torturers are more sadistic or brutal than the majority of military personnel. In fact both the testimony of victims and the testimony of torturers confirm that sadism is actively *discouraged*. The official interrogation training manual of the Khmer Rouge states that: 'The purpose of torturing is to get their responses. *It's not something we do for the fun of it* ... It's not something that's done out of individual anger, or for self-satisfaction.'[6]

As was obvious in Abu Ghraib, a sadistic torturer or a torturer motivated by hatred and anger is an inefficient torturer – one who loses control and who is less likely to achieve results. Torturers aim for efficiency, not sadism. A Brazilian victim told his interviewer that: 'Nor could [he] console himself that the men who applied the wires to his testicles were depraved. They seemed to practise sexual torture only because it was more efficient.'[7] Clearly one does not need to be a sadist – in fact one should *not* be a sadist – to be a 'good' torturer.

Perhaps torturers are fanatics driven by their commitment to the ideals of the ruling authority. Perhaps, like religious zealots or suicide bombers, they believe so strongly in their cause that they will do anything necessary to achieve its goals. That this contention is largely false is demonstrated by the studies referred to above. It is true that some torturers are fanatically committed to the ideals of the ruling authority, just as some military personnel are committed to the ideals of the ruling authority they serve. As mentioned above, military personnel who become torturers are chosen because of their reliability, obedience to the military authorities and their sympathy for the dominant political ideology. Such criteria do not describe fanatics. Many military personnel are deeply committed to military ideals but to describe all such personnel as fanatics is simply false. Many military personnel who became torturers were no more fanatical then the majority of ordinary military personnel. How do these ordinary military personnel become torturers?

From soldier to torturer

The route from ordinary combatant to torturer can occur in several different ways. Sociologist Ronald Crelinsten describes three routes through which a combatant might become a torturer: promotion, conscription, or by accident.[8] He might be promoted or assigned to special training in a unit dealing with interrogations, or he might be conscripted into the army or into the special unit directly. Finally a combatant might find himself in a torture unit almost by accident – perhaps through requesting a transfer to a different area or a different city, for example.[9] However, even in cases of conscription or 'accidental' assignments, military personnel rarely leave the torture unit. Why?

Perhaps military personnel become torturers (and remain torturers) because they fear the consequences of disobedience: court-martials, dishonourable discharge, personal reprisals, perhaps even execution. This was certainly the defence adopted by many on trial for war crimes in the Nuremberg Trials, and similar claims are found in the testimony of torturers from more recent military regimes, several of whom claimed that they would have been killed had they disobeyed orders.[10] Furthermore, it is true that torturers and indeed all military personnel are threatened with punishment for disobeying orders.[11] As we shall see, there is great official and unofficial pressure on torturers to remain with the unit – torturers are likely to undergo hazing rituals similar to those described in Chapter 6. No doubt it would require a great deal of courage and moral integrity to disobey orders to torture prisoners. However, it is not clear that the threat of punishment leaves military personnel with no choice but to obey or is so coercive a threat that it excuses obedience.

While some ex-torturers describe being threatened with death if they tried to leave there are many cases of torturers who were able to stop torturing without being severely punished.[12] One Greek soldier who 'could not stomach the torture' was simply moved to a clerical job.[13] Another was permitted to leave the unit when he presented a certificate from a doctor stating that he had 'psychological difficulties.'[14] In one Uruguayan unit, two officers (out of an intake of fourteen) refused to participate in torture and were expelled from the military.[15] Another officer in the Uruguayan army who refused to torture a man he recognized as a childhood friend was arrested and tried in a military court, but far from being killed or even imprisoned he was allowed to return to service in a different capacity.[16] In all these cases the worst that happened was the end of a military career. In practice therefore, military personnel who wish to stop torturing can find ways of doing so. Serious punishment rarely results as long as the refusal to continue torturing is couched in terms of the individual combatant's weakness or failure to be 'man enough', rather than as a direct refusal of an order.[17] Note, though, that this kind of 'escape route' leaves the morality of the torture unchallenged. Military personnel who adopt this strategy are not therefore displaying the qualities of military virtue. Instead of questioning the validity of the orders they receive, the torturers mentioned above dealt with their discomfort by taking an easy way out – a way that does not cause offence but that does not confront the immorality of torture. Very few military personnel refuse to torture on the basis that torture violates deeply held moral and professional values.

Of course the fact that disobedience may not result in serious punishment does not imply that disobedience does not come at a price. Refusing to torture in the face of extreme pressure requires great moral integrity and moral courage. As will become apparent, the intense group-oriented environment of torture units, the demand for total loyalty and obedience, and the often brutal training environment all combine to make disobedience extremely difficult.[18] Yet these features that make disobedience seem an impossible option all have their counterparts in ordinary military units, and therefore should not excuse obedience to manifestly illegal orders. As described in Chapter 6 ordinary military training is also extremely group-oriented and makes disobedience very difficult, yet this does not excuse obedience to manifestly illegal orders. The integrity and moral courage that are supposed to be the hallmarks of good military personnel only gain real currency in situations where disobedience is *hard*. It is easy to disobey when there is nothing at stake.

In summary, it is clear that military personnel who become torturers are not deviants or sadists, but are obedient, disciplined and loyal combatants. The character of such combatants does not as yet seem very different from the character of ideal military personnel. What then would convince such loyal and obedient military personnel to become torturers; to do something clearly illegal and immoral and that violates the military's regulative ideal? The answer to this question lies in understanding that torture rarely occurs as a one-off response to an extreme emergency or a dire threat to humanity. As I argued in Chapter 5, military torture is not used only in extreme circumstances when military personnel might be overwhelmed by a pressing need for information. Instead, the move from ordinary military personnel to torturer is a non-accidental process of training and initiation. Torture becomes, as Ronald Crelinsten puts it, 'embedded in a larger institutional framework'.[19] Torture is usually performed systematically as part of a larger process of information gathering and intelligence work – it is treated as a specialized area of military professional expertise. Because of this it is usually performed by elite military units.

Elite military units

Most often, military personnel become torturers through joining or being assigned to specialized 'reconnaissance or intelligence' units.[20] These units have a reputation for taking only the toughest, most courageous and most intelligent military personnel. They are 'elite units with exalted reputations within the military or police command structure. If their existence is known to the public, they are often highly respected and/or highly feared.'[21]

These units, such as Kopassus in Indonesia, the Greek ESA (Army Police Corps), the Special Air Services (SAS) in Australia and the UK, the US Army's Delta Force, and the Green Berets, are renowned for the covert nature of their operations (they are sometimes called 'secret armies'),[22] and for the extremely harsh training new recruits must undergo – very few of those who start the training finish it.[23] In fact, the severity of these units' training contributes to their exalted reputations and becomes a significant mark of pride for those who make it through. For example, the website for the John F. Kennedy Special Warfare Center states that

'The legendary green beret and the special forces tab are symbols of physical and mental excellence, courage, ingenuity and just plain stubbornness.'[24]

These units appeal strongly to the professional pride of military personnel in two ways. They emphasize the most important of the military virtues – self-sacrifice, courage, loyalty, and patriotism – and they appeal to the military goal of protecting national security. The rhetoric and reputation of these units appeals directly to combatants' professional pride: not just *any* military personnel could do what has to be done to protect the nation from the threat posed by terrorism and other modern evils. Only those military personnel who truly embody the military virtues are worthy to join these units. As the slogan for the British SAS states, joining the SAS means you will 'Be the Best!'[25] Similarly, the Greek soldiers who graduated from their extremely harsh training were constantly told that they were 'the cornerstone of the regime, the guardians of the nation, and as such they could do whatever they wanted'.[26] To be a member of these units is the highest honour.

Given that the majority of systematic torture involves these units and given that these units are involved in training other military forces in torture techniques, how do these units turn ordinary military personnel into torturers? As noted above, the prestige of these units is enhanced and maintained by the intense and often brutal training process that those who are selected or wish to join must undergo. What does this training involve?

Training to be the best

The training process of these units includes many aspects. New recruits are trained in survival skills, reconnaissance, rescue operations, jungle training and in counter-terrorism, counter-insurgency, and interrogation skills.[27] For the purposes of this section I will focus on survival training as it usually during this training that interrogation skills and interrogation/capture survival skills are taught.

Survival training refers to a gamut of different training exercises. The US *Survive, Evade, Resist, Escape* course at the John F. Kennedy Special Warfare Center and School encapsulates many of the techniques that are found in the Special Forces' training programmes of other countries. The aim of this course is to: 'give students the skill to survive and evade capture or, if captured, to resist interrogation or exploitation and plan their escape. The course includes a classroom phase, a field phase and a resistance training laboratory which simulates the environment of a prisoner of war camp.'[28]

In the 'resistance training laboratory' trainees undergo a highly realistic re-creation of the experience of being captured and interrogated by the enemy. Major Christopher Miller of the US Special Forces told an interviewer about the process of 'stress inoculation', an exercise that: 'places them [new officers] in a "resistance-training laboratory" that is, essentially, a prisoner of war camp, with guard towers, barbed-wire fences, blindfolds, putrid food, irregular sleep intervals, abusive guards and brutal interrogations ... Special Forces officers told me that torture is not practiced, though they did not deny that physical pressure is applied.'[29]

Similarly, British SAS training includes a 'Combat Survival' course where trainees: 'receive lessons and lectures in interrogation techniques from people who have been POWs, tortured or have other experiences ... At the end [of the training] every SAS man has to withstand interrogation training. The men are blindfolded, put in stress positions and interrogated for over 48 hours. White noise (sound) is also used. After a week on the run, cold, dehydrated and exhausted, the mind sometimes starts to play tricks and reality becomes blurred.'[30]

It is worth noting that the techniques of forced standing ('stress positions'), noise bombardment, blindfolding, poor food, and sleep deprivation are commonly recognized torture techniques – they form part of the 'five techniques' used by the British in 1971 in Ireland[31] and clearly meet the definition of torture as described in Chapter 5. The instructors of the Green Beret training course deny that such training constitutes torture but 'the Army will not publicly disclose what the limits [of the physical and mental pressure put on trainees in the mock POW camp] are so it can maximize the anxiety for future students'.[32]

We cannot therefore know exactly what the mock interrogations involve. However, when these techniques are applied to *others* they clearly *do* constitute torture.[33] Former Australian Defence Minister Robert Hill admitted as much when he revealed that the interrogation resistance training of Australian elite troops involved techniques such as sleep deprivation and 'psychological tricks' that were in clear violation of the Geneva Conventions.[34]

The effects of this training on trainees can be very severe. A study of Green Beret trainees found that trainees had far higher levels of cortisone and adrenaline (both associated with stress) than people undergoing major surgery.[35] A study of trainees at the Military Survival School at Fort Bragg found that 'trainees report extremely high levels of dissociative responses – even higher than in people under the influence of hallucinogenic drugs. We also found that elevations in the stress hormone cortisol and reductions in testosterone were some of the most dramatic we have ever seen.'[36]

The psychological stress of the training is combined with extremely demanding physical exercises that can have long-term health risks.[37]

Many training courses involve high stress marches, jungle training and fitness training. For example, Australian SAS trainees undertake 100 km three-day marches without sleep while they are hunted by other SAS men, immediately after which they have to solve complex mathematical and computing problems.[38] The British SAS training information site even claims that 'A couple of soldiers have died during selection ... Even the most experienced soldiers could have and did die in the treacherous mountain regions.'[39]

Other training techniques can involve brutalization and humiliation of trainees. The training of the Greek torturers, for example, was extremely harsh. Trainees were physically and psychologically brutalized, undergoing humiliating rituals as well as being forced to stand for days, denied toilet facilities and refused food.[40] The hazing rituals described in Chapter 6 also occur in these units – the Canadian Airborne Regiment discussed in that chapter was a Special Forces unit.

In summary, the training process of these specialized units involves intense, highly stressful and often brutal exercises. As well as the more conventional weapons and fitness training trainees are subjected to the techniques of psychological torture, a process that is extremely distressing, humiliating and can result in dissociation and deep anxiety. Building on the basic training outlined in Chapter 6, Special Forces training is even more effective in desensitizing new trainees to the endurance of suffering and the infliction of suffering – serving Special Forces officers are the fake 'torturers' during the stress inoculation exercises.[41] This process significantly reduces combatants' empathic reaction to the physical suffering of others, as well as their own. This loss of empathy reduces the moral sensitivity of military personnel and reduces the likelihood that they will feel guilt about harming the enemy. The desirability of such indifference is reinforced by rewards and praise – the kudos for surviving the training are reflected by the elite status of these units and the rhetoric that surrounds them.

Intense desensitization through resistance training is often combined with propaganda that dehumanizes and demonizes the enemy. Gibson and Haritos-Fatouros found that the Greek torturers were constantly told that the enemy were 'worms' and 'bloody communists.' Other common categories are 'terrorists, insurgents, or dissidents who endanger the state'.[42] Such dehumanization results in a rejection of the enemy's humanity that makes it significantly easier to harm them. As sociologist Ervin Staub argues: 'The most general condition for guilt-free massacre is the denial of humanity to the victim. You call the victims names like gooks, dinks, niggers, pinkos, and japs.'[43] Together with the appeal to the military's regulative ideal this combination of verbal dehumanization and desensitization forms a potent and highly effective training strategy. The training greatly enhances the desensitization and dehumanization of the enemy that occurred in basic military training and results in what Ronald Crelinsten describes as 'the gradual movement from one world view (human, civilian, empathetic, caring) to another (inhuman, torturer, cruel, detached). The subject (the conscript/recruit/torturer-to-be) is progressively desensitized while the object (the subversive/Communist/terrorist/victim-to-be) is progressively dehumanized, objectivized, stripped of any identity.'[44]

Not all Special Forces units systematically use torture, but the training programmes used by these units are disturbingly similar to those adopted by units that have been known to use torture. Ex-torturers from South America describe being subjected to the same kind of 'stress inoculation' used during the training of the Australian and British SAS and the American Green Berets. Like SAS and Green Beret recruits these torturers also received lectures and demonstrations in torture techniques.[45] The psychologists who studied the training of the Greek torturers interviewed many soldiers and ex-soldiers from American Special Forces units and concluded that 'all the steps in our [torture] training model were part and parcel of elite American military training'.[46] There is little difference between the training of torturers and the training processes of the elite Special Forces units.[47]

Elite military training builds on the traits and psychological dispositions already developed during basic military training. Basic military training undermines combatants' moral agency through the use of group-bonding rituals, behavioural conditioning, desensitization and dehumanization of the enemy, combined with appeals to the military's professional ideals. This training cultivates the dispositions of unreflective obedience and reduces combatants' capacity for reflective moral agency – the capacity needed for the military virtue of obedience and essential for any kind of virtuous behaviour. Elite military training continues this process. The training significantly desensitizes trainees to suffering, continues the verbal dehumanization of the enemy and cements obedience and loyalty by humiliation and group-bonding rituals. Furthermore, these units deliberately appeal to the professional pride of military personnel by claiming to be the most exclusive and elite military units – units that only accept the best military personnel. At the end of this training trainees are inured to the use of violence and are trained to inflict (and withstand) torture.

Given the rhetoric and reputation of these units, we would expect Special Forces personnel to be those who most embodied the military virtues. But as I have shown, it is these units that are most often implicated in the use of torture and the training of torturers. This blatant contradiction between rhetoric and reality is deeply troubling. While claiming to be the most professional units, Special Forces units train military personnel in such a way as to further undermine their moral agency and further develop the dispositions of unreflective obedience, dispositions inconsistent with the military's claim to professional status. The training of torturers continues to enhance the traits (loss of empathy, desensitization to suffering, dehumanization) that undermine moral reflection and that develop the dispositions of blind obedience. Furthermore the training *aims* to do so.[48] The training of torturers results in more than just a failure to embody the virtue of military obedience; it aims to pervert that virtue. It is a deliberate process that aims to instil dispositions that undermine those needed for virtuous obedience.

The training described above desensitizes trainees to the infliction and endurance of suffering, but more is needed to inure torturers to the actual process of torturing. Military torturers need to be able to manage the stress of torturing other human beings – the stress of dealing with torture victims' screams and physical suffering. Military torturers also need to accept justifications for the use of torture. They need to believe that there is a special moral permission to torture arising from the need to protect national security. This process of acceptance is aided by the use of dehumanization and the discourse of professionalism.

Dehumanization

Throughout ordinary military training and Special Forces training the enemy is verbally dehumanized. However, there is another aspect to dehumanization that takes place during the actual process of torture. The torture victim is humiliated, often naked, filthy, and terrified. The victim's physical state aids the perception of them as sub-human. They do not look and behave like fellow human beings worthy of respect. In the eyes of the torturers the victims look *disgusting* – covered in their own filth, naked and begging ('I smelled like a pig. I couldn't eat because I would lean over and my own smell would come up').[49] Torture techniques such as hooding, sleep deprivation, denial of toilet facilities and personal humiliation are designed primarily to make torture victims feel and seem less than human, thereby making it easier for the torturers and guards to treat them as if they *were* less than human. As Ronald Crelinsten writes, 'It has often been reported that the screams of torture victims no longer sound human. The irony is that to the torturer this only reinforces their dehumanization.'[50] Even the common practice (used in civilian prisons and in Australian refugee detention centres)[51] of referring to prisoners by numbers instead of their names is a part of this dehumanizing process. The Nazis also understood the dehumanizing power of losing one's name. All concentration camp inmates not only lost their names but had their heads shaved and identification numbers tattooed on their arms. Primo Levi (a prisoner in Auschwitz) describes how difficult it is to retain any sense of one's humanity under such circumstances: 'Imagine a man who is deprived of everyone he loves and at the same time of his house, his habits, his clothes, in short, of everything he possesses: he will be a hollow man, reduced to suffering and needs, forgetful of dignity and restraint, for he who loses all often easily loses himself ... It is in this way that one can understand the double sense of the term "extermination camp".'[52]

The deliberate dehumanization of torture victims is graphically revealed in the photos depicting the abuse of prisoners in the Abu Ghraib prison in Iraq. The photos reveal not only extreme brutality but deliberate humiliations such as forcing prisoners to masturbate and simulate oral sex while naked. Such acts are particularly humiliating for the prisoners because of the strict Islamic views on nudity and homosexuality.[53] The enemy is already dehumanized through the training process and they are then literally de-humanized by the process of torture itself. The photos also reveal another aspect of the process of dehumanization. The soldiers depicted in the photos are not ashamed, but proud; they are smiling and giving the thumbs-up sign – behaving as if the Iraqis were nothing more than dehumanized and despicable creatures: 'The pictures from Abu Ghraib are trophy shots. The American soldiers included in them look exactly as if they were standing next to a gutted buck or a 10-foot marlin ... The Americans in the photographs are not enacting hatred; hatred can coexist with respect, however strained. What they display, instead, is contempt: their victims are merely objects.'[54]

The dehumanization of the victim verbally and through the act of torture not only reduces the victim to a contemptible object in the eyes of the torturer, it also encourages a reduced sense of responsibility. Viewing the victim as sub-human (humiliated, stripped of identity, filthy) lessens psychological constraints against harming them and is interpreted by torturers as thereby lessening moral constraints as well. Through the dehumanizing process of torture, torturers not only find the act of torture psychologically easier but can also come to feel that the victims, by their own suffering, somehow deserve it. This belief is evident in the following quote from a US soldier involved in the abuse of prisoners in Iraq.

When watching two prisoners being forced to masturbate and simulate oral sex this soldier commented to a fellow soldier: 'Look what these animals do when you leave them alone for two seconds.'[55] The victims' suffering and humiliation (caused solely by the torture) comes to further weaken reasons against torturing them. The same process is described by Primo Levi: 'The SS escort [of train loads of Jews being sent to Auschwitz] did nothing to hide their amusement at the sight of men and women squatting where they could ... and the German passengers openly expressed their disgust: people like this deserve their fate, just look how they behave. These are not *Menschen*, human beings, but animals.'[56]

Believing that the victims 'deserve it' – are 'animals' – contributes to the belief that one is not morally responsible for harming them. In the case of Milgram's subjects the post-experiment devaluation of the learner was not encouraged or initiated by the experimenter, but appeared to be an (perhaps unconscious) attempt by the subjects to appease their feelings of guilt or unease. In the case of torturers, however, dehumanization is deliberately used to make torture psychologically easier for the torturer. Dehumanizing language and the dehumanizing process of torture itself combine to alleviate feelings of guilt and feelings of moral responsibility. This abdication of moral responsibility is further encouraged by the use of the discourse of professionalism.

The language of professionalism and the moral psychology of role-orientation play a very important role in routinizing and normalizing torture.[57] Role-orientation supported by the discourse of professionalism is used to instil a narrow moral vision in torturers – the restricted moral outlook referred to in Chapter 1. This narrow moral outlook is encouraged by certain attitudes towards torture adopted by torturers, their trainers, and the military unit as a whole. The appeal to the military's professional goals is just one part of this process. A survey of torturers' experiences strikingly highlights the current perception of the torturer's role and justifications for the use of torture. Modern military torturers consider themselves to be professionals.

The profession of torture

Like ordinary military personnel, military personnel who become torturers adopt the language and concepts of professionalism.[58] This appeal to professionalism involves more than the belief that torturers are a legitimate part of the military profession; it involves a whole set of beliefs about the character of the good professional torturer. When interviewed, torturers often claim that a good torturer should be committed to carrying out his duties professionally, with a minimum of emotional engagement. Torturers consider themselves to be fulfilling an important professional role that, while unpleasant, is a necessary extension of the role of ordinary military combatant. Like the role of ordinary military combatant, the role of torturer is justified by the need for national security and peace. As noted in Chapter 5, the military's justifications for the use of torture refer to the same goals that justify the use of military force more generally – the goals of protecting national security. The military has special moral permission to kill enemy combatants and destroy enemy military targets because those actions are necessary in order to protect national security. The permission to torture is claimed to arise from the same basis: the military has special permission to torture when the threat to national security is extreme. Torturers are doing a 'dirty' job, sacrificing their own interests for the wellbeing of the state. The act of torture is recognized as being 'bad', but the perpetrator: 'either refuses to accept the category of acts to which it is assigned ("crime" or "massacre") or presents it as morally justified'.[59]

Once the use of torture has been justified by appeals to the military's professional ideals, then the role of torturer is also taken to be justified. Indeed it is not only justified, it is a role that requires the most professional military personnel trained in units that only take the strongest, most disciplined, loyal, and trustworthy recruits.[60]

The following quotes give an indication of the prevalence of this perception of the role of torturer:

> Some people die on their torturers, without a decision having been made to kill them; this is regarded as a *professional failure*.[61]

> 'I'm here', the officer, whose name was Massini, told [the] prisoner. 'I'm a serious professional. After the revolution, I will be at your disposal to torture whom you like.'[62]

> 'Torturing became a job. If the officers ordered you to beat, you beat. If they ordered you to stop, you stopped ... When I was doing it, I didn't feel any guilt.'[63]

> 'I don't use ... violence outside the standard of my conscience as a human being. I'm a conscientious professional. I know what to do and when to do it.'[64]

> 'We didn't operate on anger or sadism or anything like that. And this is probably more horrific. It became a function. It became part of the job. It became standard operating procedure.'[65]

This appeal to professionalism is a relatively new but increasingly common attitude towards torture. The prevalence of this framework is brought into sharp relief by a study undertaken by sociologist Martha Huggins. Huggins interviewed 27 Brazilian ex-military policemen and ex-military officers, fourteen of whom had participated in or witnessed torture and murder during the military dictatorship.[66] She classified the justifications offered by these men for their actions into four categories: they diffused responsibility, blamed individuals, cited a 'just cause' or justified their violence as part of a 'worthy professionalism'.[67]

Of the fourteen men identified as torturers and/or murderers, eight assigned responsibility to other individuals or to the broad socio-political environment, ten blamed other individuals, usually the victims, six referred to a just cause (for example, that the country was in a 'state of siege', therefore justifying extreme measures)[68] and *all* interviewees cited 'Professional mandates and pressures as the causes of torture and/or murder.' Two-thirds made *two* such arguments.[69]

Since, as I argued in Chapter 5, the role of torturer cannot be a professional role justified by reference to the military profession's regulative ideal, how is the illusion of professionalism created? What is the purpose of this illusion?

Turning torture into a profession

The view that the role of torturer is a professional role governed by unique professional values contributes to the creation of psychological dispositions that aid the performance of torture and that aid torturers in managing the stress and distress caused by torturing. This occurs in several ways. Professionalism discourse is used to legitimize and normalize torture. It enables the creation of a division between professional and private morality and it encourages an abdication of responsibility. This is done primarily by making torture into a routine professional task that requires expertise, professional detachment and self-control.

Routinization

The characterization of torture as a profession contributes to what Herbert Kelman calls the process of routinization, whereby the act of torture becomes part of a routine job subject to role-specific professional standards and justifications ('standard operating procedure').[70] Kelman describes this phenomenon: 'Professionalizing the practice of torture clearly contributes to normalizing their [the torturers'] work; it also contributes to ennobling their efforts since it conveys the image of torture as a special profession dedicated to the service of the state. Like other professionals, torturers undergo professional training to prepare them for their roles.'[71]

The effectiveness of professionalism discourse in making torture seem like a routine task is evidenced in the experience of one former Uruguayan soldier. This soldier became a torturer by being transferred to the Company of Counter-information and had to attend a two month course in topics such as surveillance, tracking suspects, and interrogation. Completely unaware of what his new duties would involve and having avoided any serious military training, his experience testifies to the power of the professionalized attitude to make torture seem normal: 'The worst thing ... was that they tried to make us have a relaxed attitude about torture. They did it just by talking about it. It was an everyday matter, nothing to be ashamed of, something you just had to do. There was no question; you just had to do it.'[72]

His words demonstrate how effectively this attitude normalizes the use of torture. They also demonstrate that when this view of torture is supported by strong group pressure and appeals to military ideals, it would be very difficult for an individual torturer to avoid adopting this perspective on torture.

The language of professionalism reconfigures the act of torture from a brutal act of violence against another human being to what Kelman calls the 'routine application of specialized knowledge and skills.'[73] Huggins argues that the language of professionalism removes all reference to the infliction of violence on an actual human body. It effectively 'disembodies' violence and makes the torturers and murderers appear as 'organizational actors for human agency and physicality'.[74] The language encourages an extreme form of professional detachment by removing any acknowledgement that torture is a violent act of physical harm. So torture is almost never called by that name; it is always 'interrogation'.[75] Even the names of different torture methods are euphemistic: 'operating table', 'safe house' (torture centre), 'the grill', and 'the submarine'.[76] As I noted in Chapter 5, the term 'torture lite' is also intended to reduce awareness of what this kind of torture actually does to the victims.[77] This use of euphemisms is necessary because despite the brutality of the training, it can still take some time for torturers to get used to their work. As one Chilean ex-torturer explained: 'when you first start doing this job, it is hard ... you hide yourself and cry, so nobody can see you. Later on, you don't cry, you only feel sad ... And after ... not wanting to ... but wanting to, you start getting used to it. Yes, definitely, there comes a moment when you feel nothing about what you are doing.'[78]

This process of detachment from moral and physical revulsion is aided greatly by the dehumanization of the victims described above (pp. 170–2).[79] Such detachment was also used in Auschwitz to inure new doctors to the unpleasant tasks they had to perform. Robert Lifton describes the experiences of new doctors: 'Newcomers ... "suffered initially" at the selections, but "then it got to be routine – like all other routines in Auschwitz" ... Most SS doctors underwent ... an extraordinary individual-psychological shift from revulsion to acceptance.'[80]

Like the good Nazi doctor, the professional torturer does not get emotionally involved in his work. Unlike the unprofessional poorly trained Abu Ghraib guards, he is not sadistic or filled with hatred but governs his work by strict professional standards. In that sense he does not seem far removed from the good lawyer.[81] However, the torturer must become detached not only from the physical and emotional revulsion that he might initially feel about the prospect of torturing another human being, but also from any *moral* revulsion or doubts he may have about the permissibility of torture itself.[82] Indeed, being able to overcome such feelings comes to be seen as a mark of toughness, discipline and strength of character; another mark of pride for the elite military personnel who must carry out the dirty work of torture. Heinrich Himmler appealed to this pride in a speech he gave to SS generals, many of whom had been part of the murder squads (*Einsatzgruppen*) responsible for the shooting of thousands of Jews in Eastern Europe: 'Most of you know what it means when 100 corpses are lying side by side, or 500, or 1000. To have stuck it out and at the same time – apart from exceptions caused by human weakness – to have remained decent fellows, that is what has made us hard. This is a page of glory in our history which has never been written and is never to be written.'[83]

The ability to kill thousands of individuals and have 'stuck it out' is seen as a cause for pride, not shame: 'It is the curse of greatness that it must step over dead bodies to create new life.'[84] In this rhetoric, torturers, Nazi doctors and SS generals are all shouldering the burden of committing heinous acts for the protection of national security and 'new life'. Good torturers, like good Nazis, overcome their feelings of revulsion and doubt because they recognize the importance of their mission. This kind of detachment is very different from the normal role of professional detachment which, as explained in Chapter 2, allows professionals to control their emotional responses without becoming callous. Torturers' professional detachment is far more extreme: they are encouraged not to just control their distress but to eradicate that distress altogether.

The routinization of torture and the sense of being part of a special elite profession are enhanced by the torture unit's social and physical isolation. Such isolation is a feature of the military in general – military personnel live, work, and socialize almost exclusively within the military environment – but it is even more apparent in elite military units. Partly because of the covert nature of many of their operations, these units can almost become worlds unto themselves. For example, the Canadian Airborne Regiment implicated in human rights abuses in Somalia during 1993 'believed themselves to be part of an elite unit, a cut above the ordinary infantry soldier.'[85] This isolation from outside contact cements loyalty within the group, strengthens the sense of a special and unique status, and prevents outside perspectives from altering the group's ethos. Ronald Crelinsten describes the result of such an intense group-oriented environment: 'This socially constructed reality – the routine of torture – replaces objective reality with one that is presumed to exist. In doing so, it also supplants conventional morality, substituting in its place the ideological dictates of the authority structure within which torture occurs.'[86]

The use of the professionalism discourse further aids this distorted version of reality. New members of the group are encouraged to accept the professionalized view of torture by adopting euphemistic or morally neutral language to describe torture, by accepting the justifications given for the use of torture and by following the example of older members of the group who exemplify the detached, dispassionate attitude towards torture. As a result it is very difficult for new members to sustain any kind of opposing view. This process also occurred among the Nazi doctors in the concentration camps: 'the fact that the camps were more or less closed environments also helped to facilitate compliance ... the "Auschwitz reality" became for the doctors the "baseline for all else"; immersed in the camp's institutional structure, it grew increasingly difficult to adopt and maintain a perspective critical of its governing beliefs and values'.[87]

In summary, the use of the professionalism discourse, supported by the dehumanizing process of torture, the isolation of the torture unit and the intense group ethos enables the routinization of torture and gives an apparent justification for an extreme form of professional detachment. The result of the process is the perception of torture as 'just a job', a necessary task that should be done as professionally as possible. What impact do this kind of detachment and the routinization of torture have on torturers' beliefs about their moral responsibility?

Moral responsibility and the professionalization of torture

As we have seen, adopting the discourse of professionalism serves several interrelated functions. It gives an aura of legitimacy to the practice of torture and enables the individual torturer to feel that they are part of a valued and important profession performing unpleasant but necessary work. The professionalization of torture also encourages torturers to abdicate moral responsibility for their actions. This occurs in several interrelated ways. First, professionalizing torture enables the torturer to create a distance between their personal moral selves and their professional activities, as evidenced in the quote above ('I don't use ... violence outside the standard of my conscience as a human being. I'm a conscientious professional. I know what to do and when to do it').[88] Like the Milgram subjects who distanced themselves from their actions and claimed that if it was up to them they would not have continued shocking the learner, torturers make a distinction between their professional activities and their personal moral characters. The authorization of torture by the military authorities and the adoption of the discourse of professionalism encourage the torturer to displace moral responsibility for his 'professional' actions onto the authority and to maintain an intact positive self-image.[89] This division between the personal and the professional finds neat expression in the justification offered by one of Huggins' interviewees, a man who had been in charge of a death squad that had killed 100 people: 'he had "never killed anyone off duty"; his murders were all on-duty and "in the line of duty".'[90] In this use of the professionalism discourse, the torturer appeals to a distinction between professional ('on-duty') and personal ('off-duty') in an attempt to maintain a view of himself as essentially good.[91]

Under this view torturers' professional moral character is judged by how well they perform their tasks. However the morality of torture itself is considered to be beyond their professional jurisdiction. This distinction enables a reduced sense of personal moral responsibility because torturers feel responsible for how well they torture – how professional they are – but not for the decision to use torture or for the suffering of the victims. They are encouraged not to consider the moral import or consequences of their actions or the impact on the victim. Instead the use of the professionalism discourse encourages torturers to limit their attention and moral assessment to how well they perform the duties of their role: 'the fact that one is subjecting a human being to the worst sort of suffering is literally eclipsed by the task at hand (extracting information).'[92] Being a good torturer is equated with being a detached, efficient, reliable torturer.

Some of the professional torturers quoted earlier show pride in how well they performed their tasks – pride in the successful separation of 'justified' torture (authorized, professional, efficient, unemotional) from 'unjustified' torture ('off-duty', unauthorized, excessive, sadistic). The existence of this pride gives the lie to the separation of the personal from the professional realms. Pride, as Gerald Postema points out, requires a *personal* identification with the act performed. If there were truly a separation between the personal and the professional, then the 'personal' self could not identify with the actions of the professional – good or bad.[93]

The focus on accurate and efficient performance of professional duties echoes the 'tuning' that Milgram's obedient subjects engaged in to cope with the stress of their position. As Crelinsten explains, 'The induction of a new torturer into the worst forms of behaviour is a gradual process, and the outcome for many is this narrow focus on getting the job done.'[94] In the case of torturers, however, what was a perhaps unconscious process in the Milgram subjects is given a legitimate gloss by the deliberate use of professionalism. The fact that torture occurs in a professional setting and is governed by professional standards is taken to mean that the moral framework through which it is assessed is different, and is limited to the boundaries of the role requirements, to what Postema calls the 'moral universe' of the role.[95] The torturer and the act of torture are viewed through and judged by a narrow, role-defined moral framework. This alteration of the moral perspective is evident in the words of the torturer quoted earlier: 'I don't use ... violence outside the standard of my conscience as a human being. I'm a conscientious professional. I know what to do and when to do it.'[96] Good torturers separate the moral universe of their professional work from that of ordinary morality – they separate 'on-duty' from 'off-duty' torture, and take pride when they achieve this separation successfully.

This sense of professional pride is also evident in the attitudes of torturers towards the torture practices of other countries. Torturers often compare their level of skill and professionalism favourably against other less professional armies. John Conroy lists several examples: 'Bruce Moore-King [a Rhodesian torturer] told me ... that the tortures he administered were mild compared to what was done to people who were sent to Rhodesia's Special Branch. Hugo Garcia [a Uruguayan torturer] told me that the Argentine torturers were far worse than the Uruguayan. Omri Kochva assured me that the men of the Natal battalion had not descended to the level of the Americans in Vietnam. A former U.S. Army interrogator who served and tortured in Vietnam told me how much worse the South Vietnamese National Police were.'[97]

What seems to be occurring here is a kind of justification overkill. Torturers are taught to believe that torture is justified. However, because it is unpleasant and causes emotional stress and distress in those who must do it, it can be hard to reconcile the physical and emotional difficulty in torturing with its apparent justification. Some torturers resolve this dilemma by appealing to a version of professional integrity, against which other torturers and other countries can be judged. Torture, as we saw earlier, is characterized as a necessary evil. If it must be done, then at least it should be done *professionally*. So the appeal to professionalism aids this process by providing a set of internal standards that 'professional' torturers adhere to and which delineate 'good' torturers from 'bad' torturers.

This division of the professional from the personal encourages torturers to adopt a version of the 'fractured autonomy' already noted in the Milgram subjects. There is the agent who tortures and there is the hierarchy of authority along which the orders to torture have been transmitted. Who is responsible for the final act? The torturer did not decide the policy and his superiors did not actually commit the act.[98] The intention to harm is perceived to rest with the authority, and the act of harming rests with the torturer. As we saw with the Milgram subjects, this is a split between two aspects of what Thomas Nagel has called the 'phenomenology of action'.[99] An action involves two parts: believing the act to be justified and forming the intention to carry it out, and then physically carrying out the action. The military authority does not physically perform torture and the torturer did not form the intention or order the use of torture.[100] Neither feels fully responsible for the final act. The torturers, like Milgram's subjects, can see themselves as mere operatives, conduits for the intentions of others.

This moral psychology is very similar to that identified by Lifton in his study of Nazi doctors. In order to manage the stress caused by the awful tasks they had to perform (including choosing which prisoners would be killed, and performing experiments on living prisoners), Lifton argues that the Nazi doctors adopted a psychological mechanism called 'doubling' – they developed a separate 'Auschwitz-self' that embodied their actions in the context of the camp and that was separate from their 'normal' humane self.[101] Like the torturers, such a separation of the personal (humane) self from the professional (detached, dispassionate) self was crucial for maintaining an intact self-image and for containing the emotional distress caused by their work. This process of detachment (again similar to that used by torturers) was greatly aided by the dehumanization and demonization of the victims. Like justifications for the use of torture, the justifications used by the Nazi doctors appealed to protecting the security (racial as well as political in the Nazi ideology) of the nation-state. One doctor resolved the apparent conflict between his professional duty to heal and his support of Jewish extermination as follows: 'Of course I am a doctor and I want to preserve life. And out of respect for human life, I would remove a gangrenous appendix from a diseased body. The Jew is a gangrenous appendix in the body of mankind.'[102]

His words reveal a perverted concept of professional integrity. Far from being the antithesis of medicine's regulative ideal, the need to destroy the Jews is seen as something that is justified by that ideal. Sometimes a good doctor must cause suffering to promote health; must cut off the 'gangrenous appendix'. Similarly, appeals to the goals of national security contribute to torturers' sense of professional integrity. The torturer, like the Nazi doctor, is doing what he must (unpleasant though the work is) and doing what is required to serve the ideals of the military profession. In both cases the ideals of the profession have become grossly distorted – a distortion that serves an important psychological role. The calm, professional, unemotional approach to torture has two main aims: to make the act of torture psychologically easier and to provide torturers with a 'legitimate' professional gloss; a sense that their role is justified by the military's legitimate professional concerns.

In summary, the moral psychology of torture is instilled through the following techniques. During basic and elite military training torturers are desensitized to the infliction and endurance of suffering. They are trained to dehumanize their victims, first by the verbal dehumanization used in basic and elite training and then by the act of torture itself. Torture deliberately aims to strip the victim of humanity and torture techniques are designed to make the victim feel and appear sub-human. The use of the professionalism discourse also contributes to the dehumanizing of the victim by utilizing language intended to 'neutralize' the act of torture, by removing any reference to what torture actually does to the victim's body.

Torturers are encouraged to accept the justifications for the use of torture unquestioningly; to accept both that torture is necessary and that it is a special professional moral permission arising from the military profession's regulative ideal. As military personnel, they have a special responsibility to do what is necessary to protect national security and so the burden of torturing falls on them. They are encouraged to adopt a version of professionalism that changes the way that torture is perceived, changes torturers' beliefs about their personal and moral responsibility and delineates the limits of the moral framework within which the act is judged. All these features deliberately build on the traits identified by Milgram and Kelman and Hamilton and enhanced during basic military training. These features are almost identical to the processes of tuning, devaluation of the victim, and abdication of responsibility that were adopted (largely unconsciously) by Milgram's obedient subjects to deal with the stress of obedience and to maintain a positive self-image, and they are also characteristic of the processes of moral disengagement.

The moral psychology of torture therefore involves a combination of features that enable torturers to accept justifications for the use of torture and to overcome their physical and emotional revulsion to torture. As we have seen, the combination of role-orientation (induced by the adoption of professionalism), dehumanization of the victim, and the consequent reduced sense of responsibility are powerful psychological dis-inhibitors. Torturers are military personnel who (often) have undergone specialized, severe training, become inured to causing and receiving pain and have been encouraged to adopt a 'professional attitude' towards their work. How different are they from ordinary military personnel?

Conclusion

As most ordinary military personnel do not join elite military units, most will not undergo the extreme training of those units and will not be exposed to the distorted version of professionalism described above. Ordinary military personnel undergoing basic military training will not generally be tortured as part of that training. Neither will they be trained in the specialist counter-insurgency and counter-terrorism operations that are the forte of the Special Forces.[103] However there are clear connections between basic military training and elite military training.

In Chapter 6 I argued that ordinary military combat training instils psychological dispositions that undermine combatants' moral agency and by doing so undermine the capacity for reflective judgement that is necessary for moral integrity and honour. Through the use of desensitization, dehumanization and behavioural conditioning, ordinary military training instils the dispositions of unreflective obedience. The rhetoric of military academies and military writers encourages military personnel to see their role as a professional role justified by the military's professional ideals. Military personnel are taught to accept the claim that the military is a profession dedicated to the service of the state and that the military has special moral status because of this role. These features of ordinary military training are identical to the characteristics of elite military training and the moral psychology of torture that results. The difference between ordinary military training and elite military training is a difference of degree, not of kind. The moral psychology of torturers is not significantly different from that of ordinary military personnel. The moral psychology cultivated in elite military training, far from being a special case, is a more distilled version of that cultivated during basic military training.

After basic training the framework of the moral psychology of torture (dehumanization, desensitization, and the discourse of professionalism) is already in place and military personnel are already prepared psychologically (to some degree) for the kinds of traits that torturer training produces. Building on the framework put into place during basic military training, the training of torturers in elite military units further dehumanizes the enemy and further desensitizes military personnel to the infliction and endurance of suffering. The rhetoric and reputation of the elite military units strongly appeals to the professional pride of military personnel and the idea of special moral permissions. Ordinary military personnel are fulfilling a vital professional role but elite military forces are the best of the best. A comparison of the training of tortures and the training of ordinary military personnel reveals that: 'There is little difference between the training of soldiers in general, and the training of torturers in particular. More often than not, the second is a by-product of the first, with the act of torture becoming an integral part of one's duty; a duty that requires you to "be a man".'[104]

Far from being renegade or outlaw units, the elite military units represent the pinnacle of military training and aim to attract only the best personnel. Torturers are not 'bad apples'; they are, in the sense just outlined, the most professional of military personnel. By building on the traits identified by Milgram and Kelman and Hamilton ordinary military training lays the psychological ground work for sadistic crimes such as those committed at Abu Ghraib, but torturer training hones those dispositions to a far more systematic and efficient level.

Conclusion

Professional status and professional special moral permissions impose strict moral constraints on how professional goals may be achieved. By claiming professional status, the military is therefore accepting limitations on what it may do in pursuit of national security. These limitations are set by the laws of war and broad-based moral standards, and they cannot be conveniently disregarded when obeying them seems to conflict with the protection of national security. As part of the military profession, military personnel are supposed to be guided by professional ideals and a concept of professional integrity that will lead them to act ethically; to obey the laws of war and to carry out their duties effectively.

Yet despite this overt commitment to strict professional ethical standards, we have seen that military torture and other crimes of obedience are prevalent in the modern world. In the war against terrorism, torture is used not only as a response to extreme circumstances but as a systematic long-running policy involving military personnel of all ranks. The arguments used to justify such violations of the military's ethical commitments imply a belief that the use of torture is a special professional permission justified by the military's role as protector of the nation-state. Yet, as I have shown, the military cannot claim such permission: the use of torture cannot be justified by appeal to the military's professional ideals. The prevalence of torture demonstrates that the military is systematically violating its own professional ideals.

This systematic violation is not the result of individuals failing to live up to professional ideals and it is not the result of the 'fog of war'. Instead, it is the result of institutionalized processes that deliberately inculcate the dispositions of destructive obedience during basic military training.

Basic military training, reinforced by brutal and humiliating group-bonding rituals and given a veneer of legitimacy by rhetoric about good military character, uses the processes of dehumanization, desensitization, and tuning in order to instil unreflective obedience and to minimize combatants' moral and emotional unease about killing. Military personnel are taught to kill 'without even thinking'. This training perverts the concepts of professionalism, professional integrity and special moral permissions and undermines combatants' capacity for reflective moral agency; the very capacity that military personnel need if they are to embody the military virtues. Furthermore it aims to do so. Regardless of the success rate of this training (there are after all many military personnel – such as Captain Rockwood – who do retain strong moral integrity), the *aim* of the training is straightforward – to desensitize military personnel to the moral and physical aspects of killing and harming the enemy. That aim would be open to criticism even if it were a complete failure.

The result of this training is a moral psychology that encourages unreflective obedience. When combined with dehumanization of the enemy and desensitization to the infliction and endurance of suffering, this unreflective obedience creates a psychological framework linked to crimes of obedience such as the abuse that occurred at Abu Ghraib. The empathy of military personnel for the enemy is diminished, their moral reflection is undermined and so they are more likely to obey illegal and immoral orders and more likely to 'get creative' when carrying out ambiguous orders. Crimes of obedience occur not just when there is a *failure* to be disobedient – this could just be indicative of individual weakness – but also when there are institutional processes that aim to reduce the capacity for moral reflection and moral sensitivity.

The difference between the unprofessional, untrained torturers at Abu Ghraib and the 'professional' torturers who carry out supposedly justified torture is a matter of degree. Professional torturers are typically trained in elite military units reputed to be the most professional military forces. The training used in these units hones the dispositions cultivated during basic military training to a higher degree. The transition from ordinary military personnel to 'professional' torturer is therefore not a leap but a continuation and enhancement of already learned habits and dispositions, justified by reference to military ideals and military goals. So torturers become 'professionals' serving important 'professional' ideals and professional integrity comes to mean extreme professional detachment from both moral and emotional distress. At the same time as appealing to the military's professional status, these units are continuing a training process that undermines the capacities needed to justify that status. What are we to make of this deliberate, institutionalized corruption of the moral agency of military personnel and the corruption of the idea of professionalism?

The training I have described in this book is deeply problematic for several reasons. First, it gives the lie to the military's rhetoric about the kind of moral agent it wants military personnel to become. The military claims that it wants personnel who will be capable of moral reflection; capable of embodying and protecting the values that the military stands for. The ideal combatant is honourable and would have the courage to refuse illegal or immoral orders if the need arose. Such an ideal is just that, an ideal. But, as I have demonstrated, the cause of military torture is far more serious than the failure of individuals to live up to a professional ideal. The cause of military torture is the deliberate and systematic undermining of the very capacities needed to achieve military ideals and needed to justify the military's claim to be a profession.

The use of professionalism discourse by torturers raises further problems with the military's claim to be a profession. The reasons why we think that the military does not have a special permission to torture and why the training of torturers cannot be justified by appeal to the military's professional goals are the same reasons why we should be suspicious of the modern military's claim to be a profession. If we think that training torturers is unjustified because of the kinds of dispositions the training develops, then we should also have serious doubts about the justifiability of ordinary military training – training that cultivates those same dispositions and for the same professional goals. Our abhorrence of torture and torturers gives us reason to abhor the training that leads to those dispositions – the training of ordinary military personnel.

This training also harms military personnel. To corrupt an individual's capacity for moral reflection is one of the greatest harms you can do to them. The realization – too late – that killing is a moral issue can cause immense distress. The recognition of the psychological impact of killing and other acts of violence on the perpetrators can be severe, as we saw from the words of the soldier quoted in Chapter 6: '[I just] reali[zed] that he was another human being, just like I am. And so that's hard to deal with, but that day it was too easy. That upsets me more than anything else, how easy it was to pull the trigger over and over again.'[1]

If we accept Milgram and Kelman and Hamilton's findings, then many of us have a latent disposition to obey orders from an authority figure. If so, then developing the capacity for moral reflection and moral courage is one of the most important ways of combating these dispositions. It is even more important to cultivate reflective moral agency in the military, however, given the nature of the military's special moral permissions. The military claims special moral permission to use great destructive force against enemies of the nation. Because these special permissions involve killing, wounding, destruction of property, and destruction of the environment they *must* be properly grounded and justified by reference to the military's regulative ideal. These permissions must be constrained by the laws governing the military profession – laws to which the goverments of Australia, America and the UK have voluntarily committed themselves – and must be demonstrably necessary for the protection of national security. If these constraints seem extremely limiting, that is as it should be. Military force is too destructive and dangerous a power to permit creative licence in how and when it is used. If the military wants professional status then it must be prepared to live up to the constraints that follow from that status. If the military is not prepared to abide by those constraints, then the military is not a profession and cannot claim special moral permissions. As long as the military uses training methods that produce the dispositions of destructive obedience and as long as elite military training hones those dispositions into the moral psychology of torture, the military cannot claim to be a profession. Is the military addressing these problems?

Unfortunately, current developments indicate that the military is not prepared to abide by the constraints imposed by professional status. Far from training military personnel to be more morally sensitive, new developments in military training will simply exacerbate the problems I have identified. There are two areas of particular concern.

First, in the United States research is going ahead into chemoprophylactic drugs that would inhibit combatants' emotional reactions to killing and prevent, or at least dull, the emotional trauma associated with combat. By inhibiting the emotions associated with trauma, these drugs would prevent or diminish the formation of traumatic memories and feelings of guilt or remorse.[2] Supporters of this research argue that it could be used to treat Post-Traumatic Stress Disorder (PTSD), but it is clear that the use of such drugs would not merely be compassionate but, by inhibiting combatants' emotional responses to trauma, would also undermine in the most blatant way combatants' moral responses and sensitivity to moral issues in warfare. Indeed, such drugs would not just be taken after a traumatic event – they could be taken *before* going into combat. Such research is not limited to America. The Australian Defence Force has stated that research into these kinds of drugs was 'on the agenda'.[3]

It is of course important to help military personnel deal with the trauma associated with combat. However, these kinds of drugs would not help military personnel come to terms with the moral issues that arise in the course of their professional duties. These drugs would attempt to eradicate emotional distress and fear altogether so that there would be nothing to come to terms with. Such drugs would take the process of desensitization discussed in Chapters 6 and 7 one step further. While the aim of the training methods described in this book is to minimize combatants' emotional and moral unease about killing, the use of drugs would aim to eradicate that unease altogether.

Furthermore, the use of the drugs in the military is not just a possibility; it is already occurring. The US Air Force gives pilots amphetamines or

'Go' pills to help them stay awake during long missions. These pills were banned in 1992 after reports of addiction among pilots fighting in the First Gulf War but they have been reintroduced over the last few years. As well as keeping pilots awake, these pills have been known to heighten aggression and paranoia and their use has been linked to several 'friendly fire' incidents in Afghanistan.[4]

Second, a common method of getting military personnel into the mood for combat is the use of loud aggressive music. US tank crews in Iraq listened to music through internal stereos and headphones – heavy metal bands Guns 'n' Roses and Slayer and aggressive hip-hop being among the most popular choices.[5] When military personnel are ensconced in the tanks and bombarded with intense loud aggressive music, combat is likely to be reduced to little more than an arcade game. This would further detach military personnel from the reality of what they are doing and reduce their moral and emotional awareness of the combat situation.

The techniques discussed above have one thing in common. Drugs and loud music aim to dull if not eradicate entirely combatants' emotional responses to and moral awareness of what is happening around them. The research into drugs that would inhibit the formation of traumatic emotions and traumatic memories would only make this process more efficient. It is far from accidental or unfortunate that the basic military training I have described undermines combatants' moral agency. This undermining is a deliberate process aimed at reducing combatants' moral and emotional responses to war and killing – the use of drugs and music are just more refined techniques. As well as dulling combatants' emotional responses to combat, these techniques dull their capacities for moral reflection by distancing them from the moral implications of their actions. Far from actively trying to train military personnel to be reflective moral agents, the evidence suggests that the military is trying even harder to find ways of creating military personnel who are more like automatons than reflective moral agents. It is clear that the military is not seriously committed to training its personnel to be professionals and as a result is not seriously committed to its own stated professional ideals.

What can we conclude from this? Current military training methods undermine the ability of military personnel to embody the military's professional values. This process is being further developed through the use of drugs and other techniques. As it stands therefore, the military has no credible claim to be a profession. Even if the military serves an important human good – and there is some doubt that national security is always such a good – that is not sufficient to justify professional status if the military is not properly guided by the constraints imposed by the laws of war and its own professional values. If it is a profession, the military should be guided by its regulative ideal which incorporates the laws of war. To do this requires military personnel who are reflective moral agents capable of embodying the military virtues. By training military personnel in ways that instil the dispositions of unreflective obedience and that undermine combatants' moral agency, the military loses any justification for professional status and cannot claim professional special moral permissions.

If the military is not a profession, then it is nothing more than the tool of the civilian authority. As such, it is little better than a mercenary army. Such a conclusion may seem shocking, but it is a direct consequence of the military's training techniques and the military's blatant undermining of combatants' reflective moral agency. If the military wishes to claim professional status then it must radically alter how military personnel are trained.

There are two ways we might deal with this problem. First, we might leave military training as it is. After all, the training techniques that I have discussed seem to have produced very efficient military personnel. If we as a society desire a military force that can protect us effectively and efficiently, then perhaps we should just accept the fact that creating an effective military force requires using training techniques that are morally reprehensible and that are connected to crimes of obedience – in which case we must accept the 'dirty hands' that results, and we must concede that the military is not a profession and has no greater moral standing than a mercenary army. This might seem a plausible, if cynical, option except that a worrying consequence of adopting this view is that we would lose any moral high ground in the war against terrorism – and this is a consequence which should be avoided. This leaves us with a second possibility: we can radically rethink the nature of the military profession and military training. If we want the military to have any kind of strong moral justification, then we must alter our views about the nature of the military profession and the training of military personnel.

How might this be done? An in-depth discussion of alternative military training practices is beyond the scope of this book, but some suggestions can be made.

The first and most important step in thinking about alternatives to current military training is to challenge long-standing assumptions about the relationship between unreflective obedience and effective military functioning. The assumption that instilling unreflective obedience is the best or most important way to achieve good military functioning does not stand up to close examination.

For example, in *On the Psychology of Military Incompetence* Norman Dixon found that rigid adherence to the chain of command and a refusal to question or disobey orders was a contributing factor in major instances of military incompetence in British history, such as the Siege of Kut in World War I and the fall of Singapore in World War II. The moral, intellectual, strategic and personal failings of the military leaders of these tragedies were compounded by the ingrained tendency of their subordinates not to question orders, even when those orders were patently suicidal. Dixon also notes that the high level of incompetence demonstrated in World War I was linked to (among other things) 'A terrible crippling obedience'.[6] He quotes the historian Liddell Hart, who, in a discussion of the Third Battle of Ypres, wrote that 'It would seem that none of army commanders ventured to press contrary views with the strength that the facts demanded. One of the lessons of the war exemplified at Passchendaele is certainly the need of allowing more latitude in the army system for intellectual honesty and moral courage.'[7]

Unfortunately a more recent study suggests that need for more 'latitude in the army system for intellectual honesty and moral courage' is still pressing. A 2002 study on dysfunctional military decision-making in the United States military found that a military culture that encouraged rigid thinking and adherence to a 'groupthink' mentality lead to erroneous decision-making and to moral exclusion – the failure to consider ethical and moral principles that were directly relevant to the situation in question.[8] Using case-studies, the study used the responses of 313 military officers in order to examine their propensity to: 'prematurely implement punitive measures against a hypothetical communist government in retaliation to a costly terrorist attack against U.S. embassy personnel.'[9]

The experiment was designed to test how well the officers readjusted their recommendations in the light of new information that contradicted earlier ambiguous intelligence information and in light of what they believed other officers had decided, and to examine under what conditions officers would exhibit 'moral courage' – the ability to recognize 'the right thing to do and to follow through despite authoritative and normative pressures to do otherwise'.[10] The study found that the officers' behaviour was strongly negatively affected by groupthink – the 'suppression of critical thoughts as a result of internalisation of group norms'.[11] Groupthink was closely linked to decision-making rigidity – the refusal to re-evaluate decisions in light of new information – and to increased recommendations for aggressive responses to the hypothetical crisis.[12] An even more disturbing finding was that the decision-making process of even senior officers displayed a complete lack of awareness of any moral issues: 'not one of the sixteen 0–6's (colonels/Navy Captains – those of the highest rank tested) in the present study reported any moral or ethical considerations during their deliberations'.[13]

Jeffrey Bordin also noted that sociologists and historians have consistently found that: 'formalized and complex organisational structures restrict the ability of the organisation to learn. Historians have documented this tendency as being particularly prevalent in military organizations.'[14]

Military culture and training that promotes unreflective obedience creates effective killers but also cultivates the moral psychology of crimes of obedience and hampers imaginative and creative military thinking. It is therefore unclear that current military training does in fact produce the most efficient and effective military force, particularly in light of the military's increasing involvement in military operations other than war, such as peacekeeping.

Once we rethink what character traits and institutional culture count as good military functioning, we are in a position to consider alternative training practices that combine technical skills and psychological readiness for combat with a deep understanding of military law and ethical conduct. While many military academies require officer cadets to take some ethics and military law classes, this is not the case for the majority of military personnel, who (initially at least) are not trained in the military academies. Furthermore, the mere addition of some ethics classes does not address the fundamental problems with military training that I have identified. Given the relative time devoted to ethics and character development classes compared to that devoted to other aspects of military training and the immersion in military culture, we must question the efficacy of adding such classes to military training without also looking more closely at the impact of other aspects of military training. At the very least, far more time must be given to making sure *all* military personnel understand the laws of war and how and when they apply. Mark Osiel suggests that this could be done by rejecting the manifest illegality interpretation of combatants' responsibility to disobey illegal and immoral orders. Instead, the military should institute a culture of 'creative compliance'[15] in which military personnel are encouraged to reflect on the legality of their orders and, if in doubt, to carry out the legal interpretation of the order. This would need to take place at the level of military law and also in practice – during training and during combat. Captain Steven D. Danyluk makes a similar suggestion. He argues that ethical military behaviour must be enforced at *every* level of training. He recommends, for example, that training on the prevention and causes of atrocities should be included in military education institutes.[16]

While this would help, I argue that such methods would need to be combined with a fuller understanding of the link between military training and war crimes. However, including such courses would be an excellent start, particularly if they were combined with clear support for justified disobedience – support manifested not only in the classroom but in basic training, elite training and during combat. There must be cohesion between the rhetoric taught in ethics classes and the obedience expected in the field and in basic training. As the International Committee of the Red Cross argued in its report on violations of international humanitarian law: 'Knowledge does not suffice to induce a favourable attitude towards a norm ... Moreover, a favourable attitude – or indeed sincere acceptance – to a norm does not mean that combatants will conform to it in a real-life situation.'[17]

Giving military personnel the information they need (and that they require to be professionals) regarding their duty to disobey, combined with a concerted effort to reward disobedience when it is justified, would go some way at least to mitigating the effect of military training and military culture.

Notes

Introduction

1. *Amnesty International*, 'Stop Torture'. Available at <http://www.amnestyusa.org/stoptorture/about.html>.
2. For example, a CIA analyst sent to Guantanamo Bay in 2002 interviewed over 30 prisoners and concluded that 'we were committing war crimes in Guantanamo' (Seymour Hersh, *Chain of Command: The Road from 9/11 to Abu Ghraib* (Melbourne: Allen Lane, 2004), p. 2). An Amnesty International Report issued in October 2004 found that 'senior US military and civilian officials had set a climate, both through words and actions, conducive to torture and ill-treatment' (Amnesty International, 'Guantanamo and beyond: The Continuing Pursuit of Unchecked Executive Power', available at <http://web.amnesty.org/library/index/ENGAMR510632005>), and a February 2004 report from the International Committee of the Red Cross found that the Coalition Forces in Iraq were violating the Geneva Conventions in their treatment of prisoners (*Report of the International Committee of the Red Cross on the Treatment by Coalition Forces of Prisoners of War and Other Protected Persons by the Geneva Conventions in Iraq During Arrest, Internment, and Interrogation*, reprinted in Mark Danner, *Torture and Truth: America, Abu Ghraib, and the War on Terror* (London: Granta Books, 2004), p. 253).
3. Herbert C. Kelman, 'The Social Context of Torture: Policy Process and Authority Structure', in Ronald D. Crelinsten and Alex P. Schmid (eds), *The Politics of Pain: Torturers and Their Masters* (Boulder, Colorado: Westview Press, 1993), p. 21.

1 Professions and Professional Ethics

1. Justin Oakley and Dean Cocking, *Virtue Ethics and Professional Roles* (Cambridge: Cambridge University Press, 2001), p. 74.
2. Paul Camenisch, 'On Being a Professional, Morally Speaking', in Bernard Baumrin and Benjamin Freedman (eds), *Moral Responsibility and the Professions* (New York: Haven Publications, 1983), p. 43.
3. Michael D. Bayles, 'The Professions', in Joan C. Callahan (ed.), *Ethical Issues in Professional Life* (New York: Oxford University Press, 1988), p. 28.
4. Camenisch, p. 48.
5. For example, one of the goals of social work is the wellbeing of families, which is certainly an important human good that could count as a universal human value. However, it is not clearly an agent-neutral good.
6. Bayles, p. 2.
7. Camenisch, p. 43. Bayles makes the same point, p. 28.
8. Bayles, p. 28.
9. Camenisch, p. 45.
10. Ibid., p. 45.

11. Oakley and Cocking, p. 11.
12. Ibid., p. 117.
13. A point made by Richard Wasserstrom, in 'Roles and Morality', in David Luban (ed.), *The Good Lawyer: Lawyer's Roles and Lawyer's Ethics* (Totowa, New Jersey: Rowman & Allanheld, 1984), p. 37.
14. Michael Bayles, *Professional Ethics*, 2nd edition (Belmont: Wadsworth, 1989), pp. 22–3.
15. Wasserstrom, p. 60.
16. Within limits. Many writers (such as Richard Wasserstrom and James Rachels) think that the good of parental partiality does not justify the extent of preferential treatment (giving my children new toys when other children are starving, for example) that is common in Western societies. See Richard Wasserstrom, 'Lawyers as Professionals: Some Moral Issues', in Callahan, *Ethical Issues in Professional Life*, and James Rachels, 'Morality, Parents, and Children', in Hugh LaFollette (ed.), *Ethics in Practice: An Anthology* (Oxford: Blackwell, 1997).
17. Richard Wasserstrom, 'Lawyers as Professionals: Some Moral Issues', in Callahan, p. 59.
18. Wasserstrom, pp. 60–1.
19. Although lawyers have always had a rather problematic reputation, the role of lawyer is generally considered to be a necessary professional role, if an unsavoury one.
20. Thanks to Jeanette Kennett for this example.
21. There are limits to this claim. In one Australian court case, a woman successfully sued a medical practice for failing to make sure that she was aware her husband was HIV positive. While the judge upheld the importance of doctor–patient confidentiality, he found that the doctors were negligent in their counselling of the woman, and could have approached the Director General of Health, who has the power to breach confidentiality (Leonie Lamont, 'Payout for Wife Given HIV by Husband', *The Age*, 11 June 2003).
22. Wasserstrom, p. 60.
23. The Victorian Bar Rules of Conduct. Available at <http://www.vicbar.com.au/pdf/Current%20Bar%20Rules.pdf>.
24. Charles Wolfram, 'A Lawyer's Duty to Represent Clients', in Luban, p. 217.
25. There might be some aspects of a doctor's duties that involve such representation (perhaps when testifying in court). However, such representation is not central to the role of doctor.
26. Australian Medical Association Code of Ethics, 2004. Available at <http://www.ama.com.au/web.nsf/doc/WEEN-5WW598>.
27. Arthur Isak Applbaum, *Ethics for Adversaries: The Morality of Roles in Public and Professional Life* (Princeton, New Jersey: Princeton University Press, 1999), p. 49.
28. Applbaum, p. 50.
29. Australian Medical Association Code of Ethics.
30. Applbaum, p. 49.
31. There is much disagreement about the legitimacy of the lawyer's action in this case, but it worth noting that there is a common conception of the lawyer's role that considers such behaviour as within the bounds of proper professional behaviour for an adversarial lawyer.

32. A good example of this is the Willowbrook hepatitis study. During this study, child inmates of Willowbrook State School, a New York State institution for 'mentally defective persons', were deliberately infected with hepatitis without their consent or knowledge, in order to monitor the course of the disease and test new treatments. During the course of the study Willowbrook refused to admit new children unless the parents agreed to their participation in the studies (Office of Research Human Subjects Training, 'Willowbrook Hepatitis Study', <http://hstraining.orda.ucsb.edu/training/willowbrook.htm>).

33. Bayles, *The Professions*, p. 21.

34. Oakley and Cocking, p. 2.

35. Ibid, p. 25. For example, a Kantian or a consequentialist regulative ideal would be a conception of the motives, character, and behaviour of the good Kantian or consequentialist agent. Such a conception could then be internalized by an agent, who would use this ideal to guide their behaviour, although not necessarily in a conscious, deliberate way. The consequentialist or Kantian regulative ideal can serve (and, as many writers argue, should serve) as a criterion of rightness rather than as a conscious motive in the agent's decision procedure. This means that an agent would develop dispositions and character traits that would best promote consequentialist or Kantian moral value overall (Oakley and Cocking, pp. 40–8).

36. The ideal good friend might include traits such as loyalty, openness, and trustworthiness. For an account of the nature of friendship and a discussion of different views on friendship, see Dean Cocking and Jeanette Kennett, 'Friendship and the Self', *Ethics*, 108 (1998): 502–27.

37. Given the agent-relative nature of friendship, it seems (at first glance at least) difficult for agent-neutral moral theories to adequately accommodate the value of friendship. There have been many sophisticated attempts by utilitarians and Kantians to accommodate friendship, but it is not clear that these attempts have been successful. It is beyond the scope of this book to discuss this debate in any detail. Suffice it to say that critics of these attempts argue that trying to cash out the value of friendship in terms of agent-neutral value fails to adequately recognize the kinds of motives that govern (and *should* govern) friendship. For example, a good Kantian, even if she acts out of feelings of affection and sympathy, is constrained by duty. If being a good friend conflicts with duty, then duty wins out. Yet ending friendships for such a reason seems inconsistent with the kinds of motives that we think ought to govern friendships. For a consequentialist and a Kantian attempt respectively to accommodate friendship, see Peter Railton, 'Alienation, Consequentialism, and the Demands of Morality', *Philosophy and Public Affairs*, 13 (1984): 134–71, and Barbara Herman, Chapter 1 'On the Value of Acting from the Motive of Duty', in *The Practice of Moral Judgement* (Harvard: Harvard University Press, 1993). Nancy Sherman also makes a case for the possibility of friendships within Kantianism in *Making a Necessity of Virtue* (New York: Cambridge University Press, 1997).

38. Oakley and Cocking, p. 39.

39. Ibid., p. 63.

40. For an in-depth discussion of this issue, see Dean Cocking and Jeanette Kennett, 'Friendship and Moral Danger', *Journal of Philosophy*, 97 (2000): 278–96.

41. This similarity, however, does not imply that professional relationships should be viewed as a kind of friendship or that professionals should try to be friends with their clients, although some writers in professional ethics (for example, Charles Fried and James Drane) do take this view (Oakley and Cocking, p. 98).

42. Oakley and Cocking, p. 100.

43. This does depend on your view of friendship. If, like Aristotle, you believe in a highly moralized idea of friendship, such that the only good friendships are also morally good relationships, then there is no conflict between good friendship and morality. However, common-sense ideas of friendship seem to accept the idea that the reasons for action arising from friendship are not just a different kind of moral reason that can conflict with other moral reasons. Instead, friendship generates non-moral reasons for action that can conflict with morality *per se*.

44. Dean Cocking and Jeanette Kennett, 'Friendship and Role Morality', in C. L. Ten, Sor-hoon Tan and Kim-chong Chong (eds), *Making Sense of Community and Self* (Chicago: Open Court, 2002), p. 61.

45. Oakley and Cocking, p. 99.

46. Cocking and Kennett, 'Friendship and Role Morality', p. 63.

47. Ibid., p. 62.

48. Ibid., p. 65.

49. Indeed, if I developed too strong an affection for my client, I could be open to charges of professional misconduct. My feelings could warp the professional role in such as way as to raise the question of whether the relationship could strictly be called a professional relationship at all. As Kennett and Cocking put it: 'As a doctor, she may properly spend some time during the consultation asking after her long-term patient's adult children and chatting about their progress, but she is not given a reason to, say, go to a picnic or to the opera with her patient, just because it might be in the interests of the patient, broadly considered, for her to do so' (ibid., p. 65).

50. Ibid., p. 65.

51. Oakley and Cocking, pp. 51–2.

52. Ibid., p. 67.

53. Ibid., p. 67. Their italics.

54. Applbaum, p. 63.

55. Cocking and Kennett make a similar point, 'Friendship and Role Morality', p. 62.

56. Applbaum, p. 64. His italics.

57. See, for example, Seymour Wishman's book *Confessions of a Criminal Lawyer* (New York: Times Books, 1981). Wishman, a former defence lawyer, wrote about his experiences as a zealous advocate. He eventually came to believe that in his role of zealous advocate he had caused many blatantly unjust trial outcomes and that appeals to 'the system' as an excuse didn't change the great injustices he had been party to.

58. Oakley and Cocking, p. 97.

59. Robert Veatch, *A Theory of Medical Ethics* (New York: Basic Books, 1981), quoted in Oakley and Cocking, p. 97.

60. Richard Wasserstrom, 'Roles and Morality', in Luban, p. 29.

61. Ibid., p. 34.

62. Ibid., p. 34.

63. Gerald Postema takes this view in relation to lawyers' adoption of what he calls 'detachment strategies' (Gerald Postema, 'Self-Image, Integrity, and Professional Responsibility,' in Luban, p. 289).
64. See the website of the US Centre for Disease Control and Prevention <http://www.cdc.gov/nchstp/od/tuskegee/time.htm> for a discussion of the study.
65. Bayles discusses this in detail on page 22, *Professional Ethics*.
66. In 'Varieties of Virtue Ethics' (*Ratio*, 9 (1996): 128–52), Justin Oakley provides a succinct summary of the differences between virtue ethics, consequentialist and deontological theories.
67. I am not claiming that rival ethical theories such as consequentialism could not provide a plausible account of professional ethics. My claim is that, because Aristotelian virtue ethics is character-focused and connected to an objective account of excellent human and professional functioning, it better captures our common-sense ideas about professionals' unique responsibilities and the importance of professionals' good moral character.

2 Virtue Ethics and Professional Roles

1. As will become apparent, the account of reflective moral agency that forms the basis of Aristotelian virtue ethics is a relatively uncontroversial account that is compatible both with Kantian moral psychology and with many contemporary accounts of moral agency and virtuous action.
2. Justin Oakley and Dean Cocking, *Virtue Ethics and Professional Roles* (Cambridge: Cambridge University Press, 2001), p. 118.
3. Ibid., p. 4.
4. Brad Hooker, 'Rule-Consequentialism', *Mind*, 99 (1990): 67–77, p. 67. Many thanks to Garrett Cullity for pointing out the similarly between these two approaches to professional ethics.
5. Ibid., p. 70.
6. Ibid., p. 73.
7. Ibid., p. 74.
8. J. J. C. Smart, 'An Outline of a System of Utilitarian Ethics', in J. J. C. Smart and Bernard Williams, *Utilitarianism For and Against* (Cambridge: Cambridge University Press, 1973), pp. 10–11. Smart accuses rule-utilitarians of 'rule worship': 'the rule-utilitarian presumably advocates his principle because he is ultimately concerned with human happiness: why then should he advocate abiding by a rule when he knows that it will not in the present case be most beneficial to abide by it? The reply that in most cases it is most beneficial to abide by the rule seems irrelevant' (Smart, p. 10).
9. Hooker, p. 75.
10. Ibid., pp. 75–6.
11. Rosalind Hursthouse, 'Virtue Ethics vs. Rule-Consequentialism: A Reply to Brad Hooker', *Utilitas*, 14 (2002): 41–53, pp. 50–1.
12. It is worth pointing out that conclusions reached in this book regarding the discrepancy between the capacities needed for virtuous action and those inculcated by military training would probably hold for a dispositional rule-consequentialist approach to professional ethics, and indeed for any other

plausible theory of professional ethics. Someone who rejected the Aristotelian account may well embrace my conclusion that professional practices that undermine agents' capacities for reflective moral agency are morally problematic, at the very least. Any plausible ethical approach to professional dispositions must give pride of place to reflective moral reasoning, and the dispositional rule-consequentialist would, like the Aristotelian virtue ethicist, require the good moral agent to reflect about which dispositions would best serve the ends of the profession. The difference between the two approaches lies in when such reflection is appropriate and how such reflection relates to the meaning of the term 'virtue'.

13. There are other competing accounts of virtue ethics that I cannot discuss here. One contemporary view, primarily developed by Michael Slote in *From Morality to Virtue* (New York: Oxford University Press, 1992), rejects the *eudaimonia* account and instead attempts to derive a list of virtues from traits that we admire in other people. For example, we might look at admirable people such as Nelson Mandela and Mother Theresa, and consider the traits we most admire in them. This would then provide a reason to emulate those traits ourselves (Oakley and Cocking, p. 17). While this approach is interesting, I focus on Aristotelian virtue ethics for three reasons: it is the most developed in relation to professional ethics, it is based on a largely objective view of human flourishing and it ties virtuous action to the exercise of reflective moral agency. By connecting professions to the idea of human flourishing, Aristotelian virtue ethics is well-placed to incorporate the moral importance of professions as contributors to specific human goods – something that approaches such as Slote's might find difficult.

14. Oakley and Cocking, p. 15. Thanks to Dirk Baltzly and Fiona Leigh for their comments on this section.

15. This term is often translated as 'happiness', but it means more than simple pleasure. It does not refer to a simple emotional state, but a state of satisfaction or fulfilment (David Ross, Introduction to Aristotle, *The Nicomachean Ethics* (Oxford: Oxford University Press, 1998), p. xxvii).

16. Dirk Baltzly, 'Peripatetic Perversions', *The Monist*, 86 (2003): 3–29, p. 5.

17. Aristotle, *The Nicomachean Ethics*, I.1, I. Aristotle discusses excellent human functioning and the nature of happiness in Book 1 of *The Nicomachean Ethics*.

18. *The Nicomachean Ethics*, I.7.1097^{b}25–1098^{a}15.

19. Baltzly, p. 7. For example, a good human life is likely to include friendships, wisdom, health, and love.

20. Ibid., p. 5.

21. Aristotle, *The Nicomachean Ethics*, III.2.1111^{b}1–22.

22. Aristotle, *The Nicomachean Ethics*, II.7.1107^{a}25–^{b}17.

23. Aristotle, *The Nicomachean Ethics*, III.2.1111^{b}1–22. In this section, Aristotle discusses both what a choice is, and what it must relate to. This discussion is not central for this chapter, suffice to say that choice must be the result of deliberation and must pertain to objects that are within our power (III.3.1112^{a}11–31).

24. Rosalind Hursthouse, *On Virtue Ethics* (Oxford: Oxford University Press, 1999), pp. 108–9.

25. Christine Korsgaard, 'From Duty and for the Sake of the Noble: Kant and Aristotle on Morally Good Action', in Stephen Engstrom and Jennifer

Whiting (eds), *Aristotle, Kant, and the Stoics: Rethinking Happiness and Duty* (Cambridge: Cambridge University Press, 1996), p. 214.

26. Richard Sorabji, 'Aristotle on the Role of Intellect in Virtue', in Amelie Oksenberg Rorty (ed.), *Essays on Aristotle's Ethics* (London: University of California Press, 1980), p. 205.
27. Aristotle, *The Nicomachean Ethics*, VI.5.1140^{a}20–^{b}6.
28. Sorabji, p. 206. '*To Kalon*' is a term that captures the meaning of words such as 'beautiful', 'fine', 'noble', and 'useful'. Thanks to Dirk Baltzly for clarifying this point.
29. Korsgaard, p. 215.
30. Aristotle also notes that we should chose the action for its own sake, not just to bring about good consequences. The virtues are chosen for their own sake because they are a constitutive part of living a good human life. If we do not try to be virtuous then according to Aristotle we cannot achieve what we want: happiness. So the virtues, because they are manifestations of practical wisdom, are valuable in their own right as necessary constituents of a flourishing human life (Aristotle, *The Nicomachean Ethics*, VI.12.1143^{b}35–1144^{a}18).
31. Aristotle, *The Nicomachean Ethics*, VI.3.1144^{b}5–29.
32. Aristotle, *The Nicomachean Ethics*, VI.3.1144^{b}5–29.
33. Aristotle, *The Nicomachean Ethics*, III.2.1111^{b}1–22.
34. Aristotle, *The Nicomachean Ethics*, III.2.1111^{b}1–1112^{a}31. As Hursthouse points out, an adult might choose to act from inclination – might decide that she will just be guided by her feelings. Could she then be held responsible for her actions, if they are not expressions of her rational choice? She could, according to Hursthouse, because she is manifesting *culpable* ignorance – she has the capacity for practical wisdom, but pretends that she does not. She is therefore responsible for her actions because she has decided (made a choice), mistakenly, that acting from inclination is the best way to live (Hursthouse, p. 105).
35. One difference is that Aristotle insists that a virtuous person not only acts from reflective wisdom but also takes satisfaction in acting virtuously. Someone who experiences a conflict between their inclinations and their understanding of virtuous action is not fully virtuous (Dirk Baltzly, private communication, 19 February 2005). Hursthouse discusses other differences between them, particularly in the role of the emotions in moral action. Aristotle, unlike Kant, argued that emotions had a very important role to play in rational action (Hursthouse, pp. 119–20).
36. Kant, *Groundwork of the Metaphysics of Morals*, 4.393.
37. Korsgaard, p. 203.
38. Kant, *Groundwork of the Metaphysics of Morals*, 4.401.
39. Kant, *Groundwork of the Metaphysics of Morals*, 4.398.
40. Hursthouse, p. 101.
41. Kant, *Groundwork of the Metaphysics of Morals*, 4.393–4.
42. Kant, *Groundwork of the Metaphysics of Morals*, 4.398–9.
43. Hursthouse, p. 103. The importance of reflective moral agency for virtuous action is also found in contemporary moral philosophy. Gary Watson and Harry Frankfurt, for example, both pinpoint the capacity for moral reflection as the distinctive characteristic of persons; of moral agents. See Harry Frankfurt, 'Freedom of the Will and the Concept of a Person', and Gary Watson, 'Free

Agency', in Gary Watson (ed.), *Free Will*, 2nd edition (Oxford: Oxford University Press, 2003).

44. Randolph Clarke, 'Free Will and the Conditions of Moral Responsibility', *Philosophical Studies*, 66 (1992): 53–72, p. 55.

45. Karen Jones, 'Emotion, Weakness of Will, and the Normative Conception of Agency', in Anthony Hatzimoysis (ed.), *Philosophy and the Emotions: Royal Institute of Philosophy Supplement 52* (Cambridge: Cambridge University Press, 2003), p. 190.

46. Oakley and Cocking, p. 118.

47. Ibid., p. 86.

48. This is also case for non-professional roles. The role of parent, for example, involves a role-specific conception of excellence. Being an excellent parent is not the same as being an excellent person.

49. Oakley and Cocking, pp. 25–6.

50. Ibid., p. 27. Their italics.

51. Ibid., p. 92.

52. Ibid., pp. 92–3.

53. Ibid., pp. 92–3.

54. A good example of this can be found in the debate about euthanasia. Some doctors are concerned that if euthanasia were to be legalized it would involve the creation of new duties (directly killing patients) that would conflict with the ideals of medicine.

55. This will emerge in the discussion of the military profession in Chapter 3.

56. Oakley and Cocking, pp. 18, 129.

57. A further worry about this view is that the claim that a professional might be justified in cultivating traits that are neutral or even vicious in everyday life could in theory lead to situations where a professional can and should develop quite possibly contradictory character traits. They might be trying to remove a professional trait in their everyday life, and then seeking to cultivate it in their professional life. It is questionable if such a strategy and the split character that would result are achievable or desirable. If there is good reason not to cultivate certain traits in our everyday life because they inhibit human flourishing, we might have reason to wonder at the claim that we should actively cultivate those traits in our professional life – which is surely an integral part of the flourishing human life. The professional life does not exist in a vacuum.

58. This would not be possible under a unity of the virtues approach (the view that possessing one virtue means possessing them all). However, while this issue is not discussed in *Virtue Ethics and Professional Roles*, Oakley and Cocking reject a unity of the virtues approach (Justin Oakley, private communication, 7 April 2004. See Oakley and Cocking, pp. 18, 129). For Aristotle's view on the unity of the virtues, see *The Nicomachean Ethics*, VI.13.1144b29–1145a11 and *The Edumian Ethics*, 1144b8.

59. Oakley and Cocking, p. 129.

60. Ibid., p. 82.

61. Leslie Cannold, 'Consequences for patients of health care professionals' conscientious actions: the ban on abortions in South Australia', *Journal of Medical Ethics*, 20 (1994): 80–6, p. 80.

62. Oakley and Cocking, p. 82.

63. Cannold, p. 80.
64. Ibid.
65. Oakley and Cocking, p. 83.
66. Ibid.
67. Oakley and Cocking noted that some writers in legal ethics do not think this would be a justifiable reason to refuse to represent a client (Oakley and Cocking, p. 120).
68. Ibid., p. 125.
69. Gerald Dworkin, 'Patients and prisoners: the ethics of lethal injection', *Analysis*, 62 (2002): 181–9, p. 181.
70. Of course these operations are sometimes necessary for patient health and wellbeing in the traditional sense – for example, providing breast implants for a patient who had a mastectomy to remove breast cancer. I am referring to purely cosmetic, non-medical surgery.
71. Arthur Isak Applbaum, *Ethics for Adversaries: The Morality of Roles in Public and Professional Life* (Princeton, New Jersey: Princeton University Press, 1999), p. 48.
72. Oakley and Cocking, p. 81.

3   Professional Ethics and the Military

1. Richard Gabriel, *To Serve With Honor: a Treatise on Military Ethics and the Way of the Soldier* (Westport, Connecticut: Greenwood Press, 1982), p. 85.
2. Samuel Huntington, 'Officership as a Profession', in Malham M. Wakin (ed.), *War, Morality, and the Military Profession*, 2nd edition (Boulder, Colorado: Westview Press, 1986), p. 28. Anthony Hartle refers to these roles as 'support roles' (Anthony Hartle, *Moral Issues in Military Decision Making*, 2nd edition (Lawrence, Kansas: University Press of Kansas, 2004), p. 20). There are important issues that arise from the conflict that might occur when professionals such as doctors work for professional organizations with different and potentially conflicting goals. However this issue is beyond the scope of this book.
3. Harold Laswell, quoted by Huntington, p. 27.
4. Ibid.
5. Huntington, p. 28.
6. The other institution is the police force.
7. Gabriel, p. 82.
8. Martin L. Cook, 'Moral Foundations of Military Service', *Parameters*, 30 (2000): 117–29, p. 122.
9. Historically military forces have appealed to a concept of 'honour', but such a concept is too vague given that it is strongly linked to cultural and national ideals. The Japanese Samurai, for example, had a very different idea of honour to that of the American Confederate army during the Civil War. Thanks to Justin Oakley for this suggestion.
10. Cook, p. 126.
11. LTC Dan Zupan, 'On the Obligation to Conduct World Police Work', paper presented at the *Joint Services Conference on Professional Ethics*, Springfield, Virginia, 2002. Available at <http://www.usafa.af.mil/jscope/JSCOPE02>. For a discussion of the ethics of humanitarian interventions, see C. A. J. Coady,

The Ethics of Armed Humanitarian Intervention (Washington, DC: The US Institute of Peace, 2002).

12. Carl Ceulemans, 'Just Cause', in Bruno Coppieters and Nick Fotion (eds), *Moral Constraints on War: Principles and Cases* (Lanham, MD: Lexington Books, 2002), p. 33.

13. Elizabeth Anscombe, 'War and Murder', in Wakin, p. 285.

14. For example, in 2006 the US military budget request was $438.8 billion, 52 per cent of the discretionary budget. Education and health received only $58.4 billion and $51 billion (6.9 per cent and 6.1 per cent of discretionary budget) respectively (Anup Shah, 'High Military Expenditure in Some Places'. Available at <http://www.globalissues.org/Geopolitics/ArmsTrade/Spending.asp>).

15. Hartle, pp. 15–16.

16. Hartle notes that while it may be true that the existence of the military is seen as essential for the protection of society, it is also true that the military has often been a *threat* to established society and civilian authority. During the course of the twentieth-century military dictatorships overthrew civilian governments in Argentina, Chile, Greece, and many other countries. However, in most economically stable Western nations the military is strictly subordinate to the civilian government and does not pose a threat to that authority (Hartle, p. 16).

17. Gabriel, p. 84.

18. Ibid., p. 85.

19. Hartle, p. 13.

20. This term is related to Samuel Huntington's claim that corporateness is essential to the definition of a profession. His work *The Soldier and The State: The Theory and Politics of Civil-Military Relations* (Cambridge, Massachusetts: Belknap Press of Harvard University Press, 1967) is a classic in the field of military ethics.

21. Major T. L. Stevens, 'A Code of Professional Ethics for Army Officers: Is One Needed?', *Australian Defence Force Journal*, 111 (1995): 33–7, p. 34.

22. Stevens, p. 34.

23. Hartle, p. 21.

24. Huntington, for example, claims that 'the standards of professional military competence apply in Russia as in America, and in the nineteenth century as in the twentieth', 'Officership as a Profession', in Wakin, p. 2. In the US, the official value statements of the three services include traits such as honesty, fairness, duty, loyalty, courage, integrity, and discipline (Hartle, pp. 67–72). In the Australian military, the value statements of military academies such as the Royal Military College Duntroon and the Australian Defence Force Academy refer to traits such as respect, integrity, loyalty, and self-discipline.

25. Hartle, p. 20.

26. *Royal Military College Duntroon*, Australia. Available at <http://www.defence.gov.au/army/rmc/RMCA/RMCA-Mainpage.asp>.

27. Arthur Isak Applbaum, *Ethics for Adversaries: the Morality of Roles in Public and Professional Life* (Princeton, New Jersey: Princeton University Press, 1999), p. 3. In this quote Applbaum is talking more generally about adversarial professions, but the permission discussed also applies to roles in the military profession.

28. Samuel Huntington, 'The Military Mind: Conservative Realism of the Professional Military Ethic', in Wakin, p. 41.
29. David Luban, 'Just War and Human Rights', *Philosophy & Public Affairs*, 9 (1980): 160–81, p. 168.
30. Ibid., p. 168.
31. Michael Walzer, *Just and Unjust Wars: A Moral Argument with Historical Illustrations*, 3rd edn (New York: Basic Books, 2000), p. 54.
32. Michael Walzer, 'The Moral Standing of States: A Response to Four Critics', *Philosophy and Public Affairs*, 9 (1980): 209–29, p. 214.
33. Walzer, 'The Moral Standing of States', p. 214.
34. Walzer, *Just and Unjust Wars*, p. 90.
35. It is true that this justification has often been used in a highly debatable manner, in, for example, the American invasion of Panama and the overthrow of the Allende government in Chile. Indeed, one might argue that these invasions were unjust partly because the governments of Panama and Chile were *legitimate* – Allende, for example, had been democratically elected. It is also true that there are many blatantly illegitimate states that have *not* been overthrown by outside forces on the grounds that to do so would violate those states' rights. However, the misuse of this excuse does not render it illegitimate.
36. Huntington, 'The Military Mind: Conservative Realism of the Professional Military Ethic', pp. 46–7. There is some debate about the ideal extent of this neutrality. Morris Janowitz, for example, argued that the military should aim to embody society's values rather than become completely independent of civilian society. More recently Rebecca Schiff has argued that effective civilian control of the military depends on the cultural, social, and historical relations between the military, the political elite, and the citizenry. Whether maintaining military political neutrality is the best method of ensuring civilian control depends on cultural and historical factors that vary from country to country. However, all writers agree that the civilian authority must control the use of the military, and in democracies such as America, Australia and the UK this is best achieved by a strong separation between the military and politics. See Morris Janowitz, *The Professional Soldier: A Social and Political Portrait* (Glencoe, Illinois: Free Press, 1960) and Rebecca L. Schiff, 'Civil-Military Relations Reconsidered: A Theory of Concordance', *Armed Forces and Society*, 22 (1995): 7–18.
37. Lance Betros, 'Political Partisanship and the Military Ethic in America', *Armed Forces and Society*, 27 (2001): 501–23, p. 502.
38. Misha Schubert, 'PM Defends Digger Photos', *The Age*, 25 June 2004.
39. Huntington, 'The Military Mind: Conservative Realism of the Professional Military Ethic', p. 48.
40. Janowitz, *The Professional Soldier: A Social and Political Portrait* (Glencoe, Illinois: Free Press, 1960), p. 233, quoted in Hartle, p. 60.
41. Huntington, 'The Military Mind: Conservative Realism of the Professional Military Ethic', p. 47.
42. There is a vast literature on just war theory. For a detailed discussion of *jus in bello* and *jus ad bellum*, see James F. Childress, 'Just-War Theories: The Bases, Interrelations, Priorities, and Functions of Their Criteria', in Wakin, pp. 256–76, Michael Walzer, *Just and Unjust Wars*, 3rd edition (New York: Basic Books, 2000), and Bruno Coppieters and Nick Fotion (eds), *Moral Constraints on War: Principles and Cases* (Lanham, MD: Lexington Books, 2002).

43. Later in this chapter I discuss the relationship between the laws of war and the regulative ideal of the military in detail.
44. Justin Oakley and Dean Cocking, *Virtue Ethics and Professional Roles* (Cambridge: Cambridge University Press, 2001), p. 85.
45. Ibid., p. 90.
46. Quoted in Michael Walzer, 'Political Action: The Problem of Dirty Hands', *Philosophy & Public Affairs*, 2 (1973): 160–80, p. 167. I will elaborate on the problem of training military personnel to kill in Chapter 6.
47. Oakley and Cocking, p. 130.
48. Hartle, pp. 32–5.
49. Ibid., p. 41. The technical aspects of the combatant's role will of course vary greatly both within the three services and between them.
50. For an excellent discussion of military history and comparative military culture, see John Keegan, *A History of Warfare* (London: Pimlico, 1994).
51. See Hartle, pp. 76–100, for a discussion of these principles.
52. Martin L. Cook, 'The Proper Role of Military Advice in Contemporary Uses of Force', *Parameters*, 32 (2002/2003): 21–33, p. 26.
53. Huntington, *The Soldier and the State* (Cambridge, Massachusetts: Belknap Press of Harvard University Press, 1957), p. 73, quoted in Hartle, p. 34.
54. Hartle, p. 40.
55. Ibid., p. 59.
56. Ibid., p. 57.
57. Ibid., p. 58.
58. Captain Marc Hedhal, 'The Washington Post Test: Integrity's Last Stand', paper presented at the *Joint Services Conference on Professional Ethics*, Springfield, Virginia, 2002. Available at <http://www.usafa.af.mil/jscope/JSCOPE02>.
59. *Royal Military College Duntroon*, statement of Military Ethic. Available at <http://www.defence.gov.au/army/rmc/>.
60. A poor relationship between officers and their men was cited as one of the contributing reasons to the high rate of 'fragging' in the Vietnam War. 'Fragging' occurs when military personnel kill or attempt to kill (usually using hand grenades) their commanding officers (Joanna Bourke, *An Intimate History of Killing: Face-to-Face Killing in Twentieth-Century Warfare* (London: Granta Books, 1999), p. 197). The US Defense Department later admitted to 788 confirmed fraggings, and another 200-odd attempts involving other weapons. In total, 'over 1000 officers and NCOs were killed by their own men in Vietnam' (Bourke, p. 198).
61. Hartle, p. 57.
62. Ibid., p. 45.
63. Ibid., p. 50.
64. Ibid., p. 53.
65. Ibid., p. 54.
66. Ibid., p. 48.
67. Another source of conflict could arise if two of these basic values conflicted – if, for example, protecting freedom of political assembly conflicted with the right to free speech. Thanks to Dirk Baltzly for suggesting this idea.
68. Many officers felt (and still feel) very bitter about the extent of civilian involvement in military policy during the Vietnam War. As Martin Cook

claims: 'In the minds of most officers, Vietnam was a clear case of civilians asking the impossible of the military, both in the ends sought by the uses of military force and in the civilian micromanagement of the conduct of military operations' (Martin Cook, 'The Proper Role of Professional Military Advice in Contemporary Uses of Force', p. 23).

69. Malham M. Wakin, 'Military and Societal Values: The Relevance of Knowing and Doing', paper presented at the *Joint Services Conference on Professional Ethics*, Springfield, Virginia, 1995. Available at <http://www.usafa.af.mil/JSCO PE95>.

70. Lieutenant Colonel M. L. Phelps, 'The Australian Army's Culture: From Institutional Warrior to Pragmatic Professional', *Australian Defence Force Journal*, 123 (1997): 37–43, p. 39.

71. Ibid., p. 40.

72. The First World War and the Vietnam War are two examples of such participation.

73. Phelps, p. 40.

74. Ibid., p. 41.

75. Ibid.

76. James F. Childress, 'Just-War Theories: The Bases, Interrelations, Priorities, and Functions of Their Criteria', in Wakin, p. 257.

77. Eric S. Krauss and Mike O. Lacey, 'Utilitarian vs. Humanitarian: The Battle over the Law of War', *Parameters*, 32 (2002): 73–85, p. 79.

78. Ibid., p. 79.

79. Ibid., p. 82.

80. The distinction between customary law and treaty law is helpful in thinking about this question. Treaty law such as that in the Geneva Conventions is written law. Customary law is not written, but refers to laws that are held to be generally accepted by all states (the prohibition against killing unarmed civilians falls into this category). If the law has been generally accepted state practice in the international community, then it is binding even if some particular state practices violate such laws. Treaty law is only legally binding on states that have ratified the treaty in question, but customary law is held to be binding on all states. For further information, see the International Committee of the Red Cross website at www.icrc.org, which explains the difference between treaty and customary law in some detail.

81. Seymour Hersh, *Chain of Command: The Road from 9/11 to Abu Ghraib* (Melbourne: Penguin Books, 2004), p. 1.

82. In the Israeli Defence Force, for example, there have been several cases of military personnel (usually reservists) refusing to serve in particular military missions. For a discussion of conscientious objection in the Israel Defence Forces, see Ruth Linn, 'Soldiers with Conscience Never Die – They are Just Ignored by their Society. Moral Disobedience in the Israel Defence Forces', *Journal of Military Ethics*, 1 (2002): 57–76.

83. Michael Walzer, *Obligations* (Cambridge: Harvard University Press, 1970), p. 121.

84. Ibid., p. 128.

85. Parliament of Australia, Parliamentary Library, 'Conscientious Objection to Military Service in Australia'. Available at <www.aph.gov.au/library/pubs/rn/2002-03/03rn31.htm>.

86. Ibid.
87. For example, US servicemen Kevin Benderman was jailed for refusing to return to Iraq (he has since been released), and another servicemen, Jeremy Hinzman, fled to Canada and is appealing for refugee status. In the UK, an RAF doctor has been court-martialled for refusing to return to Iraq (Martin Halfpenny, 'RAF doctor faces court martial over stand on Iraq', *Independent Online*, <http://news.independent.co.uk/uk/legal/article351482.ece>).
88. Countries that have suffered military coups were nearly without exception in extreme civil disarray prior to the military takeover. Argentina, Brazil, Greece, Burma, and Spain were all undergoing severe economic and social upheaval prior to the military takeovers. For a discussion of the conditions that lead to military coups, see Ervin Staub, *The Roots of Evil: The Origins of Genocide and other Group Evil* (New York: Cambridge University Press, 1989).
89. Stefan Sarvas, 'Professional Soldiers and Politics: A Case of Central and Eastern Europe', *Armed Forces and Society*, 26 (1999): 99–118, p. 103.
90. Hartle, p. 10.
91. Ibid., p. 143.
92. Ibid., p. 108.

4   Obedience in the Military

1. Herbert C. Kelman and V. Lee Hamilton, *Crimes of Obedience: Toward A Social Psychology of Authority and Responsibility* (London: Yale University Press, 1989), p. xi.
2. Aristotle discusses the nature of slaves and women in Book I of *The Politics*. For example, he says that 'the slave has not got the deliberative part [of the soul] at all, and the female has it, but without full authority' (*The Politics*, I.v.6).
3. Karen Jones, 'Second-hand Moral Knowledge', *The Journal of Philosophy*, 96 (1999): 55–78, pp. 59–60
4. Ibid., pp. 65–6. For example, because an African-American is likely to have experienced racist behaviour, they are probably in a better position than a white middle-class American to tell when someone's attitudes or behaviour is racist.
5. Ibid., p. 72.
6. Ibid., p. 73.
7. Ibid.
8. Ibid., p. 75.
9. Ibid., p. 74.
10. *The Shorter Oxford English Dictionary* (Oxford: Clarendon Press, 1993).
11. David Owens, 'The Authority of Practical Judgement', unpublished paper, 2003, p. 13.
12. Ibid., p. 14.
13. Captain Christopher P. Yalanis, 'The Virtue (?) of Obedience', paper presented at the *Joint Services Conference on Professional Ethics*, Springfield, Virginia, 2001. Available at <www.usafa.af.mil/jscope/JSCOPE01>.
14. Ibid., p. 4.
15. Ibid., p. 3.
16. Thanks to Jeanette Kennett for pointing this out.

17. Yalanis, p. 4.
18. A similar problem arises in the case of loyalty. Loyalty, like obedience, involves a willingness to suspend one's judgement about the object of one's loyalty. I am not loyal to my friend because I think she is always right, or always good. My loyalty is an emotional attachment that (if genuine) should persist even when my friend acts wrongly. Indeed, loyalty can make me modify my judgement about my friend. Because I am loyal to her, I am less objective than perhaps I should be about her character and her faults, so loyalty involves, as R. E. Ewin argues in 'Loyalty and Virtues', 'a setting aside of good judgement, at least to some extent' (R. E. Ewin, 'Loyalty and Virtues', *The Philosophical Quarterly*, 42 (1992): 403–19, p. 411). Unlike obedience however, loyalty is often claimed to be an admirable trait although, like obedience, it must be a given wisely if it is to be a virtue. In the military also, loyalty must be based on deliberation about the object of loyalty – it cannot be blind loyalty.
19. In fact the judgement need not be a *moral* judgement. Obedient military personnel would accept any legitimate order from a superior officer, orders which might simply be about the correct dress code, or other practical nonmoral issues.
20. Joseph Shaw, 'The Virtue of Obedience', *Religious Studies*, 38 (2002): 63–75, p. 63. I am not going to discuss the role of obedience in other religions, suffice to say that it is likely to be considered a virtue in most mono-theistic religions.
21. Shaw, p. 64.
22. Ibid., p. 64.
23. Ibid., p. 65.
24. Gerald R. Winslow, 'From Loyalty to Advocacy: A New Metaphor for Nursing', in Joan C. Callahan (ed.), *Ethical Issues in Professional Life* (Oxford: Oxford University Press, 1988), p. 96.
25. Ibid., p. 97.
26. Ibid.
27. Isabel Robb, *Nursing Ethics*, quoted in Winslow, p. 99.
28. The prosecution (and conviction) of a nurse for carrying out a physician's orders that resulted in the patient's death (he had ordered cocaine instead of procaine) had a large impact on the justifiability of nurses' unquestioning loyalty and the supposed lack of responsibility (Winslow, p. 99).
29. A model of nursing that is finding increasing support among nurses is the advocacy model, where the nurse is seen as the patient's advocate. For a discussion of this view, see C. Willard, 'The Nurse's Role as Patient Advocate: Obligation or Imposition?', *Journal of Advanced Nursing*, 24 (1996): 60–6.
30. Justin Oakley and Dean Cocking, *Virtue Ethics and Professional Roles* (Cambridge: Cambridge University Press, 2001), p. 117.
31. As noted previously, this view has troubling consequences for the moral psychology of professionals.
32. The same criteria would also hold for the other military virtues. Loyalty, for example, exhibits at first glance some of the problems associated with obedience – loyalty to immoral causes is arguably just as problematic as obedience to immoral orders. Virtuous loyalty in the military, like obedience, must be a product of rational deliberation about the ends of the military profession

and the role that loyalty might play in promoting those ends. Interestingly, unreflective loyalty can reinforce blind obedience by making disobedience seem like disloyalty. In the heavily group-oriented military environment where lives can be at stake if group solidarity is lost, disobedient military personnel not only break the chain of command but put their own judgement above that of the group. Such disobedience, given what can be at stake, can be often interpreted as disloyalty to one's fellow combatants and even to the military or the nation as well. For example, Israeli Army reservists who refused to fight during the Intifada war zone were called 'traitors' (Linn, p. 61).

33. Michael O. Wheeler, 'Loyalty, Honor, and the Modern Military', in Malham M. Wakin (ed.), *War, Morality, and the Military Profession*, 2nd edition (Boulder, Colorado: Westview Press, 1986), p. 173.

34. Ibid., pp. 172–3.

35. Royal Military College Duntroon, <http://www.defence.gov.au/army/rmc/>; United States West Point Military Academy, <http://www.usma.edu>.

36. There are other cases in which disobedience may be justified, such as when the order-giver exceeds their authority, when the order would require the subordinate to violate internal regulations, or when the order is a general or standing order. For example, 'the town X is out of bounds until further orders' (Nico Keijzer, *Military Obedience* (Alphen aan den Rijn, The Netherlands: Sijthoff & Noordhoff, 1978), p. 86). For the purposes of this discussion, I focus on obedience to illegal orders. In such a case, the order giver may have legitimate authority over the subordinate, but the orders given violate either the laws of war or are patently immoral.

37. Rhonda M. Wheate and Lieutenant Nial J. Wheate, 'Lawful Dissent and the Modern Australian Defence Force', *Australian Defence Force Journal*, 160 (2003): 20–30, p. 20.

38. Ibid., p. 21.

39. Ibid., p. 20.

40. There may even be cases where military personnel should disobey legal orders, when obeying those orders would lead to or fail to prevent gross human rights abuses. This possibility will be discussed in Chapter 5.

41. It is accepted in a certain limited number of situations. In the *Australian Defence Force Discipline Act 1982* for example, 'the "defence of superior orders" is available where: 1. the act or omission was in execution of the law; or 2. was in obedience to a) a lawful order; or b) an unlawful order that the person did not know, and could not reasonably be expected to have known, was unlawful' (Ibid., p. 20).

42. Quoted in Sidney Axinn, *A Moral Military* (Philadelphia: Temple University Press, 1989), p. 2.

43. The Army Field Manual, quoted in Axinn, p. 3.

44. Keijzer, p. 153.

45. Mark J. Osiel, *Obeying Orders: Atrocity, Military Discipline and the Law of War* (New Jersey: Transaction Publishers, 2002), p. 48.

46. Ibid., p. 48.

47. Ibid., p. 44.

48. Ibid., p. 75.

49. The Model Penal Code #2.10 (1985) stated that 'It is an affirmative defence that the actor, in engaging in conduct charged to constitute an offence, does

no more that execute an order of his superior in the armed services that he does not know to be unlawful' (ibid., pp. 75–6).
50. Ibid., p. 49.
51. Ibid., p. 48.
52. Ibid., p. 55.
53. Ibid., p. 46.
54. Osiel, p. 46, footnote.
55. Ibid., p. 45.
56. Colonel Dennis C. Tabbernor, 'Operational Commanders, Orders, and the Right to Choose', Advanced Military Studies Course, Canadian Forces College, 1998. Available at <http://198.231.69.12/papers/amsc1/039.htm>.
57. Thanks to Dirk Baltzly for this example.
58. Osiel, p. 74.
59. Ibid., p. 55.
60. As noted earlier in this chapter, very few cases of crimes of obedience ever come to trial. Generally, only those which involve very obvious atrocities are prosecuted. However, there are many cases where crimes of obedience occur in response to orders that may not be manifestly illegal. For example in the Nuremberg trials, the International Military Tribunal claimed that orders regarding prisoner-of-war forced labour were criminal but not manifestly illegal, and so commanders who had obeyed these orders were acquitted (Osiel, p. 73).
61. Kelman and Hamilton, p. 3.
62. Many military colleges in Australia and in the United States do recognize the importance of this kind of training and most military training (particularly of officer cadets) involves classes in ethics and in military law. However, this approach does not address some fundamental problems with other aspects of military training, problems discussed in the following chapters.
63. Of course it is unrealistic to expect an exact match between the ideal of military obedience and the cases of disobedience (or obedience) that are legally punishable, just as there is not an exact match between laws of libel and our common sense ideas about the ideals of fair speech (thanks to Garrett Cullity for bringing this to my attention). However, we would expect the legal requirements on military obedience to mirror the most important features of the ideal of military obedience. So we would expect the legal code to recognize that military personnel have a legal and not just a moral duty to disobey orders that blatantly violate the laws of war. As I shall demonstrate, it is far from clear that the current legal approaches do fit even the basic tenets of ideal military obedience.
64. Anthony E. Hartle, 'Obedience and Responsibility', *Professional Ethics*, 10 (2002): 65–80, pp. 66–7.
65. Claims of torture and ill-treatment have been documented by Amnesty International, Human Rights Watch, and the International Committee of the Red Cross. See also Seymour M. Hersh, *Chain of Command: The Road from 9/11 to Abu Ghraib* (Melbourne: Allen Lane, 2004).

5   Military Torture

1. Ariel Dorfman, 'The Price we pay for Paradise is Torture', *The Australian*, 10 May 2004, p. 9.

2. George W. Bush, quoted in Mark Bowden, 'The Dark Art of Interrogation', *The Atlantic Monthly* 29 (2003).
3. This is not to deny that torture is also performed in other contexts, such as in organized crime. However, I am primarily interested in torture that is authorized by a legitimate authority, and most systematic wide-scale use of torture of this kind takes place in a military context.
4. *Convention against Torture and Other Cruel, Inhuman, or Degrading treatment or Punishment*, United Nations, 1984. Available from the website of the Office of the United Nations High Commissioner for Human Rights at <http://www.ohchr.org/english/law/cat.htm>.
5. Bowden, p. 4.
6. Ibid., p. 4.
7. John Barry, Michael Hirsch and Michael Isikoff, 'The Roots of Torture: The road to Abu Ghraib began after 9/11, when Washington wrote new rules to fight a new kind of war. A NEWSWEEK investigation', *Newsweek*, 24 May 2004, p. 26. In late 2004, the US Justice Department expanded the definition of torture to include mental suffering (R. Jeffrey Smith and Dan Eggen, 'Justice Expands "Torture" Definition', *The Washington Post*, 31 December 2004, p. A01).
8. John Conroy, *Unspeakable Acts, Ordinary People* (New York: Alfred A. Knopf, 2000), p. 6.
9. Ibid., p. 6.
10. Ibid., pp. 7–9.
11. Ibid., pp. 39–40, p. 123.
12. Ibid., p. 47.
13. One of these psychiatrists, a Dr Robert Daly, testified that the five techniques were 'refinements of a system of torture developed by the KGB' (Ibid., p. 127).
14. Ibid., p. 136.
15. Ibid., p. 178.
16. Ibid., p. 180.
17. Ibid., p. 182.
18. Stefan Priebe MD and Michael Bauer PhD, MD, 'Inclusion of Psychological Torture in PTSD Criterion A', *American Journal of Psychiatry*, 152 (1995): 1691–2.
19. Ibid., p. 1692.
20. M. Basoglu *et al.*, 'Factors Related to Long-term Traumatic Stress Responses in Survivors of Torture in Turkey', *Journal of the American Medical Association*, 272 (1994): 357–63, p. 361.
21. Mark Van Ommeren *et al.*, 'Psychiatric Disorders Among Tortured Bhutanese Refugees in Nepal', *Archives of General Psychiatry*, 58 (2001): 475–82, p. 479.
22. Conroy, p. 180.
23. It would perhaps mitigate legal claims for compensation. My point here is that it should not mitigate the belief that the act of torture was wrong *at the time it was committed*, regardless of how well the torture victim recovers after the event.
24. Thanks to Justin Oakley for this suggestion.
25. A consequentialist might argue that the moral assessment of acts such as torture and rape includes the foreseen or foreseeable consequences of those acts. So, it might be claimed, part of the reason these acts are wrong is because

they usually lead to long-term distress and suffering. This general claim about foreseeable consequences does not however lead to the conclusion that the moral status of the act is changed if those long-term consequences do not eventuate in individual cases.

26. Wolfgang Heinz, 'The Military, Torture and Human Rights: Experiences from Argentina, Brazil, Chile, and Uruguay', in Ronald D. Crelinsten and Alex P. Schmid (eds), *The Politics of Pain: Torturers and Their Masters* (Boulder, Colorado: Westview Press, 1993), p. 65.
27. Ibid., p. 72.
28. Ibid., p. 67.
29. Quoted in Heinz, p. 37.
30. Dana Priest and Barton Gellman, 'U.S. Decries Abuse but Defends Interrogations "Stress and Duress" Tactics Used on Terrorism Suspects Held in Secret Overseas Facilities', *The Washington Post*, 26 December 2002, p. A0.
31. Herbert C. Kelman, 'The Social Context of Torture: Policy Process and Authority Structure', in Crelinsten and Schmid, p. 25.
32. Major William D. Casebeer, 'Torture Interrogation for Terrorists: A Theory of Exceptions (with Notes, Cautions, and Warnings)', paper presented at the *Joint Services Conference on Professional Ethics*, Washington DC, 2003. Available at <http://www.usafa.af.mil/jscope/JSCOPE03>.
33. Heinz, p. 72.
34. Ibid., p. 67.
35. Ibid., p. 80.
36. Quoted in Casebeer, p. 2.
37. Alberto R. Gonzales, Memorandum to the President, 'Decision re Application of the Geneva Convention on Prisoners of War to the Conflict with Al Qaeda and the Taliban', reprinted in Mark Danner, *Torture and Truth: America, Abu Ghraib, and the War on Terror* (London: Granta Books, 2005), p. 84.
38. Casebeer, p. 3.
39. Henry Shue, 'Torture', *Philosophy and Public Affairs*, 7 (1978): 124–43, p. 141. For a further discussion of the problems with the 'Ticking Bomb' argument, see Jessica Wolfendale, 'Training Torturers: A Critique of the "Ticking Bomb" Argument', *Social Theory and Practice*, 32 (2006): 269–89.
40. Casebeer, p. 1.
41. Christopher Tindale, 'The Logic of Torture', *Social Theory and Practice*, 22 (1996): 349–74, p. 366.
42. Jean Maria Arrigo, 'A Utilitarian Argument against Torture Interrogation of Terrorists', *Science and Engineering Ethics*, 10 (2004): 1–30, p. 12.
43. This raises questions of how an interrogator would know definitely that the correct information had been revealed. A simple confession would need to be checked, and there is the further problem of establishing whether all the relevant information has been revealed. Arrigo outlines the problems in sorting out truth from fiction in the data gained from the use of torture (Arrigo, p. 13).
44. Tindale, p. 367.
45. Ibid.
46. Ibid., p. 350.
47. Tindale outlines these different purposes for torture (pp. 350–1), as does Henry Shue, p. 132.
48. Arrigo, p. 9.

49. Ibid., p. 22.
50. Ibid., p. 9.
51. For example 'resort to denial, psychological dissociation, alcohol, or drugs' (Ibid., p. 11).
52. Lawrence Weschler, *A Miracle, a Universe: Settling Accounts with Torturers* (New York: Pantheon Books, 1990), pp. 126–7.
53. *Amnesty International*, 'Where in the World is the U.S. Military? Who are they teaching what?'. Available at <http://www.amnestyusa.org/arms_trade/ustraining/students.html>
54. Some of these Filipino officers were trained in the United States. *Amnesty International*, 'Where in the World is the U.S. Military? Who are they teaching what?'.
55. Website of Fort Benning. Available at <http://www.benning.army.mil/fbhome>.
56. See *School of The Americas Watch*. Available at <http://www.soaw.org/new/>.
57. Arrigo, p. 18. This happened to Maher Arar, a Syrian-born Canadian citizen who was detained at JFK and then handed over to the Syrian authorities for ten months for torture and interrogation (Jane Mayer, 'Outsourcing Torture: The secret history of America's "extraordinary rendition program" ', *The New Yorker*, 14 February 2005.
58. Ronald D. Crelinsten, 'In Their Own Words: The World of the Torturer', in Crelinsten and Schmid, p. 50.
59. Arrigo, p. 10.
60. Heinz, p. 78.
61. Mark Forbes, 'Feared Kopassus to watch SAS train', *The Age*, 12 August 2003.
62. Conroy, p. 27.
63. Ibid., p. 29.
64. Kelman, p. 27.
65. David Luban, 'Liberalism, Torture, and the Ticking Bomb', in Karen J. Greenberg (ed.), *The Torture Debate in America* (New York: Cambridge University Press, 2006), p. 48.
66. Arrigo, p. 12.
67. Hersh, p. 2.
68. Ibid.
69. Neil Lewis, 'Red Cross accuses the US of Torture', *The Age*, 1 December 2004.
70. See Conroy, pp. 113–21, and Bowden, pp. 8–9.
71. Bowden, p. 7.
72. In fact, it is occurring now. The torture at Abu Ghraib is a good example of 'uncontained' torture – torture used outside the official, authorized conditions. Medics have also been implicated in the covering up of the torture and illegal homicides. See 'Abu Ghraib Medics Forced to Amputate', *The Age*, 7 February 2005.
73. Shue, p. 143.
74. It has been suggested to me that the 'ticking bomb' justification could also be a form of an argument from self-defence rather than a consequentialist argument. The self-defence argument would go something like this: torture is justified if it is absolutely necessary to avert a dire threat to the very existence of a country or a sufficiently large group of people. Indeed, the United States appealed to just such an argument in the memo prepared for Counsel to the

President Alberto Gonzales by the US Department of Justice Office of Legal Council on the use of torture. For a copy of the memo, see Dana Priest, 'Justice Dept. Memo Says Torture "May Be Justified"', *The Washington Post*, 13 June 2004. Arguments based on self-defence are discussed in pages 39–46 of the memo. However, given that the victims of torture no longer pose a direct threat, and given the epistemological requirements discussed above, it is very difficult to see how an appeal to self-defence can justify torturing people who *might* have information that *might* prevent an attack. Certainly, my right to self-defence does not permit me to torture people who I believe are plotting against me or who can tell me when and how a threat to my life will occur.

75. Casebeer, p. 3.
76. Ibid., p. 4.
77. Ibid., p. 4.
78. *Amnesty International*, 'Combating Torture: A Manual for Action', section 3.2. Available at <http://www.amnesty.org/resources/pdf/combating_torture/sections/section3-2.pdf>.
79. Ibid.
80. *Amnesty International*, 'Combating Torture: A Manual for Action', section 3.2.6. A peremptory norm is a basic principle of international law that is considered to be accepted by the international community of nation-states as a whole. Peremptory norms are binding on all states, regardless of state practices, and any treaty that required the violation of a peremptory norm would be invalid.
81. Mark Osiel, *Obeying Orders: Atrocity, Military Discipline, and the Law of War* (New Jersey: Transaction Publishers, 1999), p. 55.
82. For details, see Seymour Hersh, *Chain of Command: The Road from 9/11 to Abu Ghraib* (Melbourne: Allen Lane, 2004).
83. Joanna Bourke, *An Intimate History of Killing: Face-to-Face Killing in Twentieth Century Warfare* (London: Granta Books, 1999), pp. 178–80.
84. Quoted in Bourke, p. 187.
85. Hersh, *Chain of Command: The Road from 9/11 to Abu Ghraib*, p. 24.
86. Bourke, p. 181.
87. Former American defence secretary Robert McNamara used this phrase in the film *The Fog of War*, paraphrasing Clausewitz: 'War is the realm of uncertainty; three-quarters of the factors on which action is based are wrapped in a fog of greater or lesser uncertainty.'
88. Hilliard Aronovitch, 'Good Soldiers, a Traditional Approach', *Journal of Applied Philosophy*, 18 (2001): 13–23, p. 14.
89. Peter Maas, 'A Bulletproof Mind', *The New York Times Magazine*, 10 November 2002, p. 55.
90. Aronovitch, p. 15.
91. Ibid., p. 16.
92. Ibid., pp. 19–20.
93. Ibid., p. 21.
94. James B. Donovan and Rafael P. McLaughlin, 'United Nations Peacekeepers and International Humanitarian Law: Can There be an Affirmative Duty to Prevent War Crimes and Crimes Against Humanity?', *New England International and Comparative Law Annual*, 5 (1999).

95. Stephen Wrage, 'Captain Lawrence Rockwood in Haiti', *Journal of Military Ethics*, 1 (2002): 45–52, p. 48.
96. Ibid., p. 46.
97. Ibid., p. 45.
98. Ibid., pp. 45–51. The court held that the order not to inspect the jails was not illegal, and held that 'a soldier may only refuse to follow a direct order when it would require him to commit an illegal act' (Donovan and McLaughlin). See footnote 101 for clarification of the legal status of Rockwood's orders.
99. One of Rockwood's heroes was Chief Warrant Officer Hugh C. Thomson: 'the helicopter pilot who saw the My Lai massacre in progress, lowered his helicopter into the middle of it, and ordered the door gunner to train his machine gun on U.S. troops who were killing unarmed civilians' (Wrage, p. 47).
100. Ibid., p. 51.
101. It is unclear if he was right about this existence of this duty, as there are few clear guidelines outlining the specific duties of peacekeepers in such cases. An analysis of international law reveals little consensus about the obligations of peacekeeping forces in cases such as Haiti. However, the principles of the Geneva Conventions among others lend support to the claim that an obligation to interfere exists if known human rights violations are occurring (and the peacekeeping forces can intervene without too great a risk to their forces). As Donovan and McLaughlin argue, 'The legal obligations established in the Geneva Conventions, at Nuremberg, and as a result of the Calley affair, indicate that there is a duty to prevent acts of inhumanity that violate international humanitarian law.'
102. Major Carl D. Rehlberg, 'Implications of *Dereliction of Duty*', paper presented at the *Joint Services Conference on Professional Ethics*, Springfield, Virginia, 28–29 January 2000. Available at <http://www.usafa.af.mil/jscope/JSCOPE00>.
103. Wrage, p. 50.
104. Albert C. Pierce, 'Commentary: Captain Lawrence Rockwood in Haiti', *Journal of Military Ethics*, 1 (2002): 53–4, p. 54.
105. Osiel, p. 75.
106. Establishing such grounds would not necessarily be easy. In could be very difficult at the time and in retrospect to establish which course of action in fact best served military values. But this objection does not hold in the case of Captain Rockwood. Far from providing a reason to adopt a more lenient approach to obedience, the existence of hard cases actually supports more education and more training for military personnel so that they are better able to identify the legality and morality of their orders and have the resources for clarifying their orders, if clarification is necessary and possible. As I argued in relation to education about torture, as professionals military personnel should have professional expertise in the law regarding their duties. In the concluding chapter I outline some positive suggestions for how such education could proceed.
107. The public disgust and outrage at the events in Abu Ghraib is just one indication of the impact of these kinds of crimes on the reputation of and public support for the US Military.
108. I am not implying that military personnel should disobey when there is the slightest doubt about the legality of their orders. My point is that military

rhetoric *itself* supports the claim that military personnel should disobey illegal orders. If orders are of doubtful legality, then surely military personnel should clarify the issue (time permitting). The consequences of obeying an illegal order are so serious that it is better to risk few cases of unjustified disobedience than to risk military personnel committing war crimes. I am referring to cases where there is serious doubt about an order's legality.

109. Anthony E. Hartle, 'Obedience and Responsibility', *Professional Ethics*, 10 (2002): 65–80, p. 66.
110. Frank Walker, 'RAAF Aborted Dozens of Missions', *Sunday Age*, 14 March 2004.
111. Ibid.

6   Military Training and Moral Agency

1. Lieutenant General Robert Gard, quoted in Richard Gabriel, *To Serve With Honor: A Treatise on Military Ethics and the Way of the Soldier* (Westport, Connecticut: Greenwood Press, 1982), p. 89.
2. Samuel Huntington, 'The Military Mind: Conservative Realism of the Professional Military Ethic', in Malham M. Wakin (ed.), *War, Morality, and the Military Profession*, 2nd edition (Boulder, Colorado: Westview Press, 1986), p. 52.
3. Anthony E. Hartle, *Moral Issues in Military Decision Making*, 2nd edition (Lawrence, Kansas: University Press of Kansas, 2004), pp. 40–1.
4. In America, the vast majority of military officers identify themselves as republican (Lance Betros, 'Political Partisanship and the Military Ethic in America', *Armed Forces and Society*, 27 (2001): 501–23), p. 504.
5. Ibid., p. 505.
6. As noted in Chapter 2 there are problematic features of this account – particularly with the 'split' psychology it seems to encourage.
7. Hartle, p. 44.
8. Donna Winslow, 'Misplaced Loyalties: The Role of Military Culture in the Breakdown of Discipline in Two Peace Operations', *Journal of Military and Strategic Studies*, 6 (2004): 1–19, p. 4.
9. 'Military Culture and Ethics', *Report of the Somalia Commission of Inquiry*, 2 July 1997. Available at <www.dnd.ca/somalia/vol1/v1c5e.htm>.
10. Major E. J. Stevenson, 'Educating the Community's "Cream": Common Military Training at the Australian Defence Force Academy', *Australian Defence Force Journal*, 120 (1996): 11–18, p. 13.
11. Winslow, p. 6.
12. Josh Gordon, 'How an Army of Bullies Drove a Soldier to Suicide', *The Age*, 24 June 2003.
13. Ibid.
14. World News, 'Australia Aims to Stop Brutality by Military', *The Cambridge Reporter*, 10 February 2001. In 2006 A Learning Culture Inquiry report into ADF Schools and Training Establishments found significant progress in combating harassment and bullying, but stated that there was still 'room for improvement' (see <http://www.defence.gov.au/publications/LCIreport.pdf> for the full text of the report).

15. Winslow, p. 7.
16. Ibid., p. 5.
17. Members of these regiments were involved in black market activities, torture, sexual misconduct, and misuse of alcohol (see Winslow for details).
18. Winslow, p. 12.
19. Ibid., p. 7.
20. Ibid., p. 7.
21. It is true that this assumption is questioned in some quarters (see, for example, Captain Christopher P. Yalanis, 'The Virtue (?) of Obedience: Some Notes for Military Professionals', paper presented at the *Joint Services Conference on Professional Ethics*, Springfield, Virginia, 2001. Available at <http://www. usafa.af.mil/jscope/JSCOPE01>). However, this assumption is still by far the most prevalent attitude towards obedience and therefore must be addressed as such.
22. S. L. A. Marshall, quoted by Gwynne Dwyer in Lt. Col. David Grossman, *On Killing: The Psychological Cost of Learning to Kill in War and Society* (Boston: Little, Brown & Co, 1995), p. 250.
23. Richard Gabriel, quoted in Grossman, p. 43.
24. Grossman, p. 52.
25. Ibid., pp. 52–5.
26. Ibid., p. 59. Sailors and other naval personnel do kill of course, but generally speaking their targets are ships and airplanes, not individuals. It is easier for them to feel like 'they are not killing human beings' (quoted in Grossman, p. 59).
27. Rachel McNair, *Perpetration-Induced Traumatic Stress: The Psychological Consequences of Killing* (Westport, Connecticut: Praeger, 2002), pp. 13–31.
28. See McNair, pp. 1–13, for the definition and features of Perpetration-Induced Traumatic Stress.
29. Ibid., p. 3. She references Grossman on this issue.
30. Grossman, p. 34.
31. Ibid., p. 29.
32. In his book *Men Against Fire: The Problem of Battle Command in Future War* (Washington: Infantry Journal; New York: William Morrow, 1947) military historian S. L. A. Marshall claimed that only 25 per cent of infantry soldiers fired their weapons in battle. However, this figure has been disputed, as Marshall did not provide statistical analysis or field notes of the interviews that he claimed to have conducted (John Whiteclay Chambers II, 'S. L. A. Marshall's *Men Against Fire*: New Evidence Regarding Fire Ratios', *Parameters*, 33 (2003): 113–21, p. 113). However, the claim that military personnel are for the most part averse to killing, and must be trained to overcome that aversion, has been supported from other sources. The US Army Air Corps (now the US Air Force), for example, found that in World War II less than one per cent of fighter pilots accounted for 30 to 40 per cent of enemy aircraft destroyed in the air (Grossman, p. 30). Studies by Gwynne Dyer and Ben Shalit found similar problems (Ben Shalit, *The Psychology of Conflict and Combat* (New York: Praeger Publishers, 1988); Gwynne Dyer, *War* (London: Guild Publishing, 1985)).
33. During the Second World War films were also used to inure military personnel to the 'noise and bloody gore' of battle (Joanna Bourke, *An Intimate*

History of Killing: Face-to-Face Killing in Twentieth Century Warfare (London: Granta Books, 1999), p. 96.

34. Grossman, p. 25.
35. Firing rates refer to the percentage of bullets fired to direct hits (ibid., p. 16). This figure has been disputed, however (Michael Walzer, private communication, June 2005).
36. A Rhodesian torturer interviewed by John Conroy in *Unspeakable Acts, Ordinary People: The Dynamics of Torture* believed that his ability to torture had its roots in his experiences at the English-style boarding school he had attended. This school had an entrenched tradition of 'fagging' (where younger students effectively act as servants for the older students) involving hazing, bullying, and initiation rites in which the older students would intimidate and humiliate the younger (John Conroy, *Unspeakable Acts, Ordinary People: The Dynamics of Torture* (New York: Alfred A. Knopf, 2000), p. 90).
37. Grossman, p. 161.
38. Seymour Hersh, 'Torture at Abu Ghraib', *The Age*, 10 May 2004.
39. Jonathon Glover, *Humanity: A Moral History of the Twentieth Century* (London: Pimlico, 1999), p. 36.
40. Daniel Muñoz-Rojas and Jean-Jacques Frésard, *The Roots of Behaviour in War: Understanding and Preventing IHL Violations* (Geneva: International Committee of the Red Cross, 2004), p. 9.
41. Grossman, p. 306.
42. Ibid., p. 254.
43. Ibid., p. 255.
44. Ibid., pp. 253–4.
45. Ibid., p. 254.
46. Ibid., pp. 255–6.
47. Fred Downs, 'The Dark Side of Command', *The Washington Post*, 16 August 1987, p. D1.
48. Quoted in Grossman, p. 256.
49. Quoted in a *Frontline* interview with David Grossman. Available at <http://www.pbs.org/wgbh/pages/frontline/shows/heart/interviews/grossman.html>.
50. Ibid., p. 257.
51. Grossman, p. 260.
52. Peter Maas, 'A Bulletproof Mind', *The New York Times Magazine*, 10 November 2002, p. 52.
53. Ibid., p. 54.
54. Captain Pete Kilner, 'Military Leaders to Justify Killing in Warfare', paper presented at the *Joint Services Conference on Professional Ethics*, Washington DC, 27–28 January 2000. Available at <http://www.usafa.af.mil/jscope/JSCOPE00>.
55. Ibid., p. 4.
56. Interview with Ranger Private First Class Jason Moore for CNN/Frontline. Available at <http/www.pbs.org/wgbh/pages/frontline/shows/ambush/rangers/moore.html>, quoted in Kilner, p. 5.
57. Kilner, p. 1.
58. Ibid. His italics.
59. Ibid., p. 5.
60. Ibid., pp. 1–2.
61. Ibid., p. 5. His italics.

62. Ibid., p. 6. Many reasons might have contributed to this reduction in numbers. However, the accounts of the soldiers themselves does indicate that the killing they participated in had a long-term impact that contributed to psychological distress and guilt.

63. Rosalind Hursthouse, *On Virtue Ethics* (Oxford: Oxford University Press, 1999), p. 124.

64. Seymour Hersh, *Chain of Command: The Road from 9/11 to Abu Ghraib* (Melbourne: Allen Lane, 2004), p. 13.

65. In Rwanda the Hutu minority killed over two million of the Tutsi majority. The deaths were caused both by the army and by civilian gangs. For more information, see the Amnesty International Report on Rwanda, available from <http://web.amnesty.org/report2005/rwa-summary-eng>.

66. Jonathon Glover, in his book *Humanity: A Moral History of the Twentieth Century* (London: Pimlico, 1999) considers other factors that can lead to group violence, such as racial hatred (tribalism) and political ideologies such as Nazism.

67. Herbert C. Kelman and V. Lee Hamilton, *Crimes of Obedience: Toward a Social Psychology of Authority and Responsibility* (New Haven: Yale University Press, 1989), p. 46.

68. Arthur G. Miller, Barry E. Collins and Diana E. Brief, 'Perspectives on Obedience to Authority: the Legacy of the Milgram Experiments', *Journal of Social Issues*, 51 (1995): 1–19, p. 2.

69. Stanley Milgram, *Obedience to Authority: An Experimental View* (London: Tavistock Publications, 1974), p. 2.

70. The responses are as follows: 'Please continue', or 'Please go on'; 'The experiment requires that you go on'; 'It is absolutely essential that you continue'; 'You have no other choice, you must go on'. If the teacher refuses after the fourth prod, the experiment is discontinued (Miller, Collins and Brief, p. 2; Milgram, p. 21).

71. Thomas Blass, 'Understanding Behaviour in the Milgram Obedience Experiment: The Role of Personality, Situations, and their Interactions', *Journal of Personality and Social Psychology*, 60 (1991): 398–413, p. 399.

72. Milgram, p. 36.

73. Ibid., p. 6.

74. In order to test the importance of this factor on obedience rates, Milgram ran a version of the experiment off-campus in a room with little evidence of genuine authority. While obedience rates did decline, 48 per cent of subjects were still fully obedient (Milgram, p. 61).

75. Ibid., p. 149.

76. Ibid., p. 133.

77. Ibid.

78. John Doris, *Lack of Character: Personality and Moral Behavior* (New York: Cambridge University Press, 2002), p. 42.

79. Ibid., pp. 42–3.

80. Milgram, p. 377, quoted in Doris, p. 43.

81. Milgram, p. 146.

82. Ibid., p. 144.

83. Milgram, quoted in Herbert C. Kelman and V. Lee Hamilton, *Crimes of Obedience: Toward a Social Psychology of Authority and Responsibility* (New Haven: Yale University Press, 1989), p. 155.

84. Milgram, p. 47.
85. Douglas Lackey, 'Professional Sins and Unprofessional Excuses', in B. Baumrin and B. Freedman (eds), *Moral Responsibility and the Professions* (New York: Haven Publications, 1983), p. 245.
86. Milgram, p. 146. The fact that this was how they *felt* does not in the least imply that they were right about the level of responsibility and control they had. They were not automatons, although they may have felt that they were.
87. Ibid., p. 146.
88. There is of course an obvious inconsistency in such a belief, particularly if they took pride or responsibility in how well they performed their task. Their denial of responsibility was quite selective – a process indicative of self-deception. Gerald Postema discusses this process in relation to lawyers in 'Moral Responsibility in Professional Ethics', *New York University Law Review*, 55 (1980): 63–89, p. 79. The point here is not to discuss the validity of their beliefs about their responsibility, but to draw out the moral psychology of their obedience – to see how they saw their own actions, regardless of whether their beliefs about their responsibility are in fact justified.
89. Milgram, p. 54.
90. Elizabeth Wolgast, *Ethics of an Artificial Person: Lost Responsibility in Professions and Organizations* (Stanford: Stanford University Press, 1992), p. 66.
91. Ibid., p. 66.
92. Thomas Nagel, *The View from Nowhere* (New York: Oxford University Press, 1986), p. 180.
93. Milgram, p. 146.
94. Milgram, quoted in Conroy, p. 101.
95. I am not claiming that such cases of fractured autonomy do also result in fractured responsibility, or that the feeling of fractured autonomy points to any actual division of autonomous action. My point here is that subscribing to such a view (consciously or unconsciously) served to make the obedient subject *feel* less responsible, and so feel less guilty or distressed about their involvement in harming the learner.
96. Milgram, p. 144.
97. Ibid.
98. Ibid., p. 143.
99. Ibid., p. 38.
100. This process of tuning is similar to one explanation for why so many subjects in John M. Darley and C. Daniel Batson's study on altruistic behaviour failed to help an apparently injured man. Darley and Batson found that whether the subject stopped to help the 'injured' man on their way to give a talk was determined primarily by whether or not they were in a hurry (John M. Darley and C. Daniel Batson, ' "From Jerusalem to Jericho": A Study of Situationals and Dispositional Variables in Helping Behaviour', *Journal of Personality and Social Psychology*, 23 (1973): 100–8). It was not the case that the subjects who failed to helped noticed the distressed man and choose to ignore that information; instead, they failed to notice that the situation called for ethical decision-making at all: 'when a person is in a hurry, something seems to happen that is akin to Tolman's (1948) concept of the "narrowing of the cognitive map"... according to the reflections of some of

the subjects ... they did not perceive the scene in the alley as an occasion for an ethical decision' (Darley and Batson, pp. 107–8).

101. Jeanette Kennett, *Agency and Responsibility: A Common-Sense Moral Psychology* (New York: Oxford University Press, 2001), p. 139. Kennett also notes that this technique can be used for different purposes: 'Someone might try to evade uncomfortable feelings of guilt by counting stitches or watching a movie instead of reflecting on their actions' (Kennett, p. 139, n10).

102. The role of emotions such as repulsion, distress, sympathy, and empathy in alerting us to morally salient facts is discussed in Kennett's book and in Jonathon Bennett's article 'The Conscience of Huckleberry Finn', in Peter Singer (ed.), *Ethics* (Oxford: Oxford University Press, 1994), pp. 294–305.

103. Alfred Mele, 'Errant Self-Control and the Self-controlled Person', *Pacific Philosophical Quarterly*, 71 (1990): 47–59. Quoted in Kennett, p. 121. Mele's example is a boy who, in order to join a gang, overcomes his nerves in order to break into a house despite his belief that house-breaking is wrong (Kennett, p. 121).

104. Milgram, p. 146.

105. Ibid., p. 147.

106. Francois Rochat and Andre Modigliani, 'The Ordinary Quality of Resistance: from Milgram's Laboratory to the Village of Le Chambon', *Journal of Social Issues*, 51 (1995): 195–211, p. 203.

107. Rochat and Modigliani, p. 206.

108. Milgram, quoted in Conroy, p. 101. Emphasis added.

109. Conroy, p. 100.

110. Milgram, p. 46.

111. This massacre took place at the hamlet of My Lai on 16 March 1968. Members of 'Charlie' Company undertook a 'search and destroy' mission to wipe out members of the Viet Cong from their supposed base at My Lai. On arrival, all they found was old men, women and children. By the end of the day, up to 500 Vietnamese were killed. Lieutenant William Calley was the platoon leader (Kelman and Hamilton, pp. 1–3).

112. Ibid., p. 170.

113. Ibid., pp. 104–6.

114. Ibid., p. 113. See Kelman and Hamilton, pp. 296–302, for an in-depth discussion of these results.

115. Ibid., p. 276.

116. Ibid., p. 299.

117. Ibid.

118. Ibid, p. 305. Note, however, that the reasons for obedience and denial of responsibility would be different for each orientation. Rule-oriented individuals would obey out of a sense of powerlessness or fear of reprisal and would deny responsibility for their actions, whereas role-oriented individuals would obey because they accepted the values of their role, and because the role of soldier (or any role that included a relationship with authority) requires obedience. A role-oriented individual would deny responsibility for crimes of obedience such as Lt Calley's if obedience was part of the role requirements. They would be likely to argue that Lt Calley was just doing his job and it was not his place to assess the moral validity of the orders he received (ibid., p. 297).

119. Ibid., p. 305.

120. Moti Nissani, 'A Cognitive Reinterpretation of Stanley Milgram's Observations on Obedience to Authority', *American Psychologist*, 45 (1990): 1384–5, p. 1385.

121. John Sabini and Maury Silver, 'Lack of Character? Situationism Critiqued', *Ethics*, 115 (2005): 535–62, pp. 549–50.

122. For example, see H. J. Wim Meeus and Quinten A. W. Raajmakers, 'Obedience in Modern Society: the Utrecht Studies', *Journal of Social Issues*, 51 (1995): 155–76.

123. See Michael J. Osofsky, Albert Bandura and Phillip G. Zimbardo, 'The Role of Moral Disengagement in the Execution Process', *Law and Human Behaviour*, 29 (2005): 371–92.

124. Muñoz-Rojas and Frésard, pp. 8–10.

125. Note that this does not presuppose that killing in war is wrong. Instead, applying Milgram and Kelman and Hamilton's work to the training of military personnel draws out the similarities between the destructive obedience seen in the obedient Milgram subjects and the dispositions instilled through ordinary military training. The military claims that it wants personnel who can kill enemy combatants when it is morally right to do so, but who will disobey illegal orders. Yet the training I have described creates dispositions that make such moral reflection extremely difficult. By making killing a non-moral issue, military personnel are not encouraged to reflect upon the difference between justified and unjustified killing in warfare. The problem is not that killing in war is wrong (in most cases it is not) but that these dispositions are connected to *crimes* of obedience – obedience to illegal and immoral orders.

126. Getting 'dirty hands' refers to situations where we are 'morally sullied by doing what is morally permissible or even obligatory' (Anthony Cunningham, 'The Moral Importance of Dirty Hands', *Journal of Value Inquiry*, 26 (1992): 239–50, p. 239). For a discussion of dirty hands in politics, see Michael Walzer, 'Political Action: The Problem of Dirty Hands', *Philosophy & Public Affairs*, 2 (1973): 160–80, and C. A. J. Coady, 'Politics and the Problem of Dirty Hands', in Peter Singer (ed.), *A Companion to Ethics* (Cambridge: Blackwell, 1991).

127. Hersh, *Chain of Command*, p. 25.

128. Ibid., p. 26.

129. Army Major General Miller, who took command at Guantanamo in 2002, was given permission to use interrogation techniques such as sleep deprivation, stress positions, exposure to extreme heat and cold, and isolation (ibid., p. 14).

130. Ibid., p. 32.

131. Ibid., p. 34.

7 The Moral Psychology of Torture

1. For a comparison of this analysis of the moral psychology of torture with that suggested by Nancy Sherman in *Stoic Warriors: The Ancient Philosophy behind the Military Mind* (Oxford: Oxford University Press, 2005), see Jessica Wolfendale, 'Stoic Warriors and Stoic Torturers: The Moral Psychology of Military Torture', *South African Journal of Philosophy*, 25 (2006): 62–77, and Nancy Sherman, 'Torturers and the Tortured', *South African Journal of Philosophy*, 25 (2006): 77–88.

2. Ervin Staub, 'Torture: Psychological & Cultural Origins', in Ronald D. Crelinsten and Alex P. Schmid (eds), *The Politics of Pain: Torturers and Their Masters* (Boulder, Colorado: Westview Press, 1993), p. 106.

3. Ibid.

4. John Conroy, *Unspeakable Acts, Ordinary People: The Dynamics of Torture* (New York: Alfred A. Knopf, 2000), p. 88.

5. Janice T. Gibson and Mika Haritos-Fatouros, 'The education of a torturer; there is a cruel method to the madness of teaching people to torture. Almost anyone can learn it', *Psychology Today*, 20 (1986): 50–8, p. 50.

6. Herbert C. Kelman, 'The Social Context of Torture: Policy Process and Authority Structure', in Crelinsten and Schmid, p. 35. Emphasis added.

7. Ronald D. Crelinsten, 'In Their Own Words: The World of the Torturer', in Crelinsten and Schmid, p. 37.

8. Ibid., p. 45.

9. Ibid.

10. Ibid., p. 59.

11. Punishment for disobedience of *legal* orders can include a court-martial, being relieved of formal duties, or informal sanctions depending on the severity of the offence (Mark J. Osiel, *Obeying Orders: Atrocity, Military Discipline and the Law of War* (New Jersey: Transaction Publishers, 2002), p. 250). As noted previously, disobedience of an *illegal* order should not, in theory at least, result in punishment.

12. Crelinsten, p. 59. It is important to note that torturers' accounts of being threatened with death may well be self-serving, particularly when there is the possibility that they will be charged with war crimes. It is unlikely that they would admit that they could have ceased torturing voluntarily.

13. Ibid., p. 48.

14. Conroy, p. 106.

15. Ibid., p. 108.

16. Crelinsten, p. 59.

17. It is interesting how similar these 'exit strategies' are to those adopted by Milgram's subjects who disobeyed the experimenter's orders. As we saw in Chapter 6 many of the disobedient subjects explained their disobedience by reference to personal failings rather than criticizing the morality of the experimenter's orders.

18. Crelinsten, pp. 58–60.

19. Ibid., p. 43.

20. Ibid., p. 44.

21. Ibid., p. 45. Michael Walzer pointed out to me that some military officers regard the Special Forces as worthy of contempt because they operate outside the bounds of morality and law (private communication, June 2005). However, such an attitude is not reflected in the military's official representations of the Special Forces, as found in military publications and websites.

22. Entries from Richard M. Bennett, *Elite Forces: The World's Most Formidable Secret Armies* (London: Virgin Books, 2003).

23. For example, only one trainee in four completes the training course for the Green Berets. See the *John F. Kennedy Special Warfare Center and School* website. Available at <http://www.training.sfahq.com/survival_training.htm>.

24. *John F. Kennedy Special Warfare Center and School* training information.

25. Website of the *British Special Air Services*. Available at <http://www.geocities. com/sascentre>.
26. Conroy, p. 95. Gibson and Haritos-Fatouros describe the training of the Greek torturers on page 50.
27. For example, see the websites of the *British Special Air Services* and the *John F. Kennedy Special Warfare Center and School*.
28. Website of the *John F. Kennedy Special Warfare Center and School*.
29. Peter Maas, 'A Bulletproof Mind', *The New York Times Magazine*, 10 November 2002, p. 52.
30. Website of the *British Special Air Services*.
31. Conroy, p. 6.
32. Website of the *John F. Kennedy Special Warfare Center and School*.
33. Detainees from the Guantanamo Bay military camp have claimed that while in detention they were 'forcibly injected, denied sleep and forced to stand for hours in painful positions' (Tania Branigan, 'Former terror detainees accuse US of ill-treatment', *The Age*, 20 August 2003, p. 9).
34. 'Solders Exposed to Torture, says Hill', *The Age*, 14 February 2005.
35. Website of the *John F. Kennedy Special Warfare Center and School*.
36. Website of the *John F. Kennedy Special Warfare Center and School*.
37. A study of the effects of Australian SAS training found that ' "In particular, development of the counter-terrorist capacity of the SAS in the late 1970s and early 1980s involved the development of new skills and expertise, which brought exposure to risks associated with experimentation and intense periods of enhanced hazard." The study found that SAS personnel encountered lead on indoor firing ranges, high levels of teargas, coloured smoke and masking agents as well as explosions and high levels of physical trauma and stress' (Max Blenkin, *The Age*, 9 March 2004).
38. Tom Wright, 'Band of Brothers', *The Bulletin*, 19 February 2003.
39. Website for the *British Special Air Services*.
40. Conroy, pp. 94–5.
41. For example, the Greek torture trainees were beaten and humiliated by older servicemen (Haritos-Fatouros, 'The Official Torturer: A Learning Model for Obedience to the Authority of Violence', in Crelinsten and Schmid, p. 143). Also, the Green Beret trainees held in the mock prisoner of war camp were interrogated by already serving Green Berets.
42. Gibson and Haritous-Fatouros, p. 50.
43. Ervin Staub, *The Roots of Evil: The Origins of Genocide and other Group Evil* (New York: Cambridge University Press, 1989), p. 61.
44. Crelinsten, p. 48.
45. Ibid., p. 50.
46. Gibson and Haritous-Fatouros, p. 55.
47. Ibid., p. 50.
48. Of course, the training described in this chapter is not clearly training in obedience. It is also training in physical and emotional endurance, in the techniques of interrogation, in weapons handling, in unconventional warfare and in other diverse skills. However, when I claim that Special Forces training develops a form of obedience that is very different from the military ideal of obedience, I do not mean simply that the training aims *solely* at making obedient military personnel. My point is that the character traits and psychological

dispositions generated first through ordinary military combat training and then enhanced in elite military training (such as the dehumanized attitude towards the enemy and the desensitization to the infliction and endurance of pain) undermine combatants' capacity for the moral reflection that is essential for virtuous obedience. As explained in Chapter 2, a virtuous agent does not merely have the right emotions; she governs them by practical wisdom. Therefore, in order to embody the virtues an individual must be a reflective moral agent, with the capacities to reflect upon the nature and ends of virtuous action, whose actions are manifestations of rational deliberation.

49. Torture victim Irena Martinez, quoted in Conroy, p. 171.
50. Crelinsten, p. 41.
51. Children held in detention centres talk about how the officers only refer to them by their prisoner numbers, never by their names. See 'National Inquiry into Children in Immigration Detention'. Available at <http://www.hreoc. gov.au/human_rights/children_detention/submissions/seminar_uws.html>.
52. Primo Levi, *If This is a Man* (London: Abacus, 1987), p. 33.
53. 'Homosexual acts are against Islamic Law and it is humiliating for men to be naked in front of other men.' Seymour M. Hersh, 'Torture at Abu Ghraib', *The Age*, 10 May 2004.
54. Luc Sante, 'Tourists and Torturers', *New York Times*, 11 May 2004.
55. Seymour Hersh, *Chain of Command: The Road from 9/11 to Abu Ghraib* (Melbourne: Allen Lane, 2004), p. 24.
56. Primo Levi, *The Drowned and the Saved* (London: Harper Collins, 1988), pp. 88–9, quoted in Jonathon Glover, *Humanity: A Moral History of the Twentieth Century* (London: Pimlico, 2001), p. 342.
57. The terms 'normalization' and 'routinization' come from Kelman, p. 30.
58. As I argued in Chapter 5, they are not justified in adopting the framework of professionalism. But the use of the language and concepts of professionalism serves a very distinct psychological purpose.
59. Quoted in Martha Huggins, 'Legacies of Authoritarianism: Brazilian Torturers' and Murderers' Reformulation of Memory', *Latin American Perspectives*, 27 (2000): 57–78, p. 60.
60. Kelman, p. 23.
61. This quote comes from an interrogator's manual from the main prison facility of the Khmer Rouge (Crelinsten, p. 41). Emphasis added.
62. Crelinsten, p. 56.
63. Gibson and Haritos-Fatouros, 'The education of a torturer; there is a cruel method to the madness of teaching people to torture. Almost anyone can learn it', p. 8.
64. Huggins, p. 63.
65. Conroy, p. 92.
66. Huggins, p. 59.
67. Ibid., p. 58.
68. Ibid., p. 60.
69. Ibid.
70. Kelman, p. 30.
71. Ibid. This is confirmed by the fact (noted in Chapter 5) that there is significant international involvement in the training and use of torture (for example, the presence of American instructors in South America).

72. Conroy, p. 3.
73. Kelman, p. 31.
74. Huggins, p. 61.
75. Crelinsten, p. 40. As I noted in Chapter 6, this kind of language is also used in more general military culture in order minimize the violence of military action.
76. Ibid., p. 41.
77. The Nazis were so aware of the power of language to change perceptions of reality that they invented a whole terminology to describe the activities of the Holocaust – the term 'Final Solution' was part of this terminology. So thorough was this re-definition of language that one Holocaust scholar mentioned by Lifton 'told of examining "tens of thousands" of Nazi documents without once encountering the word "killing" until, after many years, he finally did discover the word – in reference to an edict concerning dogs' (Robert Jay Lifton, *The Nazi Doctors: Medical Killing and the Psychology of Genocide* (New York: Basic Books, 1986), p. 445).
78. Quoted in Crelinsten, p. 51.
79. As I discussed in Chapter 2, certain kinds of detachment are necessary for professionals, and there are many arguments relating to the moral justifications for such detachment (and the different kinds of detachment) which are beyond the scope of this book to explore. For the purposes of this chapter, it is enough to note that the kind of detachment engaged in by torturers would not find a justification in theories of professional ethics.
80. Lifton, pp. 194–5.
81. As explained in Chapter 2 the good lawyer is expected to develop professional detachment in the sense that they are expected to refrain from judging the justness of the cases they take on, and they are expected to be detached from the distress they might cause to witnesses they cross-examine, as well as the impact of their client's case on the wellbeing of others.
82. This is a problem that can arise in the case of the lawyer as well (Elizabeth Wolgast, *Ethics of an Artificial Person: Lost Responsibility in Professions and Organizations* (Stanford, California: Stanford University Press, 1992), p. 71).
83. Heinrich Himmler, quoted in Jonathan Bennett, 'The Conscience of Huckleberry Finn', in Peter Singer (ed.), *Ethics* (Oxford: Oxford University Press, 1994), p. 299.
84. Heinrich Himmler, quoted in Bennett, p. 300.
85. Donna Winslow, 'Misplaced Loyalties: The Role of Military Culture in the Breakdown of Discipline in two Peace Operations', *Journal of Military and Strategic Studies*, 6 (2004): 1–19, p. 9.
86. Crelinsten, p. 54.
87. John Doris, *Lack of Character: Personality and Moral Behavior* (Cambridge: Cambridge University Press, 2002), pp. 56–7.
88. Huggins, p. 63.
89. This kind of deep split between private and professional selves is inconsistent with the ideal of reflective moral agency. The good professional, as outlined in Chapters 1 and 2, is reflective about the kinds of dispositions they develop as part of their professional duties. They do not attempt to divorce their professional moral character from their private moral character.
90. Huggins, p. 63.

91. As I noted in Chapter 1, the belief that professionalism alters the moral assessment of both roles and specific acts is common to many accepted theories of professional ethics and is also subject to much criticism. However, this should not be taken as condoning torturers' adoption of these concepts. The point here is not to comment on whether torturers are justified in adopting the moral framework of professionalism (or even if they are adopting it correctly), but to draw out the moral psychology of torturers – the framework that they appeal to in attempting to justify, rationalize, and live with their actions. It would be interesting to explore whether torturers' use of the professionalism discourse to generate certain psychological coping mechanisms and to mask moral and emotional distress has an echo in the use of this discourse in far more 'legitimate' professions. There are some uncomfortable similarities with the moral psychology adopted by some lawyers, for example. For a discussion of this see Gerald Postema, 'Moral Responsibility in Professional Ethics', *New York University Law Review*, 55 (1980): 63–89.
92. Crelinsten, p. 51.
93. Gerald Postema, 'Self-Image, Integrity, and Professional Responsibility', in David Luban (ed.), *The Good Lawyer: Lawyers' Roles and Lawyers' Ethics* (Totowa, New Jersey: Rowman & Allanhead, 1983), p. 301.
94. Crelinsten, p. 52.
95. This term comes from Gerald Postema, 'Moral Responsibility in Professional Ethics', p. 71.
96. Huggins, p. 63.
97. Conroy, p. 112.
98. Kelman, p. 22.
99. Thomas Nagel, *The View from Nowhere* (New York: Oxford University Press, 1986), p. 180.
100. This feeling of divided responsibility is not limited to torturers of course: it could also be a feature of actions taken in any hierarchically organized institution. For a discussioon of this issue see Elizabeth Wolgast's book *Ethics of an Artificial Person: Lost Responsibility in Professions and Organizations*.
101 Lifton, p. 427.
102. Ibid., p. 16.
103. Some of the *unofficial* 'initiation' rituals discussed in Chapter 6 might fit the definition of torture. For example, cadets at the School of Infantry in Australia were involved in the very brutal and humiliating 'hazing' of new trainees – one of whom committed suicide (Josh Gordon, 'How an Army of Bullies Drove a Soldier to Suicide', *The Age*, 27 August 2003).
104. Quoted in Crelinsten, p. 44.

Conclusion

1. Captain Pete Kilner, 'Military Leaders to Justify Killing in Warfare', paper presented at *Joint Services Conference on Professional Ethics*, Washington DC, 27–28 January 2000. Available at <http://www.usafa.af.mil/jscope/JSCOPE00>, p. 5.
2. Erik Baard, 'The Guilt-Free Soldier', *The Village Voice*, 22–28 January 2003. Available at <http://www.villagevoice.com/issues/0304/baard.php>.

3. Richard Kerbaj, 'Pill may reduce troop trauma', *The Age*, 19 October 2003.
4. See Michael Buchanan, 'Drugs involved in friendly fire deaths', BBC News World Edition, 20 December 2002. Available at <http://news.bbc.co.uk/2/hi/americas/2595641.stm> and 'Need for Speed: Did Amphetamines Play a Role in Afghanistan Friendly Fire Incident?', *abcNEWS.com*, 20 December 2002.
5. Cath Dwyer, interview with George Gittoes, maker of the documentary 'Soundtrack to War', Radio National, 30 June 2004.
6. Norman Dixon, *On the Psychology of Military Incompetence* (London: Jonathan Cape, 1976), p. 82.
7. B. H. Liddell Hart, *History of the First World War* (London: Pan Books, 1972), p. 332, quoted in Dixon, p. 82. Passchendaele (known as the Third Battle of Ypres) cost more than 2000 lives a day (Dixon, p. 89). At the end of the battle, the British and empire forces had lost more than 250,000 men and advanced only five miles.
8. Jeffery Bordin, 'On the Psychology of Moral Cognition and Resistance to Authoritative and Groupthink Demands during a Military Intelligence Analysis Gaming Exercise', paper presented at the *Joint Services Conference on Professional Ethics*, Springfield, Virginia, 24–25 January 2002. Available from <http://www.usafa.af.mil/jscope/JSCOPE02>.
9. Bordin, p. 3.
10. Ibid.
11. Ibid.
12. Ibid., p. 26.
13. Ibid., p. 28.
14. Ibid., p. 5.
15. Mark Osiel, *Obeying Orders: Atrocity, Military Discipline and the Law of War* (New Jersey: Transaction Publishers, 2002), p. 315.
16. Capt. Steven D. Danyluk, 'Preventing Atrocities', *Marine Corps Gazette*, 84 (2000): 36–8, p. 38. Danyluk, however, fails to identify military training as a source of the moral psychology of destructive obedience. Instead, he identifies the causes of atrocities as '(1) external pressure, (2) a breakdown in small unit leadership, and (3) an overpowering sense of frustration' (p. 37). While these factors may of course lead to atrocities, they are far from the sole or primary cause, as this book as demonstrated.
17. Daniel Muñoz-Rojas and Jean-Jacques Frésard, *The Roots of Behaviour in War: Understanding and Preventing IHL Violations* (Geneva: International Committee of the Red Cross, 2004), p. 8.

Selected Bibliography

Books

Applbaum, Arthur Isak. *Ethics for Adversaries: the Morality of Roles in Public and Professional Life* (Princeton, New Jersey: Princeton University Press, 1999).

Aristotle. *The Nicomachean Ethics.* Translated by David Ross, *Oxford World's Classics* (Oxford: Oxford University Press, 1998).

—— *The Politics.* Translated by H. Rackham (Cambridge, Massachusetts: Harvard University Press, 1977).

Axinn, Sidney. *A Moral Military* (Philadelphia: Temple University Press, 1989).

Bayles, Michael D. *Professional Ethics,* 2nd edn (Belmont: Wadsworth, 1989).

Bennett, Richard M. *Elite Forces: The World's Most Formidable Secret Armies* (London: Virgin Books, 2003).

Bourke, Joanna. *An Intimate History of Killing: Face-to-Face Killing in Twentieth-Century Warfare* (London: Granta Books, 1999).

Bowden, Mark. *Black Hawk Down: A Story of Modern War* (New York: Atlantic Monthly Press, 1999).

Coady, C. A. J. *The Ethics of Armed Humanitarian Intervention* (Washington DC: The US Institute of Peace, 2002).

Conroy, John. *Unspeakable Acts, Ordinary People: The Dynamics of Torture* (New York: Alfred A. Knopf, 2000).

Dixon, Norman. *On the Psychology of Military Incompetence* (London: Jonathan Cape, 1976).

Doris, John. *Lack of Character: Personality and Moral Behavior* (New York: Cambridge University Press, 2002).

Gabriel, Richard. *To Serve with Honor: a Treatise on Military Ethics and the Way of the Soldier* (Westport, Connecticut: Greenwood Press, 1982).

Glover, Jonathon. *Humanity: A Moral History of the Twentieth Century* (London: Pimlico, 1999).

Grossman, Lt Col David. *On Killing: The Psychological Cost of Learning to Kill in War and Society* (Boston: Little, Brown & Co, 1995).

Hartle, Anthony E. *Moral Issues in Military Decision Making,* 2nd edn (Lawrence, Kansas: University Press of Kansas, 2004).

Herman, Barbara. *The Practice of Moral Judgement* (Harvard: Harvard University Press, 1993).

Hersh, Seymour M. *Chain of Command: The Road from 9/11 to Abu Ghraib* (Melbourne: Allen Lane, 2004).

Hursthouse, Rosalind. *On Virtue Ethics* (Oxford: Oxford University Press, 1999).

Janowitz, Morris. *The Professional Soldier: A Social and Political Portrait* (Glencoe, Illinois: Free Press, 1960).

Kant, Immanuel. *Groundwork of the Metaphysics of Morals.* Translated by Mary Gregor, *Cambridge Texts in the History of Philosophy* (Cambridge: Cambridge University Press, 1998).

Keegan, John. *A History of Warfare* (London: Pimlico, 1994).

Keijzer, Nico. *Military Obedience* (Alphen aan den Rijn, The Netherlands: Sijthoff & Noordhoff, 1978).

Kelman, Herbert C. and Hamilton, V. Lee. *Crimes of Obedience: Toward A Social Psychology of Authority and Responsibility* (London: Yale University Press, 1989).

Kennett, Jeanette. *Agency and Responsibility: A Common-Sense Moral Psychology* (New York: Oxford University Press, 2001).

Levi, Primo. *If This is a Man* (London: Abacus, 1987).

Lifton, Robert Jay. *The Nazi Doctors: Medical Killing and the Psychology of Genocide* (New York: Basic Books, 1986).

McNair, Rachel. *Perpetration-Induced Traumatic Stress: The Psychological Consequences of Killing* (Westport, Connecticut: Praeger, 2002).

Milgram, Stanley. *Obedience to Authority: An Experimental View* (London: Tavistock Publications, 1974).

Muñoz-Rojas, Daniel and Frésard, Jean-Jacques. *The Roots of Behaviour in War: Understanding and Preventing IHL Violations* (Geneva: International Committee of the Red Cross, 2004).

Nagel, Thomas. *The View from Nowhere* (New York: Oxford University Press, 1986).

Oakley, Justin and Cocking, Dean. *Virtue Ethics and Professional Roles* (Cambridge: Cambridge University Press, 2001).

Osiel, Mark J. *Obeying Orders: Atrocity, Military Discipline & the Law of War* (New Jersey: Transaction Publishers, 2002).

Sherman, Nancy. *Stoic Warriors: The Ancient Philosophy behind the Military Mind* (Oxford: Oxford University Press, 2005).

Slote, Michael. *From Morality to Virtue* (New York: Oxford University Press, 1992).

Staub, Ervin. *The Roots of Evil: The Origins of Genocide and other Group Evil* (New York: Cambridge University Press, 1989).

Walzer, Michael. *Just and Unjust Wars: A Moral Argument with Historical Illustrations*, 3rd edn (New York: Basic Books, 2000).

—— *Obligations* (Cambridge: Harvard University Press, 1970).

Weschler, Lawrence. *A Miracle, a Universe: Settling Accounts with Torturers* (New York: Pantheon Books, 1990).

Wishman, Seymour. *Confessions of a Criminal Lawyer* (New York: Times Books, 1981).

Wolgast, Elizabeth. *Ethics of an Artificial Person: Lost Responsibility in Professions and Organizations* (Stanford: Stanford University Press, 1992).

Collections

Baumrin, B. and Freedman, B (eds). *Moral Responsibility and the Professions* (New York: Haven Publications, 1983).

Callahan, Joan C (ed.). *Ethical Issues in Professional Life* (New York: Oxford University Press, 1988).

Coppieters, Bruno and Fotion, Nick (eds). *Moral Constraints on War: Principles and Cases* (Lanham, MD: Lexington Books, 2002).

Crelinsten, Ronald D. and Schmid, Alex P (eds). *The Politics of Pain: Torturers and Their Masters* (Boulder, Colorado: Westview Press, 1993).

Engstrom, Stephen and Whiting, Jennifer (eds). *Aristotle, Kant, and the Stoics: Rethinking Happiness and Duty* (New York: Cambridge University Press, 1996).

Greenberg, Karen J (ed.). *The Torture Debate in America* (New York: Cambridge University Press, 2006).

Hatzimoysis, Anthony (ed.). *Philosophy and the Emotions: Royal Institute of Philosophy Supplement 52* (Cambridge: Cambridge University Press, 2003).

Luban, David (ed.). *The Good Lawyer: Lawyer's Roles and Lawyer's Ethics* (Totowa, New Jersey: Rowman & Allanheld, 1984).

Rorty, Amelie Oksenberg (ed.). *Essays on Aristotle's Ethics* (London: University of California Press, 1980).

Smart, J. J. C. and Williams, Bernard. *Utilitarianism For and Against* (Cambridge: Cambridge University Press, 1973).

Ten, C.L., Tan, Sor-Hoon and Chong, Kim-chong (eds). *Making Sense of Community and Self* (Chicago: Open Court, 2002).

Wakin, Malham M. (ed.). *War, Morality, and the Military Profession*, 2nd edn. (Boulder, Colorado: Westview Press, 1986).

Watson, Gary (ed.). *Free Will*, 2nd edn (Oxford: Oxford University Press, 2003).

Articles

Anscombe, Elizabeth. 'War and Murder', in Malham M. Wakin (ed.), *War, Morality, and the Military Profession*, 2nd edn (Boulder, Colorado: Westview Press, 1986).

Aronovitch, Hilliard. 'Good Soldiers, a Traditional Approach', *Journal of Applied Philosophy*, 18 (2001): 13–23.

Arrigo, Jean Maria. 'A Utilitarian Argument against Torture Interrogation of Terrorists', *Science and Engineering Ethics*, 10 (2004): 1–30.

Baltzly, Dirk. 'Peripatetic Perversions', *The Monist*, 86 (2003): 3–29.

Barry, John; Hirsch, Michael, and Isikoff, Michael. 'The Roots of Torture; The road to Abu Ghraib began after 9/11, when Washington wrote new rules to fight a new kind of war. A NEWSWEEK investigation', *Newsweek*, 26 (2004).

Basoglu, M; Paker, M; Ozmen, E; Tasdemir, O. and Sahin, D. 'Factors Related to Long-term Traumatic Stress Responses in Survivors of Torture in Turkey', *The Journal of the American Medical Association*, 272 (1994): 357–63.

Bayles, Michael D. 'The Professions', in Joan C. Callahan (ed.), *Ethical Issues in Professional Life* (New York: Oxford University Press, 1988).

Bennett, Jonathan. 'The Conscience of Huckleberry Finn', in Peter Singer (ed.), *Ethics* (Oxford: Oxford University Press, 1994).

Betros, Lance. 'Political Partisanship and the Military Ethic in America', *Armed Forces and Society*, 27 (2001): 501–23.

Blass, Thomas. 'Understanding Behaviour in the Milgram Obedience Experiment: The Role of Personality, Situations, and Their Interactions', *Journal of Personality and Social Psychology*, 60 (1991): 398–413.

Bordin, Jeffery. 'On the Psychology of Moral Cognition and Resistance to Authoritative and Groupthink Demands during a Military Intelligence Analysis Gaming Exercise', paper presented at the *Joint Services Conference on Professional Ethics*, Springfield, Virginia, 2002. Available at http://www.usafa.af.mil/jscope/JSCOPE02.

Bowden, Mark. 'The Dark Art of Interrogation', *The Atlantic Monthly*, 29 (2003).

Camenisch, Paul. 'On Being a Professional, Morally Speaking,' in Bernard Baumrin and Benjamin Freedman (eds), *Moral Responsibility and the Professions* (New York: New Haven, 1983).

Cannold, Leslie. 'Consequences for Patients of Health Care Professionals' Conscientious Actions: the Ban on Abortions in South Australia', *Journal of Medical Ethics*, 20 (1994): 80–6.

Casebeer, Major William D. 'Torture Interrogation for Terrorists: A Theory of Exceptions (with Notes, Cautions, and Warnings)', paper presented at the *Joint Services Conference on Professional Ethics*, Washington D.C., 2003. Available at http://www.usafa.af.mil/jscope/JSCOPE03.

Ceulemans, Carl. 'Just Cause', in Bruno Coppieters and Nick Fotion (eds), *Moral Constraints on War: Principles and Cases* (Lanham, MD: Lexington Books, 2002).

Chambers, John Whiteclay II. 'S. L. A. Marshall's *Men Against Fire*: New Evidence Regarding Fire Ratios', *Parameters*, 33 (2003): 113–21.

Childress, James F. 'Just-War Theories: The Bases, Interrelations, Priorities, and Functions of Their Criteria', in Malham M. Wakin (ed.), *War, Morality, and the Military Profession*, 2nd edn (Boulder, Colorado: Westview Press, 1986).

Clarke, Randolph. 'Free Will and the Conditions of Moral Responsibility', *Philosophical Studies*, 66 (1992): 53–72.

Coady, C.A.J. 'Politics and the Problem of Dirty Hands', in Peter Singer (ed), *A Companion to Ethics* (Cambridge: Blackwell, 1991).

Cocking, Dean and Kennett, Jeanette. 'Friendship and Role Morality', in C. L. Ten, Sor-Hoon Tan, and Kim-chong Chong (eds), *Making Sense of Community and Self* (Chicago: Open Court, 2002).

—— 'Friendship and the Self', *Ethics*, 108 (1998): 502–27.

—— 'Friendship and Moral Danger', *Journal of Philosophy*, 97 (2000): 278–96.

Cook, Martin L. 'Moral Foundations of Military Service', *Parameters*, 30 (2000): 117–29.

—— 'The Proper Role of Military Advice in Contemporary Uses of Force', *Parameters*, 32 (2002/2003): 21–33.

Crelinsten, Ronald D. 'In Their Own Words: The World of the Torturer', in Ronald D. Crelinsten and Alex P. Schmid (eds), *The Politics of Pain: Torturers and their Masters* (Boulder, Colorado: Westview Press, 1993).

Cunningham, Anthony. 'The Moral Importance of Dirty Hands', *The Journal of Value Inquiry*, 26 (1992): 239–50.

Danyluk, Capt. Steven D. 'Preventing Atrocities', *Marine Corps Gazette*, 84 (2000): 36–8.

Darley, John M. and Batson, C. Daniel. '"From Jerusalem to Jericho": A Study of Situationals and Dispositional Variables in Helping Behaviour', *Journal of Personality and Social Psychology*, 23 (1973): 100–8.

Donovan, James B. and McLaughlin, Rafael P. 'United Nations Peacekeepers and International Humanitarian Law: Can There be an Affirmative Duty to Prevent War Crimes and Crimes Against Humanity?', *New England International and Comparative Law Annual*, 5 (1999).

Dworkin, Gerald. 'Patients and Prisoners: The Ethics of Lethal Injection', *Analysis*, 62 (2002): 181–9.

Ewin, R. E. 'Loyalty and Virtues', *The Philosophical Quarterly*, 42 (1992): 403–19.

Frankfurt, Harry G. 'Freedom of the Will and the Concept of a Person', in Gary Watson (ed.), *Free Will*, 2nd edn (Oxford: Oxford University Press, 2003).

Gibson, Janice T. and Haritous-Fatouros, Mika. 'The Education of a Torturer; there is a cruel method to the madness of teaching people to torture. Almost anyone can learn it', *Psychology Today*, 20 (1986): 50–8.

Haritos-Fatouros, Mika. 'The Official Torturer: A Learning Model for Obedience to the Authority of Violence', in Ronald D. Crelinsten and Alex P. Schmid (eds), *The Politics of Pain: Torturers and Their Masters* (Boulder, Colorado: Westview Press, 1993).

Hartle, Anthony E. 'Obedience and Responsibility', *Professional Ethics*, 10 (2002): 65–80.

Hedhal, Captain Marc. 'The Washington Post Test: Integrity's Last Stand', paper presented at the *Joint Services Conference on Professional Ethics*, Springfield Virginia, 2002. Available at http://www.usafa.af.mil/jscope/JSCOPE02.

Heinz, Wolfgang. 'The Military, Torture and Human Rights: Experiences from Argentina, Brazil, Chile, and Uruguay', in Ronald D. Crelinsten and Alex P. Schmid (eds), *The Politics of Pain: Torturers and Their Masters* (Boulder, Colorado: Westview Press, 1993).

Hooker, Brad. 'Rule-Consequentialism', *Mind*, 99 (1990): 67–77.

—— 'The Collapse of Virtue Ethics', *Utilitas*, 14 (2002): 22–40.

Huggins, Martha. 'Legacies of Authoritarianism: Brazilian Torturers' and Murderers' Reformulation of Memory', *Latin American Perspectives*, 27 (2000): 57–78.

Huntington, Samuel. 'Officership as a Profession', in Malham M. Wakin (ed), *War, Morality, and the Military Profession*, 2nd edn (Boulder, Colorado: Westview Press, 1986).

—— 'The Military Mind: Conservative Realism of the Professional Military Ethic', in Malham M. Wakin (ed), *War, Morality, and the Military Profession*, 2nd edn (Boulder, Colorado: Westview Press, 1986).

Hursthouse, Rosalind. 'Virtue Ethics vs. Rule-Consequentialism', *Utilitas*, 14 (2002): 41–53.

Jones, Karen. 'Emotion, Weakness of Will, and the Normative Conception of Agency', in Anthony Hatzimoysis (ed.), *Philosophy and the Emotions: Royal Institute of Philosophy Supplement 52* (Cambridge: Cambridge University Press, 2003).

—— 'Second-hand Moral Knowledge', *The Journal of Philosophy*, 96 (1999): 55–78.

Kelman, Herbert C. 'The Social Context of Torture: Policy Process and Authority Structure', in Ronald D. Crelinsten and Alex P. Schmid (eds), *The Politics of Pain: Torturers and Their Masters* (Boulder, Colorado: Westview Press, 1993).

Kilner, Captain Pete. 'Military Leaders to Justify Killing in Warfare' paper presented at *Joint Services Conference on Professional Ethics*, Washington, DC, 2000. Available at http://www.usafa.af.mil/jscope/JSCOPE00.

Korsgaard, Christine. 'From Duty and for the Sake of the Noble: Kant and Aristotle on Morally Good Action', in Stephen Engstrom and Jennifer Whiting (eds), *Aristotle, Kant, and the Stoics: Rethinking Happiness and Duty* (New York: Cambridge University Press, 1996).

Krauss, Eric S. and Lacey, Mike O. 'Utilitarian vs. Humanitarian: The Battle over the Law of War', *Parameters*, 32 (2002): 73–85.

Lackey, Douglas. 'Professional Sins and Unprofessional Excuses', in B. Baumrin and B. Freedman (eds), *Moral Responsibility and the Professions* (New York: Haven Publications, 1983).

Linn, Ruth. 'Soldiers with a Conscience Never Die – They are Just Ignored by their Society. Moral Disobedience in the Israel Defence Forces', *Journal of Military Ethics*, 1 (2002): 57–76.

Luban, David. 'Just War and Human Rights', *Philosophy & Public Affairs*, 9 (1980): 160–81.

——. 'Liberalism, Torture, and the Ticking Bomb', in Karen J. Greenberg (ed.), *The Torture Debate in America* (New York: Cambridge University Press, 2006).

Meeus, H. J. Wim and Raajmakers, Quinten A. W. 'Obedience in Modern Society: the Utrecht Studies', *Journal of Social Issues*, 51 (1995):155–76.

Mele, Alfred. 'Errant Self-Control and the Self-controlled Person', *Pacific Philosophical Quarterly*, 71 (1990): 47–59.

Miller, Arthur G., Collins, Barry E. and Brief, Diana E. 'Perspectives on Obedience to Authority: the Legacy of the Milgram Experiments', *Journal of Social Issues*, 51 (1995): 1–19.

Nissani, Moti. 'A Cognitive Reinterpretation of Stanley Milgram's Observations on Obedience to Authority', *American Psychologist*, 45 (1990): 1384–5.

Oakley, Justin. 'Varieties of Virtue Ethics', *Ratio*, 9 (1996): 128–52.

Osofsky, Michael J., Bandura, Albert, and Zimbardo, Phillip G. 'The Role of Moral Disengagement in the Execution Process', *Law and Human Behaviour*, 29 (2005): 371–92.

Owens, David. 'The Authority of Practical Judgement,' unpublished paper, 2003.

Phelps, Lieutenant Colonel M.L. 'The Australian Army's Culture: From Institutional Warrior to Pragmatic Professional', *Australian Defence Force Journal*, 123 (1997): 37–43.

Pierce, Albert C. 'Commentary: Captain Lawrence Rockwood in Haiti', *Journal of Military Ethics*, 1 (2002): 53–4.

Postema, Gerald. 'Self-Image, Integrity, and Professional Responsibility', in David Luban (ed.), *The Good Lawyer: Lawyer's Roles and Lawyer's Ethics* (Totowa, New Jersey: Rowman & Allanheld, 1984).

—— 'Moral Responsibility in Professional Ethics', *New York University Law Review*, 55 (1980): 63–89.

Priebe, Stefan and Bauer, Michael. 'Inclusion of Psychological Torture in PTSD Criterion A', *The American Journal of Psychiatry*, 152 (1995): 1691–2.

Railton, Peter. 'Alienation, Consequentialism, and the Demands of Morality', *Philosophy and Public Affairs*, 13 (1984): 134–71.

—— 'Indirect Consequentialism, Friendship, and the Problem of Alienation', *Ethics*, 106 (1995): 86–111.

Rehlberg, Major Carl D. 'Implications of *Dereliction of Duty*', paper presented at the Joint Services Conference on Professional Ethics. Springfield, Virginia, 2000. Available at www.usafa.af.mil/jscope/JSCOPE00.

Rochat, François and Modigliani, Andre. 'The Ordinary Quality of Resistance: from Milgram's Laboratory to the Village of Le Chambom', *Journal of Social Issues*, 51 (1995): 195–211.

Sabini, John and Silver, Maury. 'Lack of Character? Situationism Critiqued', *Ethics*, 115 (2005): 535–62.

Sarvas, Stefan. 'Professional Soldiers and Politics: A Case of Central and Eastern Europe', *Armed Forces and Society*, 26 (1999): 99–118.

Shaw, Joseph. 'The Virtue of Obedience', *Religious Studies*, 38 (2002): 63–75.

Sherman, Nancy. 'Torturers and the Tortured', *South African Journal of Philosophy*, 25 (2006): 77–88.

Shue, Henry. 'Torture', *Philosophy and Public Affairs*, 7 (1978): 124–43.

Smart, J. J. C. 'An Outline of a System of Utilitarian Ethics', in J. J. C. Smart and Bernard Williams (eds), *Utilitarianism For and Against* (Cambridge: Cambridge University Press, 1973).

Sorabji, Richard. 'Aristotle on the Role of Intellect in Virtue', in Amelie Oksenberg Rorty (ed.), *Essays on Aristotle's Ethics* (London: University of California Press, 1980).

Staub, Ervin. 'Torture: Psychological and Cultural Origins', in Ronald D. Crelinsten and Alex P. Schmid (eds), *The Politics of Pain: Torturers and Their Masters* (Boulder, Colorado: Westview Press, 1993).

Stevens, Major T.L. 'A Code of Professional Ethics for Army Officers: Is One Needed?', *Australian Defence Force Journal*, 111 (1995): 33–7.

Stevenson, Major E. J. 'Educating the Community's "Cream": Common Military Training at the Australian Defence Force Academy', *Australian Defence Force Journal*, 120 (1996): 11–18.

Tabbernor, Colonel Dennis C. 'Operational Commanders, Orders, and the Right to Choose', *Advanced Military Studies Course* Canadian Forces College 1998. Available at <http://198.231.69.12/papers/amsc1/039.htm>

Tindale, Christopher. 'The Logic of Torture', *Social Theory and Practice*, 22 (1996): 349–74.

Van Ommeren, Mark; de Jong, Joop T. V. M.; Sharma, Bhogendra; Komproe, Ivan; Thapa, Suraj B.; Cardeña, Etzel. 'Psychiatric Disorders Among Tortured Bhutanese Refugees in Nepal', *Archives of General Psychiatry*, 58 (2001): 475–82.

Wakin, Malham M. 'Military and Societal Values: The Relevance of Knowing and Doing', paper presented at the *Joint Services Conference on Professional Ethics*, Springfield, Virginia, 1995. Available at http://www.usafa.af.mil/jscope/ JSCOPE95.

Walzer, Michael. 'Political Action: The Problem of Dirty Hands', *Philosophy & Public Affairs*, 2 (1973): 160–80.

Wasserstrom, Richard. 'Roles and Morality', in David Luban (ed.), *The Good Lawyer: Lawyer's Roles and Lawyer's Ethics* (Totowa, New Jersey: Rowman & Allanheld, 1984).

—— 'Lawyers as Professionals: Some Moral Issues', in Joan C. Callahan (ed.), *Ethical Issues in Professional Life* (New York: Oxford University Press, 1988).

Watson, Gary. 'Free Agency', in Gary Watson (ed.), *Free Will*, 2nd edn (Oxford: Oxford University Press, 2003).

Wheate, Rhonda M. and Wheate, Lieutenant Nial J. 'Lawful Dissent and the Modern Australian Defence Force', *Australian Defence Force Journal*, 160 (2003): 20–30.

Wheeler, Michael O. 'Loyalty, Honor, and the Modern Military', in Malham M. Wakin (ed.), *War, Morality, and the Military Profession*, 2nd edn (Boulder, Colorado: Westview Press, 1986).

Willard, C. 'The Nurse's Role as Patient Advocate: Obligation or Imposition?', *Journal of Advanced Nursing*, 24 (1996): 60–6.

Winslow, Donna. 'Misplaced Loyalties: The Role of Military Culture in the Breakdown of Discipline in Two Peace Operations', *Journal of Military and Strategic Studies*, 6 (2004): 1–19.

Winslow, Gerald R. 'From Loyalty to Advocacy: A New Metaphor for Nursing', in Joan C. Callahan (ed.), *Ethical Issues in Professional Life* (Oxford: Oxford University Press, 1988).

Wolfendale, Jessica. 'Training Torturers: A Critique of the "Ticking Bomb" Argument', *Social Theory and Practice*, 32 (2006): 269–289.

—— 'Stoic Warriors and Stoic Torturers: The Moral Psychology of Military Torture', *South African Journal of Philosophy*, 25 (2006): 62–77.

Wolfram, Charles. 'A Lawyer's Duty to Represent Clients', in David Luban (ed.), *The Good Lawyer: Lawyer's Roles and Lawyer's Ethics* (Totowa, New Jersey: Rowman & Allanheld, 1984).

Wrage, Stephen. 'Captain Lawrence Rockwood in Haiti', *Journal of Military Ethics*, 1 (2002): 45–52.

Yalanis, Captain Christopher P. 'The Virtue (?) of Obedience', paper presented at the *Joint Services Conference on Professional Ethics*, Springfield, Virginia, 2001. Available at www.usafa.af.mil/jscope/JSCOPE01.

Zupan, LTC Dan. 'On the Obligation to Conduct World Police Work', paper presented at the *Joint Services Conference on Professional Ethics*, Springfield, Virginia, 2002. Available at http://www.usafa.af.mil/jscope/JSCOPE02.

Websites

Amnesty International, http//:www.amnesty.org.

Australian Defence Force Academy, http://www.defence.gov.au/adfa.

British Special Air Services, http://www.geocities.com/sascentre.

Fort Benning, https://www.benning.army.mil/infantry.

Human Rights Watch, http://www.hrw.org.

John F. Kennedy Special Warfare Center and School, http://www.training.sfahq.com.

Royal Military College Duntroon, Australia, http://www.defence.gov.au/army/rmc.

Office of the United Nations High Commissioner for Human Rights, http://www.ohchr.org.

United States West Point Military Academy, http//:www.usma.edu.

Index